Celebrity in the Time of Covid

ALSO BY CHRISTINA S. BECK

*Celebrity Health Narratives and
the Public Health* (McFarland, 2015)

Celebrity in the Time of Covid

*Fandom and the Influence
of Pandemic Messaging*

CHRISTINA S. BECK

McFarland & Company, Inc., Publishers
Jefferson, North Carolina

ISBN (print) 978-1-4766-8492-5
ISBN (ebook) 978-1-4766-4760-9

LIBRARY OF CONGRESS AND BRITISH LIBRARY
CATALOGUING DATA ARE AVAILABLE

Library of Congress Control Number 2022027137

© 2022 Christina S. Beck. All rights reserved

No part of this book may be reproduced or transmitted in any form or by any means, electronic or mechanical, including photocopying or recording, or by any information storage and retrieval system, without permission in writing from the publisher.

Front cover photograph by Gennadiy Kravchenko (Shutterstock)

Printed in the United States of America

*McFarland & Company, Inc., Publishers
Box 611, Jefferson, North Carolina 28640
www.mcfarlandpub.com*

To my husband,
Roger Aden,
and our daughters,
Ellie-Kate, Emmy, Chelsea, and Brittany.

A global pandemic was not fun,
but we managed to make the most
of our moments in quarantine.

I love you all!

Acknowledgments

I am forever grateful to God for blessing our family with safety, security, and good health during a once-in-a-century global pandemic. Especially after my research for this book over the past nearly two years, I realize that not everyone was nearly so fortunate.

I deeply appreciate the support of the Ohio University Honors Tutorial Program and its Undergraduate Research Fund that supported the work of my two research assistants during the summer of 2020, Will Bower and Nora McKeown. Thank you for the data that you collected and the wonderful conversations that we had during initial phases of this project.

To my family, thank you for your patience as I invested considerable time and energy in this project. I'm incredibly glad for all of the special moments that we had together as we sheltered in place and then slowly but surely reentered the world. To Roger, thanks for all of your support! I could not have completed this work without you! To our girls, Brittany Nicole, Chelsea Meagan, Emmy Grace, and Ellie-Kate—I am so blessed and honored to be your mom, and I treasure your support and encouragement.

Contents

Acknowledgments	vi
Introduction: Are We All Really "In This Together"? Fandom, Celebrity, Politics and Covid-19	1
CHAPTER 1. Framing Our Stories through Fandom	19
CHAPTER 2. Through the Window of Sports	35
CHAPTER 3. Fandom as Key to Politicization of Covid-19	55
CHAPTER 4. Celebrity Contributions to Public Narratives About Covid-19	89
CHAPTER 5. Heroes on the Frontlines of a Global Pandemic	135
References	149
Index	189

Introduction
Are We All Really "In This Together"?
Fandom, Celebrity, Politics and Covid-19

You can count Julia Roberts in as a fan of Dr. Anthony Fauci (para. 1). Roberts couldn't contain her excitement at speaking to Fauci before his arrival [on her social media during the "#PassTheMic" campaign in which celebrities shared their social media platforms with experts on the coronavirus for a day], saying, "How rad that we have maybe the coolest man on the planet right now" (para. 3). "Oh this is such a thrill," Roberts told him. "This is a thrill for me because there are very few experts of anything in the world and you truly have emerged as a personal hero for me. Just to have this little corner of your time for us is such a joy" [A. Fernández, 2020, para. 5].

The idea of glamorous movie star Julia Roberts starstruck by an elderly, unassuming scientist prompted me to chuckle as I closed out of Facebook on my phone and then logged in to check email in my makeshift home office. We had been homebound for just over a few months at that point, and we had settled into a new normal, filled with fulfilling work and school obligations before family game nights and dinner at home (as opposed to leaving the office and grabbing dinner on the road after as we shuttled our youngest daughter to softball practices and games).

On March 13, 2020, we were scheduled to be driving from Ohio to Indiana for an indoor softball tournament. Instead, that day marked the start of nine weeks in our house without leaving our property, due to Covid-19. According to the BBC, by late March 2020, nearly three out of four Americans had been directed to stay home (2020). That same article emphasized that "[s]ome 245 million people are already under orders to stay at home.... Almost two-thirds of states have issued directives for their citizens to stay put, while the remaining states have localised orders in effect" (para. 5–6). Just six months later, Schoenberg (2020) wrote that "[a]lready, COVID-19 has killed more people than World War I and Vietnam combined ... [and] pushed the unemployment rate to levels not seen since the Great Depression" (para. 1). Worldwide, by September 2020, Covid-19 had claimed more lives "than HIV. More than dysentery. More than malaria, influenza, cholera, and measles—combined" (Pérez-Peña, 2020, para. 1).

Social media and television provided our windows into the world. I admit to more time than usual on Facebook during those early days of the pandemic, scrolling and searching for information. As a communication scholar who previously authored another book on celebrity health narratives (see Beck et al., 2015), I noticed the heavy attention given to celebrities such as Tom Hanks and Rita Wilson, who disclosed their battle with Covid-19 just before my family started to shelter in place. Sperling (2020) reported in the *New York Times* that, "[w]ith the seriousness of the pandemic still being debated in some corners of the media, learning that Mr. Hanks, the star of films like 'Saving Private Ryan' and 'Apollo 13,' has been stricken may make the situation seem much more tangible to some Americans" (para. 6). As Sperling continued, "Ann Curry, a journalist and former host of NBC's 'Today,' said on Twitter: 'Ok, now we all have someone we love diagnosed with #coronavirus'" (para. 7).

Still seeking more details about this mysterious new virus, I tuned in for daily press briefings by President Trump and his team at the White House and by Ohio governor Mike DeWine and New York governor Andrew Cuomo. I wasn't alone. As individuals stayed home at unprecedented levels, they sought to know what was happening, prompting dramatic spikes in ratings for what used to be mundane governmental updates.

Grynbaum (2020) dubbed President Trump as "a ratings hit" (para. 1), observing that "Mr. Trump and his coronavirus updates ... attracted an average audience of 8.5 million on cable news, roughly the viewership of the season finale of 'The Bachelor'" (para. 2). In Cuomo's case, viewership increased from "a few thousand" to "a peak of 961,700 ... not counting cable television" (Weiner, 2020, para. 4, 6). LaGatta (2020) noted that, in Ohio, "people left housebound by the virus are ... turning on their local news channels at an uncharacteristically high rate" (para. 8). According to LaGatta, "The numbers tell a story of self-isolated Ohioans who are making DeWine's regular briefings usually around 2 p.m. a routine part of their days. Some viewers even tune in with a glass of cabernet sauvignon and munchies on hand, sharing the experience on Twitter with the hashtags #WineWithDeWine and #SnackinWithActon" (para. 9).

Introduction

As I describe in this book, the Covid-19 pandemic of 2020 became more than public health efforts to control a potentially deadly disease. Instead, it morphed into a complicated conundrum of confusing, contradictory messages advanced and interpreted by adamant stakeholders with myriad agendas. When I first proposed this book project to McFarland in late March of 2020, I envisioned a book that would spotlight celebrities encouraging their fans to take the virus seriously as well as homebound individuals gravitating to government and public health officials as objects of their fandom. (Yes, I have a "Wine with DeWine" goblet now sitting on a shelf in my dining room.) I wanted to chronicle the touching, powerful, fan-like practices by grateful citizens in celebrating exhausted health care workers.

However, especially in the United States, fandom turned out to be more than a lighthearted dimension or fun distraction of the 2020 pandemic. In this book, I argue that fandom framed how individuals socially constructed their understanding of Covid-19 and their reactions to it, proving consequential for public health and individual well-being.

Here I introduce Covid-19 as the first pandemic in the postmodern era. After briefly highlighting the dramatic scope of this worldwide public health crisis, I will preview the confounding information crisis that extended from (and, in some cases, became exacerbated by) fan activity. I conclude this introduction with an overview of the book.

A Dismal Response

Just over 100 years ago, the world faced its last pandemic (see Arnold, 2020; Barry, 2018; Crosby, 2010). In his account of the "Great Influenza" (also commonly referenced as the "Spanish flu," even though it did not originate in Spain), Barry described the United States as a country with a formal public health infrastructure still in its infancy in terms of research capacity, authority to make policy recommendations, and even certification of medical professionals.

The 1918 influenza outbreak occurred as the United States was in the process of modernizing medicine (see Barry, 2018). However, 103 years later, the ineffective handling of Covid-19, particularly in the United States—with, arguably, one of the most highly sophisticated and advanced systems of medical expertise—shocked the world (Achenbach et al., 2020; Branswell, 2021; Gamillo, 2021; Lipton et al., 2020; Meyer, 2020; Osterholm & Kashkari, 2020; T.C. Williams, 2020). In July 2020, Meyer asserted that "[t]he American pandemic is careening out of control … with more than 52,000 new cases of the coronavirus, setting a new all-time daily record" (para. 1). Seven months later, the United States passed the grim milestone of over 500,000 deaths from the virus (Galocha & Berkowitz, 2021). Yong (2020, para. 2) argued that "[d]espite ample warning, the U.S. squandered every possible opportunity to control the coronavirus. And despite its considerable advantages—immense resources, biomedical might, scientific expertise—it floundered." In September 2021, the death toll for Covid-19 exceeded deaths during the 1918 Spanish flu, and the deaths continue to mount as I complete this book (Branswell, 2021; Gamillo, 2021).

According to Achenbach et al. (2020, para 17–18), "The death rate from covid-19 in the United States looks like that of countries with vastly lower wealth, health-care resources, and technological infrastructure. America's mishandling of the pandemic has defied most experts' predictions." Beech (2020, para. 4) reported reactions from global spectators, including one mayor in Canada who commented that "[p]ersonally, it's like watching the decline of the Roman Empire." As Beech explained, "Amid the pandemic and in the run-up to the presidential election, much of the world is watching the United States with a mix of shock, chagrin and, most of all, bafflement" (para. 5). Stunned, the world heard the White House economic adviser to the Trump administration remark that "we just have to live with" rampant spread of the virus (Mathis-Lilley, 2020, para. 3), and President Trump himself admitted during an Axios interview that the death toll simply "is what it is" (https://www.youtube.com/watch?v=tfbreIXsgIs; https://www.theguardian.com/us-news/2020/aug/04/donald-trump-interview-axios-covid-19-epstein-john-lewis).

The World Health Organization solemnly reported on October 15, 2021—22 months after the first cases in Wuhan became public—that nearly five million individuals around the world have died from Covid-19, with over 239 million individuals who have been diagnosed with the disease (https://covid19.who.int/), with health consequences ranging from those with life-altering, long-term effects and others who never experienced any symptoms at all (Hendrix, 2020). According to the Centers for Disease Control and Prevention, over 776,000 individuals have died from Covid-19 (with nearly 48 million cases) in the United States alone as of November 28, 2021 (https://covid.cdc.gov/covid-data-tracker/#trends_dailycases).

In all, the weak and inconsistent U.S. response disrupted hundreds of thousands of American lives in multiple ways. As Covid-19 permeated the country, it illuminated health disparities, especially in minority communities, and it underscored deep divides, with devastating consequences.

Disrupted Lives

The emotional, physical, economic, and educational impacts of the Covid-19 pandemic on American seniors, workers, families, and children cannot be understated. As individuals dealt with death, fear, and loss during the pandemic, mental health challenges increased (see Abbott, 2021), and they encountered restrictions on access to routine and preventative care as health care facilities tried to determine how to care for patients without spreading the virus (Chen & McGeorge, 2020). Chen and McGeorge argued that "[d]elayed or forgone care may already be driving alarming health trends, including excess deaths not attributed to COVID-19" (para. 2). Perhaps the most troubling and revealing statistic came with updated life expectancy projections in the United States falling "by a full year during the first half of 2020, a staggering decline that reflects the toll of the covid-19 pandemic as well as a rise in deaths from drug overdoses, heart attacks and diseases that accompanied the outbreak" (Bernstein, 2021, para. 1).

Beyond the catastrophic physical and mental toll, the pandemic thrust the United States into a dramatic economic decline (Irwin, 2020), closing businesses and catapulting millions into financial crisis and personal despair as they lost jobs and faced hunger and even eviction. The entertainment, travel, and food service industries (and their respective employees) struggled to survive as Covid restrictions kept many potential customers from buying theater or movie tickets, booking flights or staying in hotels, going to theme parks, or dining in restaurants (see AP News, 2020; P. Cohen, 2020). Bremmer (2020, para. 9) reported in *Time* that "the monetary-policy report submitted to Congress in June by the Federal Reserve noted that the 'severity, scope, and speed of the ensuing downturn in economic activity have been significantly worse than any recession since World War II'" (for related arguments, see also Barry, 2020; Long & Siegel, 2020).

In December 2020, Lange bemoaned that "[d]aily life may be unrecognizable from 10 months ago; we wear masks in stores, have kids learning on laptops at home, we pass more and more empty storefronts on Main Street" (para. 8). Children who cheered in the past for an occasional snow day in the winter found themselves at home for over a year. Teachers reimagined their classrooms as online spaces, a situation that exposed a vast digital divide—wherein some in the United States still lack consistent internet access—as well as the reliance on schools for childcare and, in some cases, food, nutrition, and safety (see, for example, Hodges, 2020). The debate over returning students and teachers to in-person learning sparked enormous discussions amid steep stakes—the need to rekindle the economy and restore preferred methods of instruction (and socialization and social support for students) versus public health concerns about how to do so safely (see, e.g., Linker, 2020; Strauss, 2021).

Health Disparities

In the United States, Covid-19 also illuminated considerable institutional and societal vulnerabilities, including the tragic handling of the virus in nursing homes. According to Hochman (2020, p. 8), "Residents of long-term care facilities constitute less than 1 percent of the U.S. population, yet 43 percent of all COVID-19 deaths through June occurred in those places. The number has changed little since."

The pandemic also took a terrible toll on communities of color (Batchlor, 2021; Bernstein, 2021; Conger et al., 2020; Haque, 2020; Khazan, 2020; Lee, 2020; Nirappil, 2020; Sacchetti, 2020; Wallis, 2020; Wilder, 2020; Yong, 2020). Wallis argued that "COVID-19 is cutting a jarring and unequal path across the U.S. The disease is disproportionately killing people of color, particularly Black Americans, who have been dying at more than twice the rate of white people" (para. 1). According to Bernstein, life expectancy for Black and Latino Americans fell between two and three times as much as their White counterparts. In her article, Wallis reported an interview with Dr. Camara Jones, a former president of the American Public Health Association, who asserted:

> Race doesn't put you at higher risk. *Racism* puts you at higher risk. It does so through two mechanisms: People of color are more infected because we are more exposed and less protected. Then, once infected, we are more likely to die because we carry a greater burden of chronic diseases from living in disinvested communities with poor food options [and] poisoned air and because we have less access to health care [para. 5].

Disparities also stem from distrust of the medical community. For example, Rusoja and Thomas (2021) pointed to "a historical legacy of exploitation and persecution at the hands of the US healthcare system which has affected generations of Black communities" (para. 4). Resulting skepticism has contributed to hesitancy regarding the Covid-19 vaccine. According to Rusoja and Thomas, "Early signs from the current vaccine rollout show Black Americans nationwide are receiving COVID vaccinations at half the rates of White Americans" (para. 2).

Deep Divides

This virus swept through families, church congregations, schools, factories, and towns (see, e.g., Levin, 2020; Levin & Taylor, 2020; Seiger, 2020). It made its way from New York City to Los Angeles, from the Midwest to the Gulf Coast, and from nursing homes to the White House (Gowen & Bailey, 2020). Covid-19 infected millions (see, e.g., Carino, 2020; Joyce, 2020). Countless people experienced no symptoms at all; others continue to suffer months after infection; hundreds of thousands died (Ables, 2020; Bernstein, 2020).

We will likely never know the names of all who contracted Covid-19, but some happened to be famous. Although those more prominent, wealthy individuals, including President Trump, tended to fare better with surviving, not all did (such as 41-year-old Broadway star Nick Cordero). Covid-19 took and touched lives across the globe and, especially, as it mercilessly and repeatedly spiked in the United States for over 18 months. Yet, as I will detail throughout this book, initial, hesitant efforts at a unified approach shattered quickly, cratering into deep divides amid ideological, economic, political, and religious constructions of a virus, with dire physical consequences (see, e.g., Leonhardt, 2021). Accordingly, individuals across the country encountered starkly varied lived realities across the United States as some heeded warnings about ICUs filled with Covid patients while others sought to continue life as it had always been pre–Covid.

Lange posed the following question in December of 2020: "[s]o why does everything feel so ... normal? Or perhaps not normal, but at least the same.... For many it seems increasingly difficult to muster genuine concern—at least if the pandemic has not touched you or your immediate loved ones directly and significantly" (para. 2). As Khazan (2020) sadly reflected, "'compassion fade' sets in when victims are no longer individuals but statistics" (para. 3).

Haque (2020) concurred, observing that "Americans seem to have largely tuned all this out" (see also Bellafante, 2020). As Brulliard reported, "A record-breaking surge in U.S. coronavirus cases is being driven to a significant degree by casual occasions that may feel deceptively safe ... dinner parties, game nights, sleepovers and carpools"—activities that wouldn't be risky at all, if not for a global pandemic (para. 1).

To revisit Lange's question, in the context of rampant death and economic devastation, why did some Americans continue life as it had been before without apparent concerns for personal or public health while others sheltered in place and canceled holiday celebrations? As I'll detail throughout this book, many factors contributed, but one key consideration merits foregrounding now—it depended on which voices that they chose to value.

The First Postmodern Pandemic

Winston Churchill cautioned that "those who fail to learn from history are likely doomed to repeat it." Sadly, even though we learned a great deal about public health in the 100 years that separated the influenza and Covid-19 pandemics, Americans did not seem to benefit from the haunting lessons from 1918 that should have underscored the importance of consistent, clear messaging as instrumental for preventing the spread of Covid-19 in the United States.

Echoes from 1918

Back in 1918, public health officials sought to communicate through means available at the moment—newspapers, handbills, and word of mouth (Arnold, 2018, Barry, 2018; Crosby, 2003). Arnold recounted that "[o]ver in Manchester, resourceful Chief Medical Officer of Health Dr. James Niven tackled the influenza epidemic with a formidable mixture of clinical experience and public information" (pp. 67–68). Arnold explained that Niven ordered "35,000 handbills printed and distributed to local factories and businesses, with information and instructions in clear plain English" (p. 68).

Crosby (2003, p. 19) recalled that "the United States didn't have the network of effective, well-financed federal, state, and local public health departments to put together what data did exist on influenza and pneumonia in the spring of 1918 to provide even a sketch of the epidemic." Instead, various officials across the country attempted to deal with desperate, dire local outbreaks amid meager and misleading federal influences.

Barry (2018) described mass illness, death, and despair in Philadelphia as "the city began to implode in chaos and fear" (p. 329). According to Barry, "The need was not only for medical care but for care itself.... There was no trust, no trust, and without trust all human relations were breaking down" (p. 330). Yet, the federal government persisted in "efforts to preserve 'morale'" (p. 333), not because of the pandemic but rather the U.S. involvement in World War I.

Although initially reluctant to send troops, after he decided to do so, President Woodrow Wilson swiftly shifted focus to demanding support for the war effort and American soldiers. Barry explained that "since the war began, morale—defined in the narrowest, most short-sighted fashion—had taken precedence in every public utterance" (2018, p. 334). According to Barry, "newspapers reported on the disease with the same mixture of truth and half-truth, truth and distortion, truth and lies with which they reported everything else. And no national official ever publicly acknowledged the danger of influenza" (p. 334).

Meanwhile, as influenza rates surged in San Francisco, local health officials desperately sought to emphasize the stressors on the overwhelmed health system and to enforce a mask mandate. They did so even though the "California State Board of Health announced that the flu situation wasn't serious enough to require such extraordinary measures as masking" (Crosby, 2003, p. 109). Crosby acknowledged that some 90 percent of residents in San Francisco refused to comply and that the local newspaper "allowed that nobody wanted to die, but was the death rate really high enough to justify remasking? Really, wasn't this return of flu mostly normal seasonal colds, plus 'scare'? And wasn't it probable that an order to wear masks would 'increase the scare'?" (p. 109).

As I read through accounts of the 1918 pandemic while concurrently living through the United States' response to Covid-19, I felt stunned and saddened. From government denials and deception to individual mask-wearing aversion ... from terror as the disease swept through communities to disbelief by other collections of citizens that Covid even exists, I realized that the United States had, indeed, been destined to repeat a long-forgotten public health crisis, rather than to have prepared by learning from it.

Problematizing "Truth"

Over 100 years after the influenza pandemic, many more methods of communicating exist, but, lacking clear and consistent messaging, communication about Covid-19 clouded understanding and confused those who happened to hear or read what had been shared. As this novel coronavirus spread through the city of Wuhan in China and then Europe and then the rest of the world, medical professionals, public health officials, political leaders, and citizens around the globe struggled to figure out how to prevent and treat Covid-19. From the very outset, though, for a plethora of political, organizational, and personal reasons, individuals sought to stifle, shape, embrace, and ignore information about this disease. I argue that, at the core, people in the United States struggled to discern what constituted "truth" about Covid-19.

Of course, the nature of "truth" has likely been a point of dispute for generations. However, the obstacles to understanding and processing information has arguably never been more challenging than in the postmodern era and, even more so now, given the advent of social media. Gergen (1991, p. 7) contended:

> The postmodern condition more generally is marked by a plurality of voices vying for the right to reality—to be accepted as legitimate expressions of the true and the good. As the voices expand in power and presence, all that seemed proper, right-minded, and well understood is subverted.... Under postmodern conditions, persons exist in a state of continuous construction and reconstruction; it is a world where anything goes that can be negotiated.

This societal context of fragmented, multiple realities proved especially problematic as various stakeholders fought over public platforms on which to proclaim "facts" about Covid-19, even as they tried to determine what they truly knew about the disease, how they wanted to frame that knowledge, and how they decided to respond. Indeed, as Gergen (1991, p. 134) continued, "[c]laims to truth and right … are more reasonably viewed as the constructions of communities with particular interests, values, and ways of life."

As I will detail in Chapter 1, in a related classic work, Fish (1980) argued that readers interpret texts based not on their unique perspectives as individuals but as members of "interpretive communities." Extending from Fish and Gergen, I suggest that such communities contextualized understandings of Covid-19 as individuals tried to discern what to make of this health situation and how to respond to it.

Quite notably, those communities did so in the context of competing messages that proved compelling, given messengers who got treated as trustworthy. As Cloud (2018, p. 33) argued persuasively, "truth is a function of standpoint or perspective in a system of power." In an era wherein prominent people routinely get paid to function as "influencers," others strive to attract as many social media "followers" as possible, and still others seek to position and persuade for political gain, it's no wonder that communities with shared "interests, values, and[/or] ways of life" (Gergen, 1991, p. 134) clashed over conflicting approaches and perspectives, especially in the void of consistent messaging from government officials. I agree with Cloud that "we can recognize the partial perspective different groups have on the truth and … hold rhetoric accountable to realities that are not universally shared but rather mutually debated" (p. 22).

As I reflect back on collecting data over the past year and a half, I'm struck by how the story of the Covid 19 pandemic emerged, evolved, and fractured as various people grappled with what to believe and what to do. Early disputes and discrepancies in the scientific community worked to fuel confusion (and then conspiracy theories) about whether the virus was airborne (Klein, 2020; Klepper, 2020; Mandavilli, 2020; L.C. Marr, 2020), whether masks really work to mitigate spread (AP, 2020; Rinker, 2020), whether anti-malaria drugs could be viable treatments (Gabler & Rabin, 2020), and, eventually, whether vaccines for Covid-19 should be considered as safe and effective (see, e.g., Chiu & Bever, 2021; Stecklow & MacAskill, 2021).

In the U.S., the CDC, "long considered the world's premier health agency, made early testing mistakes that contributed to a cascade of problems.... It failed to provide timely counts of infections and deaths, hindered by aging technology and a fractured public health reporting system. And it hesitated in absorbing the lessons of other countries, including the perils of silent carriers spreading the infection" (Lipton et al., 2020, para. 6). According to Lipton et al., "In communicating to the public, its leadership was barely visible, its stream of guidance was often slow and its messages were sometimes confusing, sowing mistrust" (para. 7). (Notably, as I detail in Chapter 3, the House Select Subcommittee on the Coronavirus Crisis released emails, records, and testimony that document Trump White House influence that constrained the CDC's messaging about Covid-19; see Banco, 2021; Viglione, 2021.)

Noar and Austin (2020, p. 1735) argued that "[a] well-crafted national message had the potential to build unity around the goal of defeating the virus through behavior change, preferably with clear, unambiguous recommendations of what actions to take. Unfortunately, no such federal effort was undertaken, which amounted to a missed opportunity to galvanize public will to prevent the spread of the virus." As in a garden that has not been diligently tended, a plethora of voices sprang up to fill the void of clear, consistent messaging from scientific and government officials (see Harrington, 2020; Noar & Austin, 2020). Conspiracy theories suggested that the Covid-19 death toll had been exaggerated (Durkee, 2020), that Covid-19 vaccines will cause great harm (Pleat, 2020), and that hydroxychloroquine cures Covid (Novak, 2020). A video named "'Plandemic' went online May 4 ... gathered steam in Facebook pages dedicated to conspiracy theories and the anti-vaccine movement ... tipped into the mainstream and exploded" (Frenkel et al., 2020, para. 4). According to Frenkel et al., "Just over a week after 'Plandemic' was released, it had been viewed more than eight million times on YouTube, Facebook, Twitter and Instagram, and had generated countless other posts" (para. 5).

Another video then surpassed "Plandemic" by featuring a group of individuals who declared themselves to be "America's Frontline Doctors" and promoted the effectiveness of hydroxychloroquine and discouraged mask-wearing (Andrews & Paquette, 2020; Frenkel & Alba, 2020; Robins-Early et al., 2020). According to Frenkel and Alba, "It went viral, shared largely through Facebook groups dedicated to anti-vaccination movements and conspiracy theories such as QAnon, racking up tens of millions of views. Multiple versions of the video were uploaded to YouTube, and links were shared through Twitter" (para. 2). Harrington (2020, p. 1715) acknowledged the long history of conspiracy theories but asserted that "their potential spread and impact on public opinion and public health in light of the coronavirus pandemic seem far worse today."

Although mainstream, traditional news outlets (such as CBS, ABC, NBC, CNN, Fox News) certainly reported on the pandemic (see Head et al., 2020a, 2020b), coverage varied (Budak et al., 2021). Based on their analysis of that coverage, Budak et al. concluded that "Fox News covered the virus's origins, consequences and treatments differently than the other two cable networks." As Stelter (2020, p. 294) reported, "Fox's overarching storyline was set: The damn Democrats were unfairly using the virus as a cudgel against Trump." Stelter argued that "[t]his 'coronavirus is being weaponized' message whipped all around right-wing media, from Rush Limbaugh's radio show to Donald Trump Jr.'s Twitter feed and back to *Fox & Friends* and *Hannity*. Some Trump allies accused [other] news outlets of covering the coronavirus just to wound Trump" (p. 294). As just one example, Chiu (2020) reported that "[j]ust hours after World Health Organization officials said they are preparing for a 'potential pandemic' as coronavirus cases increase worldwide, conservative radio host Rush Limbaugh told his listeners [that] 'It looks like the coronavirus is being weaponized as yet another element to bring down Donald Trump'" (para. 1–2).

After President Biden's inauguration in January 2021, Dr. Anthony Fauci admitted on *Face the Nation* that "I think if we had had the public health messages from the top right through down to the people down in the trenches be consistent, that things might have been different" (West, 2021, para. 1). Instead, the hesitancies, inconsistencies, and, in some cases, downright lies ignited the postmodern explosion of contradictory and erroneous messages across myriad platforms (see, e.g., Guynn, 2020; Sullivan, 2020; Weise & Weintraub, 2020). Weiss and Weintraub reported that "scientists and physicians reacted with words such as 'aghast,' 'despicable' and 'outrageous' ... as news spread that White House appointees interfered with a basic national public health report when it conflicted with President Donald Trump's coronavirus messaging" (para. 1). As Cloud (2018, p. 24) noted, "[b]eyond the recognition that social scientists could be better persuaders, a number of social theorists have pointed out that 'facts' are social constructs that aid the powerful in the exertion of their interests."

Soon after Julia Roberts experienced her "fan girl" moment over Dr. Anthony Fauci, the medical community began its fight for credibility against its own federal government, with American lives on the line. Harrington (2020) argued:

> We are in the midst of a global pandemic, with no end in sight. We are facing an onslaught of misinformation and disinformation in both mainstream and social media sources about the virus that has caused the pandemic. And we have to convince a fearful, uncertain, and often ignorant public to accept evidence-based guidelines for protecting their health and stopping the spread of the virus—when a large segment of this public seems immune to facts and reason [p. 1715].

Unfortunately, of course, the problem involved the co-definition of what constitutes "facts," "reason," "evidence," and "truth." With so many competing and even convincing voices, how do individuals decide what "rings true"? (see W. Fisher, 1984, p. 8). If those with whom we align (i.e., our interpretive communities) provide purportedly "reasonable" alternate information (or, in the words of one Trump adviser, "alternative facts"), why not trust it as opposed to the so-called experts? According to Cloud (2018, p. 17), "rhetoric moves claims about reality and truth into the prevailing social constructs of reality and enables different groups' knowledge to register as common sense in the public imagination."

As I'll detail throughout this book, fandom played an instrumental role in how Covid-19 unfolded in the United States because certain communities elevated celebrities—including President Trump, media personalities, actors, athletes, musicians, etc.—as credible sources for medical information over actual public health experts. Moreover, even as Covid cases soared and as hospitals filled and people died, claims still filled the public sphere to the contrary. As just one illustration, Limbaugh led the way in downplaying Covid-19 soon after the first case was noted in the United States, assuring millions of daily listeners that "[t]he coronavirus is the common cold, folks" on his February 24, 2020, radio broadcast (Chiu, 2020, para. 2; see also Moser, 2021).

Even after President Trump had to be hospitalized due to a serious case of Covid-19 eight months later, that narrative remained unchanged. According to Haberman and Thomas (2020, para. 4), "Mr. Trump did his best to play down the virus's effects." As Aronson and Tavris (2020, para. 2) noted, "when the facts clash with their preexisting convictions, some people would sooner jeopardize their health and everyone else's than accept new information or admit to being wrong." Gergen (1991, p. 94) explained:

> Thus, we find steadily mounting suspicion of the objective truths of science, or of any other group that proclaims the truth of its language. To claim superiority of position on the basis of factual accuracy is specious, for accounts of "the way the world is" don't grow from nature but from the application of a socially shared perspective.... What is "objectively" true depends, then, not on what is the case, but on the community in which one happens to participate. And in light of the increasing availability of "other voices," we find an increasing range of "other truths."

Consequences of Covid Convictions

Those truths—actually, "our" truth (what we believe to be true)—about Covid have inspired commitment and investment as individuals behave in ways that align with their beliefs. As D. Park (2020, para. 5) described, "This feels so personal—because no matter what side your beliefs fall on right now, you feel threatened." She continued by noting that "I have a close friend who is breaking my heart right now. She keeps talking about how things aren't really that bad ... and the doctors are handling this all wrong, because 'what's really killing all these COVID-19 patients are the ventilators they're being put on'" (para. 7).

Clinically, a person does not need to "believe in" Covid-19 in order to die from it. Froelich (2020) reported that "[a] Texas millennial died after attending a 'COVID party' and later contracting the virus. 'I thought it was a hoax,' the patient who was in their 30s, told their nurse moments before passing away" (para. 1–2). Jodi Doering, an emergency room nurse in South Dakota, tweeted about her experience with patients who remain in denial about Covid (and then appeared in subsequent interviews on news outlets such as CNN). Falk (2020) reported:

> People severely ill with COVID-19 are flooding her hospital, suffering also from an extreme case of cognitive dissonance: They'd been told the pandemic was a concoction of the fake news media. "They tell you there must be another reason they are sick," an exhausted Doering recounted on Twitter this week. Even while gasping for breath, she says, the patients insist they don't have COVID because it's not real. The delusional talk only stops when these patients get intubated or die. "It's like a f—ing horror movie that never ends," Doering says [para. 1].

Overview of Book

This book tells the story of how people came to believe and behave as they did through the lens of fandom (and interpretive communities that emerged through fan activity). As this introduction has explained, especially in this era, the near-constant bombardment of messages on a multiplicity of diverse mediated platforms permeated our respective and collective worlds at a time when many could not be out in the world.

Two undergraduate research assistants (who worked with me during Summer 2020 on special research grants through the Ohio University Honors College) and I collected over 500 popular press articles as well as over 1,500 pages of social media posts on Twitter, Facebook, and Instagram. We searched for media accounts of reactions to public officials as they issued policies, guidelines, recommendations, and even pleas to their constituents. We followed leads of those reactions and searched for social media posts about those public officials and explored fan Facebook pages that admirers established for them (such as "Wine with DeWine" for Governor DeWine in Ohio and "Dr. Birx's Scarves" for Dr. Deborah Birx, who served as the coronavirus response coordinator for the White House Coronavirus Task Force). In all, we collected data about individuals at the international level (such as leaders from New Zealand, Great Britain, Canada, South Korea, and Brazil), national level (such as President Trump, Dr. Fauci, Dr. Redfern, the surgeon general, Dr. Birx), governors, state public health directors, judges, and local public health officials with policies or practices regarding Covid-19 covered in the news. I also read relevant books that have been released pertaining to Covid 19, public officials, and news outlets.

Notably, we followed similar search strategies for identifying and documenting media coverage of and social media posts about nonpublic official celebrities (such as actors, singers, performers, athletes, etc.) who hosted fundraising events, shared their personal experiences with Covid-19, and/or engaged in support or advocacy efforts. Finally, we also pursued popular press and social media activity pertaining to fandom of first responders and frontline workers.

I value the contributions of Will Bower and Nora McKeown, the undergraduate research assistants, during Summer 2020, and I invited both to continue to work with me as we entered the fall semester of 2020. Will elected to do an independent study with me during Fall 2020, and we coauthored a convention paper that focused on U.S. government officials, which we presented at the 2021 Central States Communication Association convention. That paper served as the foundation for what eventually expanded into Chapter 3 of this book. I asked both Will and Nora to join me as coauthors of this book, but both opted to focus on other projects and interests and declined my invitation. I appreciated the weekly conversations that we had via Zoom that summer as well as the data that they collected during the initial months of the pandemic.

Acknowledging that Covid-19 has been a deeply personal and emotional experience for each of us and that it also became politically charged, we engaged in reflexivity and discussed our own reactions to the data throughout that summer. As the project continued beyond Fall 2020, I thought often about how much that I missed talking with Will and Nora about the emergent Covid-19 public health narratives.

Because the story of how Covid-19 unfolded in the United States took a distinctive turn from other locations in the world, this book focuses on the implications of celebrity and fandom for competing public health narratives about Covid-19 that got constructed and perpetuated in the United States from March 2020 to November 2021. Stories about the development of concurrent Covid-19 narratives in other parts of the world should be told, and I hope to do so in a subsequent project.

Chapter 1 provides a foundation for understanding fan communities as socially constructed, dynamic, emergent collections of individuals who admire a person, show, or team. The immediacy of social media has worked to intensify parasocial relationships between fans and objects of their fandom, blurring boundaries and bolstering allegiances.

In Chapter 2, I begin our exploration of fandom and Covid-19 by spotlighting sports. As I'll detail, the saga of sports during the pandemic mirrored prevalent societal reactions to the virus, and sports organizations, teams, and prominent athletes provided powerful contributions to the emerging discourse on dealing with this disruption to life as we had known it prior to Covid.

In Chapter 3, I describe how the pandemic became politicized and explicate the consequential role of then-president Donald J. Trump (a former reality TV star) in framing Covid-19 for his millions of Twitter followers and fans. The politicalization of Covid-19 dramatically impacted the approaches of other government officials at national, state, and local levels in addressing the virus and encouraging public health initiatives. I argue that the treatment of public officials as objects of fandom fueled not only emergent narratives but also the deep divide as a function of anti-fandom.

In Chapter 4, I delve into the important contributions of celebrities to public conversations about Covid-19. Powerful personal accounts from celebrities such as Tom Hanks and Rita Wilson drew attention to this brand-new health threat. Other celebrities sought to raise money for those who were impacted or to bring some simple joy to those who were stuck at home and missing major life milestones. Still others tried to educate and inspire health practices that would mitigate the disease. Importantly, their contributions both indicated their own status as members of a particular interpretive community and encouraged fans to embrace the preferred perspective.

I close the book by offering final reflections about how fandom and celebrity became such an integral part of the story of Covid-19, extending beyond those who sought the public spotlight to those who, quite literally, worked tirelessly behind secure doors to save lives. Medical practitioners and public health professionals scrambled to figure out how to deal with the disease and prevent its spread, and, as the pandemic ensued, a grateful public hailed them as heroes for helping to save lives. Yet, I will detail, we also witnessed the "dark side" of fandom as all too many eventually left their jobs as health care providers, exhausted by fighting not only the virus but also rampant misinformation.

CHAPTER 1

Framing Our Stories through Fandom

In her book, Amanda Kloots, a fitness expert (and subsequently co-host of CBS' *The Talk* and contestant on *Dancing with the Stars*), tells the story of her life with and loss of her husband, Nick Cordero, a Tony-nominated Broadway star (Kloots & Kloots, 2021). In mid–March 2020, Kloots posted a happy family photo of herself, Cordero, and their infant son, Elvis, on Instagram. Only a few weeks later, Cordero—a healthy, fit, 41-year-old actor who danced and sang his way through theatrical productions on a daily basis—landed in the hospital, struggling to breathe (Messer & Kindelan, 2020).

Covid interjected itself into their lives as they were moving from New York to Los Angeles, and she confided that "[w]e had been through a lot physically, emotionally, and even mentally while trying to decide whether it was safe to fly back to LA. We were jet-lagged and exhausted. When Nick first said that he was feeling fatigued on Friday morning, I thought, *Yeah—me too*" (Kloots & Kloots, 2021, p. 9). Kloots explained that their experience during the pandemic mirrored that of others at first: "We watched the news every evening, like everyone else in the world. It was the first time in modern history when everyone, everywhere, was going through the same thing.... We found ourselves glued to the news—just waiting for more information" (p. 9). She confided that "information seemed reputable. 'Tired' wasn't a symptom. It was daily reassurance that Nick was safe" (p. 9)—until the day that he passed out and she had to drop him at the entrance to the hospital.

Still, even though they chose for Nick to get checked out at the hospital, neither was prepared for what would happen next. Kloots confided:

> It was clear he had something, but we weren't thinking that there was any possibility of his being admitted. We thought that I was dropping him off

for an hour, maybe two. I had no idea that would be the last time I would ever see him as *him*. He was never the same again. He woke up, but he never really came back [Kloots & Kloots, 2021, p. 13].

For a little over four months, Amanda Kloots chronicled her husband's battle with Covid-19. On April 1, 2020, Kloots posted on Instagram that "he is scared, in the ICU, and now unconscious so his body can get enough oxygen ... this has gone from bad to worse" (https://www.instagram.com/p/B-cCAl_gjtC/?hl=en). In another Instagram post on May 8, 2020 (that garnered over 121,000 reactions to date), Kloots shared:

> What this man has gone through.... He went to the ER on March 30 and intubated on a ventilator on April 1. Since then he has suffered an infection that caused his heart to stop, he needed resuscitation, he had two mini strokes, went on ECMO, went on dialysis, needed surgery to [remove] an ECMO cannula that was restricting blood flow to his leg, a [fasciotomy] to relieve pressure on the leg, an amputation of his right leg, an MRI to further investigate brain damage, several bronchial sweeps to clear out his lungs, a septis infection causing septic shock, a fungus in his lungs, holes in his lungs, a tracheostomy, blood clots, low blood count and platelet levels, and a temporary pacemaker to assist his heart. He has spent 38 days now in the ICU. [https://www.instagram.com/p/B_8qYEogmw7/?hl=en]

Through her posts, Kloots confided anguishing details about her husband's medical saga (as well as heartwarming videotaped "Nick stories") with her over 654,000 followers on Instagram that got referenced in related media coverage of Cordero's illness saga (see, e.g., Kloots & Kloots, 2021; Lenthang & Johnson, 2020; Messer & Kindelan, 2020; Pasquini & Chung, 2020; Truitt, 2020; K.J. Wu, 2000). Sadly, on July 5, Kloots revealed that "God has gained another angel in heaven now.... I am in disbelief and hurting everywhere," a post that has attained nearly 603,000 reactions thus far (https://www.instagram.com/p/CCSBM89Axt_/?hl=en).

Through Kloots's quite public and raw disclosures, she spotlighted Nick Cordero's tragic illness narrative by bringing it out of a lonely hospital room and onto center stage as fans and followers interacted about their own experiences, collectively mourned his loss, and supported his widow and young son. Cordero's story mattered, not just for himself and Kloots and little Elvis, but for many who heard and connected with it. I begin this chapter by describing the importance of health narratives, in general. I then provide a theoretical argument about the consequentiality of celebrity health narratives (especially amid postmodern fandom and celebrity culture) for public conversations about health.

The Significance of Health Narratives

As I was researching this book, I spent some time on Kloots's Instagram, and I was especially drawn to the "Nick stories" (https://www.instagram.com/stories/highlights/17947586530341559/). For example, in one video, Amanda recounted how Nick had never figured out how to jump rope, something important to her, given her fitness work. They had broken up, and he wanted to get back together so he made a point of learning how to jump rope. As Kloots told the story, she became emotional. She presented that memory as a powerful moment in their relationship; it communicated something about Nick and about her and about them. It didn't just happen; it came to symbolize something for them and for her. In this section, I describe narratives as pervasive and impactful as well as consequential in health contexts.

Narratives as Pervasive and Impactful

In his description of the narrative paradigm, Walter Fisher (1984) argued that humans are implicitly storytellers as "symbols are created and communicated ultimately as stories meant to give order to human experience" (p. 6). Fisher contended that "human communication should be viewed as historical as well as situational, as stories competing with other stories for good reasons, as being rational when they satisfy the demands of narrative probability and narrative fidelity, and as inevitably moral inducements" (p. 2).

We experience and craft myriad stories as we go through a day—the one about a workplace conversation, the one about a noteworthy interaction with an especially kind customer service representative, the one in reaction to stories that we saw or read in the news. Our processing and recounting of those moments reveal and reflexively shape who we are and our relationships to others (see, e.g., Brockmeier & Carbaugh, 2001a, 2001b; Gubrium & Hostein, 2009; Hostein & Gubrium, 2000; Langellier & Peterson, 2004).

Moreover, as Brockmeier and Carbaugh (2001a, p. 12) stressed, "stories are collective or collaborative productions that not only take place under particular social conditions, but are social actions." As such, individual stories implicitly become embedded in broader narratives of our individual lives and, potentially, flavor those of communities as the stories, in and of themselves, function powerfully in a plethora of ways. Details of a story can affirm or alter preferred identities, define or perpetuate relationships, share information, and, along with that other communicative work, even contribute to and shape emergent, concurrent narratives in community or public spheres (see, e.g., Beck et al., 2015; Harter et al. 2005a, 2005b). To extend from Sigman's (1995, p. 1) assertion that "[c]ommunication matters," I argue that stories matter greatly too, especially in the health context.

Health Narratives as Consequential

In the late 1990s, I experienced a health crisis following a wrist reconstruction. As I detail in my book, that saga comprised not only one that threatened my health and jeopardized my life; my fight to survive the ensuing staph infection (a postoperative complication) became one in which I sought agency, control, and voice (Beck, 2001). After over a decade of studying health communication by then, during that months long saga, I realized more than ever about the integral nature of each detail, every interaction, all choices that factored into the emergent narrative that enveloped my life as I fought for it. That realization fueled my interest in telling my story and helping others to understand contemporary acute health care as a set of medical mazes.

Until I became immersed in a medical situation in which doctors could not explain symptoms and attempted to characterize them as imagined, I truly had no context for grasping the terror and frustration of others in defining mental and physical states as I simply sought help in returning to what had felt "normal" for me.

My story mattered. The framing of details as I experienced the recovery process mattered. The medical, identity, and relational work that became embedded into that health narrative mattered. Both as I lived that story and then told it afterword, I came to understand even more that my voice mattered. I would not allow for it to be silenced by institutional policies, procedures, practices, or preferences (see Beck, 2001). As Frank (1995, p. 18) explained, "the storyteller seeks to reclaim her own experience of suffering. As she seeks to turn that suffering into testimony, the storyteller engages in moral action."

Regardless of the extent to which a storyteller shares that story with broader audiences, the details and implications of the story matter for the person and for that individual's health and well-being (see, e.g., Beck et al., 2015; Frank, 1995; Harter et al., 2005a, 2005b; Hoppin, 2016; Kleinman, 1988; Segal, 2005). Extrapolating health care experiences from the commitments to a more modernist, biomedical model, Frank argued that "[t]he postmodern divide is crossed when people's own stories are no longer told as secondary but have their primary importance.... Postmodern illness is an experience, a reflection on body, self, and the destination that life's map leads to" (p. 7). Embracing the importance of health narratives shifts agency and power to the individual who is experiencing a health challenge—someone who does not need to be relegated to the role of "patient" with a body part to be repaired but instead as a whole person crafting the meaning of the health issue within the context of the person's life and lived reality (see Frank, 1995; Harter et al., 2005a, 2005b).

Although not the person undergoing treatment for Covid-19, Amanda Kloots narrated not only her husband's journey with the disease but also her own as partner and caregiver (see, e.g., Kloots & Kloots, 2021; Lenthang & Johnson, 2020; Rosman, 2021). As I noted earlier, Kloots chronicled the physical complications of Cordero's illness as well as stressed the emotional toll as a central component of their story. How could an extremely healthy, active, fit person be stricken so hard? How could these developments be part of their life story?

She considered these questions and others on Instagram, inviting thousands and then millions into her story as well. In so doing, a friend commented that "Amanda was waking up the world to what was happening. In the prime of his life, a man who did eight shows a week with strength and vigor could be taken down by this disease" (Rosman, 2021, para. 33). As Frank (1995, p. 17) explained, "People tell stories not just to work out their own changing identities, but also to guide others who will follow them. They seek not to provide a map that can guide others—each must create his own—but rather to witness the experience of reconstructing one's own map." Rosman noted that "[o]n Instagram, for hundreds of thousands of people glued to their phones and searching for guidance, Ms. Kloots gave voice to the agonies, anxieties and isolation suffered by those whose loved ones were infected by the virus" (para. 5).

The Significance of Celebrity Health Narratives for Covid-19

Kloots's story provides a compelling example of a health narrative. It also exemplifies a special sort of one—a celebrity health narrative. In our prior book on celebrity health narratives, my colleagues and I asserted that "celebrities have long captivated public attention, and, with ever expanding and diversified mediated accessibility to public figures, those in the spotlight must implicitly wrestle with what to share, what to conceal, and why and how to do so" (Beck et al., 2015, p. 5). Building on that earlier work, this book details how celebrity health narratives played a central role in shaping emergent (and, often, competing) public health narratives about Covid-19.

Before examining individual stories that combined to construct those more master narratives later in this book, though, I devote the remainder of this chapter to providing an essential theoretical foundation for just how those stories became so impactful and integral during the progression of the disease and public interpretation of it. I begin by explaining the notion of interpretive communities. I then describe how fans constitute members of interpretive communities and conclude the chapter by discussing the implications of celebrity fandom for framing health decision-making for members of their respective interpretive fan communities.

Interpretive Communities

Fish (1980, p. 284) wisely observed that "[a] sentence is never not in a context. We are never not in a situation. A statute is never not read in the light of some purpose. A set of interpretive assumptions is always in force. A sentence that seems to need no interpretation is already the product of one." As individuals make sense of their world (and the myriad minute moments and details of it), they necessarily engage in the process of interpreting and sense-making. My mom used to routinely comment, "Well, that's just common sense." Fish would likely counter that "common sense" depends greatly on what happens to be "common to" particular people at certain times in specific situations.

An integral part of a person's sense-making framework involves what Fish (1980) referred to as "interpretive communities" (pp. 14–16). Extending from Fish, I suggest that such communities can comprise individuals who share values, beliefs, interests, perspectives, and/or goals. For example, members of a religious community likely share convictions; children from a close family might hold similar perspectives about the value of education or work ethic, and members of a sports team might enact common treatment of practice or approach to a game. According to K. Gergen (1994, p. 74), "participants in each community develop their own practices, rituals, or patterns of relationship. Within one community certain 'events' are selected out, given names, and treated in various ways." Thus, drawing from Gergen, through their language selections and actions, those in a community socially construct "facts," preferences, and meaning. As one illustration, some media scholars have discussed the implications of interpretive communities for audiences of mediated texts (see, e.g., related arguments by Ang, 1996; Lindlof, 1988; Livingston, 1990).

However, I would argue that the notion of "interpretive communities" should not be envisioned as singular or static. In contemporary life, we likely align with multiple interpretive communities as we experience our hectic, multifaceted lives, juggling various (and not always fully compatible) roles and enacting multiple, often fragmented identities. Indeed, perhaps "community" has never been so convenient or so complicated as in the era of social media. With the click of a key, we can connect, quite literally, with others around the globe (see, e.g., Shumow, 2015; Van Dijck, 2013). Of course, as Shumow observed, we also continue to communicate concurrently with others in physical spaces as well. According to Shumow, "[t]he spaces we occupy and to which we give meaning have not lost relevance or contextual complexity in the digital age. In many ways, they are more important than ever as the lines between the virtual and the real become blurred" (p. 7).

In this postmodern era, we straddle multiple contexts, exploring various dimensions of ourself and participating in multiple simultaneous communities, both on and off-line (see, e.g., Baym, 2010; Bennett & Robards, 2014; boyd, 2014; K. Gergen, 1991; Gray et al., 2017; Highfield et al., 2013; Jenkins, 2008; Jenkins et al., 2016; Shumow, 2015). According to Gergen, "The technologies of social saturation expose us to an enormous range of persons, new forms of relationship, unique circumstances and opportunities, and special intensities of feelings" (p. 69), giving us insight into "knowing how" (p. 70) others envision the world that can then inform our own perspectives and choices. As Gergen explained, "In memory we carry others' patterns of being with us. If the conditions are favorable, we can place these patterns into action" (p. 71). By understanding our process of knowledge construction as (a) not considering "facts" as external truths and (b) not contingent on strictly one interpretive community, we can appreciate diverse potential influences on the sense-making process, with varying weight depending on which identity that we opt to highlight at any given time under fluid circumstances.

Fan Communities

In this book, I argue that fans constitute unique and important interpretive communities (for related work, please see Barton & Lampley, 2014; Baym, 2000; Booth, 2015; Duffett, 2013; Gray et al., 2017; Hellekson & Busse, 2006; Hills, 2002; Hinck, 2019; Jenkins, 2013; Stanfill, 2013; Stein, 2015), especially with the ways in which the Covid-19 pandemic unfolded in the United States. As Sandvoss et al. (2017, p. 5) argued, "fans' interpretive communities (as well as individual acts of fan consumption) are embedded in existing social and cultural conditions." Subsequent chapters in this book will elaborate how objects of fandom, particularly celebrities, powerfully contributed to public dialogues about Covid-19, infusing information (and, sometimes, misinformation) and perspectives that worked to influence how fan communities came to understand the virus as well as the viability of responses to it. Sandvoss et al. asserted that "[f]andom has emerged as an ever more integral aspect of lifeworlds, and an important interface between the dominant micro and macro forces of our time" (p. 6).

Relational Nature of Fandom

I maintain that fandom became even more consequential during the pandemic because of its implicitly *relational* nature. In other words, being a "fan" does not merely entail admiration of something, even though, of course, it includes such activity. Hills (2002, p. ix) explained that "[e]verybody knows what a 'fan' is. It's somebody who is obsessed with a particular star, celebrity, film, TV programme, band; somebody who can produce reams of information on their object of fandom, and can quote their favoured lines or lyrics, chapter and verse." However, Hills also underscored that "[f]ans interpret media texts in a variety of interesting and perhaps unexpected ways. And fans participate in communal activities—they are not 'socially atomised' or isolated viewers/readers" (p. ix).

As such, fans' engagement with texts (which I would build on Hills's characterization by defining more broadly as any mediated print material, physical artifact, or public performance) constitutes a process of relating in the context of being a "fan." For example, our family loves Disney. When we visit "the Most Magical Place on Earth," we dive wholeheartedly into a land wherein we enthusiastically embrace the honor of meeting royalty when gaining an audience with a Disney princess, and we love opportunities to "talk with" Mickey and Minnie, never questioning the experience of encountering approximately five-feet-tall mice. Notably, we gain affirmation of our preference to "not kill the magic" (i.e., ruin the moment by referencing "reality") from thousands of other like-minded guests who also journey through the Magic Kingdom behaving similarly toward our Disney "friends," adorning their heads with creatively decorated ears, wearing Disney-themed attire, and eating an assortment of food items in the shape of a Mickey head.

Booth (2015, p. 3) noted that "[t]raditionally, scholars have tended to understand fandom either as an identity (fans are people who have an emotional attachment to a media text) or as a practice (fans are people who produce their own meanings and texts)." However, Sandvoss et al. (2017, p. 11) observed "duality of community *and* identity" as a hallmark of the "third wave of fan studies." Yes, individuals consider themselves to be fans, with implications for part of their respective, unique identities, *and* that fandom positions fans as part of a collection of like-minded people who engage with the object of fandom with similar perspectives and actions.

Because fans relate to and with the object of their fandom, the act of fandom encompasses more than a simple appreciation of it. Of course, not all fandom involves actions as immersive as wearing Mickey ears around a theme park or attending a Comic-Con or *Star Trek* convention in character, but it does imply an investment beyond merely not changing the channel if *Toy Story 2* or an episode of *Star Trek* pops up on the television screen. Importantly for this project, being a fan of something—whether a sports team, a radio show, a celebrity, or even a politician—both suggests and requires identification (see related work by K. Burke, 1950/1969) *as* a particular sort of fan through the corresponding actions, activities, connections, reactions, and reflections deemed appropriate to and by those in that fan community (see related work by Fish, 1981; Goffman 1959). As K. Burke noted, "A is not identical with his colleague, B. But insofar as their interests are joined, A is *identified* with B" (p. 20).

For example, as sports fans enthusiastically cite facts about a preferred sports team (see, e.g., Aden, 2007) or soap opera fans recall the rich history of a decades-old daytime drama (see, e.g., Baym, 2000), they make themselves available to other fans of those respective teams or soap operas (as well as to themselves and to nonfans) *as* legitimate fans through the display of knowledge and behaviors consistent with the particular fan community (see related work by Fish, 1980; Goffman, 1959). These socially constructed performances work rhetorically to reify what constitutes "knowledgeable," "committed," and "true" for that fan community as well as situates members in broader contexts (see related work on social constructionism by K. Gergen, 1994, 1999). Hills (2002, p. xi) argued that "fandom ... is ... always performative; by which I mean that it is an identity which is (dis-)claimed, and which performs cultural work. Claiming the status of a 'fan' may, in certain contexts, provide a cultural space for types of knowledge and attachment."

Anti-Fandom

As I will detail throughout the remainder of this book, being a "fan" in a particular fan community mattered for the ways in which individuals oriented toward both Covid-19 as well as to others who held diverse perspectives. I argue that the expressions of deep opposition to divergent Covid approaches extend from involvement in an interpretive community with a polar-opposite position than another. Drawing from Burke (1950/1969), "[i]dentification is affirmed with earnestness precisely because there is division.... For one need not scrutinize the concept of identification very sharply to see, implied in it at every turn, its ironic counterpart: division" (pp. 22–23).

Thus, just as some individuals align based on their mutual admiration for a person or text, others share a common dislike of that same person or text (see, e.g., Blodgett, 2020; Click, 2019; Dutton et al., 2011; Geraghty, 2018; Gray, 2005; Gray et al., 2017; Proctor, 2018; Proctor & Kies, 2018; Reinhard, 2018; Serazio & Thorson, 2020). According to Gray, "Hate or dislike of a text can be just as powerful as a strong and admiring, affective relationship with a text, and they can produce just as much activity, identification, meaning, and 'effects' or serve just as powerfully to unite and sustain a community or subculture" (p. 841).

Indeed, as I elaborate regarding Covid-19, expressions of support for mask-wearing or vaccinations got advanced through interpretive communities comprising celebrities and fans. Implicitly (and, often, explicitly) those same expressions became also constructed as critiques of the counter position, and both perspectives got fueled as mediated messages by various proponents on both sides went "viral." Click (2019, p. 7) argued that "[t]he emergence of digital culture, or what Henry Jenkins calls 'convergence culture,' has facilitated the growth and visibility of public expressions of dislike and hatred as well as the growth and visibility of anti-fans themselves." Hills (2018, para. 15) labeled such negativity as "toxic fandom" and contended that it could "render explicit, visible and conscious, logics of disparagement and (de-)legitimation that are structured into the very relationality of fan identities." In short, by "othering" those who advance a divergent viewpoint, fan communities implicitly solidified their own stance, symbolically "digging in their heels."

Celebrity Fandom

In her October 11, 2021, Instagram post, Kloots previewed her performance for Disney night on *Dancing with the Stars*:

> Tonight we dance the rumba to "You'll Be in My Heart" by Phil Collins. This song is about protection and love. It's said that Phil started writing it as a lullaby for his daughter before finishing it for the movie Tarzan. You can imagine how much I relate to this song and the lyrics. Raising Elvis unexpectedly alone created a bond between us that "can't be broken." The first time I saw Elvis after Nick passed I grabbed him in my arms and told him,

"It's just the two of us now. You and me." We then fell asleep together and cuddled for three hours straight. He didn't move from my side, I didn't move from his.

There's an unspoken language between us. We are a team, in this fight together. I will always do anything and everything I can for him. He is my hero [https://www.instagram.com/p/CU5P-YZpiTL/?hl=en].

One fan commented on the post that "I lost my husband when my son was 1 and this has always been my song for him. Right after the accident, I clung to him in the exact same way, it was like we were survivors together and our bond is still so strong and completely [its] own because of it. Good luck, with the dance & your beautiful boy!" Another commiserated that "[m]y mom passed away from cancer when I was about 8 years old. I remember seeing this movie in theaters with her. And even though it's been almost 20 years, I still cry when I hear this song, because her presence is so prevalent. I love that this is the song you got!"

Although celebrities have long captivated fans, social media has intensified the fan experience by extending opportunities for engagement and increasing at least the illusion of intimacy between celebrities and the many who follow them online, in the press, and through the activities for which they are famous (see, e.g., Gunter, 2014; Madere, 2018). As illustrated through the reactions to Amanda Kloots's posts on Instagram, fans routinely express concern and support while also empathizing by sharing their own stories. In so doing, they rhetorically affirm common ground (see K. Burke, 1950/1969) and connection through their respective loss. Although I'm not sure that any of the individuals who commented on Ms. Kloots's Instagram posts since she began documenting her husband's battle with Covid (and then her own journey as she recovered from his loss) will ever actually meet her in person, their engagement in the digital space comprises a form of relationship with potentially impactful implications.

Parasocial Relationships

Soukup (2006) argued that "fandom is communal and often built upon a shared identification with a media object or celebrity" (p. 322). In Soukup's related work on fansites, he asserted that, "[w]hile it is highly unlikely that the celebrity would actually visit one of his/her specific fansites, the fansite gives the fan an opportunity to publicly express stories and pictures that reflect a perceived closeness between the fan and the celebrity" (p. 331). In the case of a celebrity's social media accounts, the celebrity may or may not personally write and upload posts (see Duboff, 2016), but that person's Facebook, Instagram, or Twitter certainly give the illusion that posts come from the celebrity, further fostering the impression of interaction with fans. As Kim and Song (2016, p. 570) contended, "With easy access to direct and interactive communication methods with celebrities, fans following celebrities through social media may feel like they 'know' the celebrity and experience increased intimacy and a strong parasocial relationship."

Even before the advent of social media, though, Horton and Wahl (1956) proposed the notion of parasocial relationships—feelings of familiarity or connection with a character or person observed through the media (see also Dibble et al., 2016; Meyrowitz, 1985). However, arguably, the more engaged nature of social media can intensify those perceptions (see, e.g., Baek et al., 2013; Escalas & Bettman, 2017; Frederick et al., 2012; Kim & Song, 2016). In their study, Kim and Song determined that "when celebrities share their life and directly communicate about these experiences, fans tend to feel as if those celebrities were socially present in their life" (p. 574). Moreover, Baek et al. concluded that "reciprocal SNS (social network sites) mediated relationships contribute to increases in social trust and belongingness, in the same way that face to face relationships do" (p. 516). In their research, Frederick et al. noted that "the realization that one shares the same interests and likes the same things as an idolized professional athlete could certainly heighten one's feelings of being involved in the athlete's life" (p. 496).

Although celebrities (or whoever posting for a celebrity on a given account) can "retweet" or share or like a fan's post, such exchanges don't always happen between celebrities and the thousands (and sometimes millions) of fans who attempt to engage with them online. Yet, social media has made direct exchanges more possible, enhancing perceived connection with or closeness to a celebrity that, in turn, holds the potential to influence purchases (see, e.g., Aw & Labrecque, 2020; Burnasheva & Suh, 2020; Chung & Cho, 2017; Escalas & Bettman, 2017; Hwang & Zhang, 2018; Reinikainen et al., 2020; Schouten et al., 2019; Yuan & Lou, 2020), political choices (see, e.g., Abutaleb, 2020; Dean, 2017; Harvey, 2017; Hinck, 2019; Wheeler, 2013; Wright, 2020), and, as I will detail shortly, health-related decisions. According to Escalas and Bettman (2017, p. 306), "Despite the reality of not truly knowing celebrities, people feel as if they do know them intimately, often forming intense emotional and psychological connections to them.... Thus, in the same way that consumers trust friends' recommendations, they trust the advice of a celebrity with whom they have a parasocial relationship."

Madere (2018, p. 1) explained that "[t]his fascination with celebrities from chefs to athletes to people who are only famous for being non-celebrities in a reality TV show permeates how Americans view themselves: how they vote, the causes they give to and care about, the products they buy, their health concerns, and even how they view motherhood." Gunter (2014) agreed, asserting that while "[c]elebrities are iconic figures that others are curious about, they are also role models with the power to create social trends or to trigger specific actions among members of the public" (p. 10; see also M. Gergen, 2001, for related discussion of social ghosts).

Influences on Health

Nearly 50 years ago, long before Twitter and Facebook became household names, First Lady Betty Ford transformed a personal health saga into a public health opportunity as she used her platform to bring awareness to breast cancer (see Rosenthal, 2011). According to Rosenthal, "Jimmie C. Holland, MD, founder of the field of psycho-oncology ... often refers to Betty Ford's breast cancer revelation as one of the watershed events in public acceptance of cancer" (para. 13). As Rosenthal reported, "others had brought breast cancer into the public consciousness before Betty Ford allowed photographers into her hospital room in 1974, [but] it was the former First Lady who really opened the floodgates of cancer awareness" (para. 22). Ford also offered hope.

> Susan G. Komen for the Cure Founder and CEO Nancy G. Brinker ... said that when her sister Susan G. Komen (in whose memory and honor the organization was created) was first diagnosed in 1977 with the breast cancer that would claim her life, Susan found great inspiration from watching Betty Ford a few years earlier when photographers captured her throwing a football to the president following her surgery. "Susan told me that if Betty could do it, then she could do it" [Rosenthal, para. 4, 6–7].

Betty Ford's decision to disclose her diagnosis and to engage in public advocacy marked a moment when she prioritized public health over preferences for privacy. That choice not only worked to destigmatize breast cancer. It also emboldened other women to orient toward breast cancer as something to be battled and treated, rather than hidden, ignored, or unnamed (Wu, 2012). According to Wu, "Ford's candor brought breast cancer into the public sphere. After her diagnosis and treatment, the number of women getting breast exams increased dramatically, as did the number of women willing to talk about their own diagnoses. The silence around the disease had ended—thanks in large part to Ford" (para. 6).

At the very least, when celebrities confide a health concern to their fans, they elevate awareness in a most personal way—i.e., sharing that "this health situation has happened to me" (Beck et al., 2015). Because fans care about the object of their fandom, they recognize the life event, at a minimum, but likely beyond that surface level, fans want the celebrity to get better and to experience minimal health challenges. However, beyond that, knowing that a celebrity with whom they have a parasocial relationship faces some health-related issue might well prompt empathy and commiseration if the fan has gone through something similar and/or prompt the person to consider screenings or learn more about the medical issue (see related work by Beck et al., 2015; Brown & Basil, 1995, 2010; Cram et al., 2003; Francis, 2018; Gunter, 2014; Kosenko et al., 2015; Kresovich & Noar, 2020; Wong et al., 2017).

Gunter (2014, pp. 10–11) suggested that public figures "are not simply role models, but act out social narratives that both entertain and educate us in terms of life courses for ourselves, and learning how to behave or not behave in different settings ... celebrities gain social status and prestige and this can bestow upon them powers to influence others." For example, after tragically losing her husband to colon cancer, then-host Katie Couric allowed her own colonoscopy to be filmed and aired on NBC's *Today* as she launched an awareness campaign about the need for screening (see Cram et al., 2003). Cram et al.'s investigation noted "the Couric effect ... an immediate and sustained increase in colon cancer screening" (p. 1604). According to Cram et al., "these findings support the premise that healthy celebrity spokespersons can enhance the adoption of proven preventive interventions for a specific disease" (p. 1604). Another prominent example involves actress Angelina Jolie's announcements about decisions to undergo elective surgery for the removal of her breasts and, later, ovaries and fallopian tubes after receiving results of genetic testing, inspiring other women to seek genetic testing as well (Kosenko et al., 2015; Tetteh & Upadhyaya, 2018)—a reaction dubbed as the "Angelina Effect" (A. Park, 2013).

These examples and many others illustrate the power of personal celebrity stories to become part of their fans' respective life narratives by inspiring them to take action regarding their own health. As Gunter (2014) noted, "Further evidence has emerged from the United States and from Australia about ... the power of celebrity capital in this context [cancer] to motivate people to get their own health checked out" (p. 181). In their meta-analysis of research about celebrity health narratives, Kresovich and Noar (2020) concluded that "across a variety of health contexts, those who most feel a sense of attachment or affinity for a celebrity or media personae are most likely to modify their behavioral intentions in the wake of a celebrity health event" (p. 508).

The Case of Covid-19

As with Katie Couric and Angelina Jolie, celebrity health narratives prior to Covid-19 involved relatively singular instances of a celebrity who received a diagnosis (or suffered a personal tragedy), confided it to fans, and encouraged fans to take some sort of personal action. For example, Michael J. Fox raised money for Parkinson's research (see Beck, 1995); Magic Johnson elevated awareness about HIV/AIDS (Brown & Basil, 1995).

However, Covid-19 constituted the first time in the era of social media that nearly everyone—both celebrities and noncelebrities—had to ascertain and navigate possible risks and implications of the same disease simultaneously. Moreover, due to lockdowns, business closings, and restrictions on travel and activities, many who did not work in what got labeled as "essential" roles stayed home, relying increasingly on technology for information, communication, and connection. This context cultivated the sharing of personal reactions to and perceptions of the pandemic in perhaps an even more dialogic manner than ever before.

Unlike responses to prior celebrity health narratives that got disclosed and discussed singularly, celebrity and noncelebrity experiences during the pandemic became part of messy, confusing, fragmented public health narratives that lacked focus, clarity, or structure. The Covid-19 pandemic in the United States reflected writings about postmodernism as multiple, conflicting messages abounded in a plethora of platforms; individuals struggled to manage competing tensions and obligations as they sought to make sense not only of the disease but also of various physical, emotional, financial, and social risks; perhaps most significantly, people picked through sticky, stuffy, heavy, overwhelming webs of information and claims, seeking to identify whom to trust, whom to believe, and what to do. According to Harter et al. (2005b, p. 21), "our lives are embedded within larger narrative landscapes, times, and spaces that shape our lives and the stories we tell of them."

That landscape includes interactions with family, guidance from faith communities, and conversations with friends. It encompasses favorite television shows, radio programs, movies, and media outlets, and it involves posts from all of those whom we follow online. As individuals tried to figure out how to proceed during the pandemic and then how to make sense of what would become politicized, polarizing positions and choices, they necessarily sought those whom they came to trust the most and what narratives resonated most with them. Harter et al. (2005b, p. 21) explained that "[p]ublic discourses of health and healing are narratively constructed.... These narratives draw on and reinforce personal and organizational narratives and function as public 'mindsets,' the boundaries within which health and healing are interpreted and discussed. Such master narratives embody sociocultural beliefs, values, hopes, and fears."

I argue that celebrities played a central role in crafting two distinct and competing master narratives, both officially and unofficially, as they also personally bought into one or another (see, e.g., Abutaleb, 2020; Ives, 2021; Sherfinski, 2020; Shevenock, 2021). One narrative extends from an appreciation of science, while the other advances a position of skepticism about science-based recommendations, and the extent to which people gravitated toward one or the other depended on what rang "more true" to them (see W. Fisher, 1984) in the context of their respective interpretive communities.

Indeed, Covid-19 illuminated the pivotal nature of those communities for both framing interpretations about what individuals held to be "real" or "true" and, also importantly, about what they did not believe to be "real" or "true." Fish (1980, p. 15) provided the following useful explanation:

> Members of the same community will necessarily agree because they will see (and by seeing, make) everything in relation to that community's assumed purposes and goals; and conversely, members of different communities will disagree because from each of their respective positions the other "simply" cannot see what is obviously and inescapably there ... [thus] the explanation for the stability of interpretations among different readers (they belong to the same community). It also explains why there are disagreements and why they can be debated in a principled way: not because of a stability in texts, but because of a stability in the makeup of interpretive communities and therefore in the opposing positions they make possible.

Chapter 2

Through the Window of Sports

On March 9, 2020, Utah Jazz player Rudy Gobert made a point of spreading his fingers and touching all of the microphones on the table before walking out of his post-shootaround interview. Although unimaginable now in the post–Covid era, Gobert could not envision how impactful those actions, purportedly intended to be humorous, would come to be interpreted (Golliver, 2020; Young, 2020). Gobert recalled that "[i]t was the first day that we found out that the media was not going to be able to interview us, right next to us, and, you know, we obviously didn't know as much as we know now, and I only did that to try to liven the mood a little bit" (Young, para. 4). According to Golliver, "The clip was viewed millions of times on social media, leading angry and fearful observers to conclude that Gobert was making light of the NBA's early social distancing guidelines and putting others at risk" (para. 10).

Ironically, Gobert became "Patient Zero" in the sports world for Covid-19 just two days after the infamous microphone incident (Golliver, 2020, para. 6) with his positive Covid-19 test on March 11, sending shockwaves that reverberated through professional and amateur sports communities. According to Golliver, "Medical officials abruptly called off the Jazz's game against the Thunder that night, and within hours, [NBA Commissioner] Silver had indefinitely suspended the NBA season. The NHL, MLB, and MLS followed suit in short order, leaving fans and television networks with empty calendars" (para. 8).

Gobert faced the twin challenges of suffering through symptoms of the disease—some that lingered for months—while, at the same time, dealing with the ramifications of being the initial catalyst for a cascade of cancellations. Of course, those cancellations would have inevitably still happened that March as someone else would have become the first professional athlete to test positive for this novel coronavirus. For his part, Gobert "moved quickly to make amends in March, issuing an apology, filming a public service announcement and donating $500,000 to support coronavirus efforts in Utah, Oklahoma, and his home country of France" (Golliver, 2020, para. 11).

As I'll share throughout this chapter, the world of sports was uniquely situated to spotlight issues pertaining to Covid-19 that extended far beyond arenas and playing fields. Individual athletes, team coaches, and league commissioners struggled to ascertain the actual risk of the disease, especially in early March 2020, just as people not associated with organized sports sought to do. Collectively and individually, they wrestled with determining what constitutes a "responsible" response as opposed to an "overreaction." As time ensued, those same stakeholders increasingly struggled to figure out the ways in which a "responsible" response in terms of individual and public health should/ must be juxtaposed with the economic impacts of halting play—i.e., the loss of revenue from ticket sales and media coverage due to cancellations followed by the rapid domino effects of subsequent layoffs. Particularly in the United States, with its "show must go on" philosophy, the tug between staying safe and carrying on proved challenging and consequential.

I begin by describing how sports provided an influential platform for contributing to broader societal conversations such as the emergent Covid-19 narrative. I then delve into how sports—a complex, multifaceted industry comprising many diverse and often high-profile stakeholders—mirrored the public's dual struggle to reclaim all that had been so abruptly and unexpectedly ripped away in March 2020 while reckoning with the realities of an unpredictable virus.

The Influential Platform of Sports and Athletes

For the first four months of Covid, I understood the gravity of the disease on a cognitive level. Watching the news and working on this book impressed upon me the need to take precautions, adhere to recommendations, and avoid risk. Fortunately, extended family members and close friends also took the situation seriously, and my husband and I were personally blessed to teach from home. I managed to go four months without experiencing personal concern about a friend or acquaintance who was suffering from Covid-related symptoms.

In mid–July 2020, my husband and I traveled from Ohio to Alabama with our daughter Ellie-Kate for softball nationals. We still avoided dining in restaurants and socializing indoors, but we deemed the risk of our healthy, athletic, 12-year-old center fielder playing an outdoor sport to be within our comfort zone, and we deliberately set up our seats much farther than the recommended six feet from other spectators. About halfway through the tournament, I got bored between two games and started scrolling on Facebook. One post caused me to pause and stare at the screen. The post asked Facebook friends to pray for someone who was in the hospital with Covid-19—the very first person whom I would know to have Covid-19.

A Personal Connection

I became acquainted with Keven Lightner because his daughter used to be in my Girl Scout troop. I remember talking with him when he would come to pick her up from Girl Scout sleepovers. I recall laughing together about something that our daughters had said or done. Although I knew that he worked at the time as a football coach for the Ohio University Bobcats, to me, he was just a fellow parent with whom I casually chatted in the doorway of my home as he waited on his daughter to collect her belongings, someone whom I had come to know because we both happened to have daughters in the same kindergarten class and then Girl Scout troop.

Truth be told, my husband, Roger, was a little more in awe. To my diehard Nebraska-football-fan husband, Keven wasn't "just another dad"; he was a legend who towered in our entryway, not merely because of his physical stature but even more due to his long list of accomplishments as an offensive tackle for the Nebraska football team. Well known in the Nebraska football community, Keven Lightner had been considered Nebraska's "strongest-ever player, having recorded a 441-pound bench press while squatting 756 pounds" back in 1987 (Sipple, 2020a, para. 6). Well before the moments that we shared at cute kindergarten events and Girl Scout activities, like other Husker fans, Roger knew of Keven Lightner because he had watched him play and recalled him as an outstanding part of the team.

Now, admittedly, Roger isn't completely like all other Nebraska fans. In addition to adorning his office with Nebraska furnishings and artwork, he also wrote *Huskerville*, a book about Nebraska football fans (Aden, 2007). In it, he argued that those fans constitute a very unique, invested, zealous community, a perspective enthusiastically echoed by others who also authored books about Nebraska fans (Babcock, 1988; S. Smith, 2015; Wolfe, 2010)—even though dedicated fans of other teams might beg to differ (see Dohrmann, 2018). As Roger explained in his book, "With apologies to the devoted fans of other sports programs, then I think the Nebraska difference is this: while other teams, to use Michael Novak's word, *represent* a place and its people, we believe that the Huskers *are* Nebraska and its people" (p. 44). He quoted a local radio host who noted that "[i]f you have ties to this university, they'll stick with you.... You're one of us. You'll always be one of us" (Aden, p. 52).

When Keven ended up in the hospital with Covid-19 in July 2020, Erin, his ex-wife (with whom he co-parents their two children), realized that many would care beyond their immediate family—certainly, his extended Nebraska Husker community would want to know and help in any way that they could. Erin confided his diagnosis and progress in a series of Facebook posts, and news then spread to local and national media outlets about his situation. Now 55 years old (and a professional football coach in Japan), Keven Lightner was still big, still strong, still fit, but not invincible.

Near the beginning of his time in the hospital for Covid-19, according to Erin, Lightner "had enough wherewithal to sit up in his bed even though he was restrained and break through his restraints, and pull (the ventilator) out on his own" (Sipple, 2020a, para. 10). Erin told a reporter that "it required nine hospital staff members to restrain the former Husker," confiding that "they said it was like the Incredible Hulk.... He's super-strong, super-fit. He had no underlying conditions. He works out six days a week" (Sipple, para. 11–12).

Still, Lightner fought for his life for nearly a month and battled symptoms for an extended time thereafter. Lightner shared in a November 2020 KETV interview that he continued to struggle with complications from Covid (https://www.ketv.com/article/lightner-survives-covid-19-scare/). According to Sipple (2020b, para. 5), Lightner revealed that "[d]octors told him that he won't return to full strength for six months to a year."

Erin explained that "we are OK with putting all this out there because we encourage people to wear masks, wash hands and practice social distancing.... If this can happen to us, it can happen to anyone" (Sipple, 2020a, para. 18). In a subsequent article, Sipple (2020b, para. 14) noted that Lightner "admits that before his illness, he didn't take COVID-19 seriously enough. He knows plenty of people who think it's all a government scam. He hopes those people notice his story and maybe put their guards up." In his October article, Sipple commented that "[h]igh-level coaches I've known throughout the years almost always are highly accountable.... In that regard, Lightner's frank talk about his general lack of respect for the virus makes sense. He obviously respects it now" (para. 26).

Moreover, the ways in which Keven Lightner communicated about his personal experience with Covid-19 suggests that he hopes others will come to respect it too. Lightner's prominence in the sports world warranted coverage of his experience by reporters, particularly those who cover Nebraska football. Further, the incongruity between a prominent public health narrative that Covid affects only the weak and Lightner's reputation as extremely strong made his story an especially compelling and intriguing one. If Covid could affect someone like Keven Lightner, the disease could suddenly seem more threatening. His connection with Nebraska fans and others in the extended college football community personalized the message that someone they know (or, at least, whom they feel that they know)—particularly someone who is athletic—struggled to recover from this very real, dangerous, and impactful virus and now encourages them to take the threat seriously.

Impacting Perspectives and Actions

As I discussed in Chapter 1, being a celebrity does not necessarily translate to always being persuasive or influential, but they can (and do) attract the attention of fans who feel a connection with them and even those who merely know their name (see Harvey, 2017; Wright, 2020). For example, advertisers recognize the potential value of an athlete's endorsement of a product, from the Olympians who grace a Wheaties box to the Super Bowl MVP who grins and shouts, "I'm going to Disney World!" (see, e.g., https://www.nielsen.com/us/en/insights/report/2019/power-of-one-athletes-as-endorsers/; for related research, please see Burnasheva & Suh, 2020; Chung & Cho, 2017; Hwang & Zhang, 2018; Schouten et al., 2020; Yuan & Lou, 2020). Athletes' voices and actions can also raise awareness about societal issues certainly of more consequence than a bowl of cereal or vacation destination—such as police brutality, Black Lives Matter, and gender equality (see, e.g., S.M. Anderson, 2020; Butterworth, 2020; Cassilo & Sanderson, 2019; Cooky & Antunovic, 2020; Coombs & Cassilo, 2017; Frederick et al., 2017; Galily, 2018; Harvey, 2017; Jackson et al., 2020; Rugg, 2020; Schmidt et al., 2019; Schmittel & Sanderson, 2014; Towler et al., 2019; Williams et al., 2015). Jackson et al. (2020, p. 441) asserted:

> sport per se is replete with examples through history of leading athletes from traditionally marginalized groups seizing on their visibility to highlight issues of inequality and discrimination through innovative, mediated, and highly symbolic forms of protest—from Tommie Smith and John Carolos's Black Power Salute at the 1968 Mexico City Olympics to Colin Kaepernick's kneeling protest in 2016.

As Beck et al. (2015) observed, individuals involved in sports (such as Arthur Ashe, Magic Johnson, Scott Hamilton, Pat Summitt, Chris Spielman, Boomer Esiason, and Jim Valvano) have also engaged in health advocacy by raising awareness about health concerns. One of the ways in which they do so involves telling fans (and those who happen to pay attention to sports) about their own personal illness or injury narratives (see also Brown & Basil, 1995; Brown et al., 2003; Brown & De Matviuk, 2010). Beck et al. asserted that "athletes captain different sorts of teams—collections of individuals striving for a cure ... the chance to live (if not play) another day ... competing on a new, unfamiliar playing field for precious medical and financial resources" (p. 124). Thus, such disclosures go beyond updating an interested fan base about a personal situation; instead, athlete health narratives can work to educate about an illness/condition and encourage action such as donating money for research or engaging in preventive care.

For example, when former North Carolina State University basketball coach and then ESPN commentator Jim Valvano passionately spoke during his 1993 ESPY speech about the need for more funding for research about cancer and the desire to find a cure, he referenced his personal battle with the disease. He then went further, striving to "build his team" by urging viewers to donate to the V Foundation, the organization that he had just established to support cancer research. Valvano pleaded, "We need your help. I need your help. We need money for research. It may not save my life. It may save my children's life. It may save someone you love. And it's very important ... try if you can to support ... so that someone else might survive, might prosper, and might actually be cured of this dreaded disease" (Meah, n.d., para. 26). Valvano used the prime-time stage of accepting the Arthur Ashe Award to inspire attention to cancer and the need for a cure, and, in so doing, rallied his fans into caring about cancer and contributing resources. It worked—since 1994, the V Foundation has raised and granted over $260 million to fund cancer research (https://www.v.org/about/the-impact-and-benefit-of-cancer-research/).

Such prior instances of athlete advocacy regarding a health-related issue or illness have featured one individual sharing a personal illness or injury experience. With Covid-19, sports fans did not just witness a passionate speech on a prominent network by one person affected by a serious illness or chronic condition. Instead, they got bombarded by a plethora of messages on myriad platforms by multiple affected athletes, in addition to observing the real-life, real-time implications of a pandemic on the sports industry as well as individual sports teams. Further, unlike other diseases (such as cancer), Covid quickly became not only politicized but also confounded by unclear public health messaging, complicating what constituted "appropriate" or "reasonable" responses on individual and organizational levels. Accordingly, stakeholders (athletes, coaches, team owners, league officials, and even fans) faced complicated, messy choices about what to share, when to post, and how to proceed as they navigated presenting and responding to Covid-related illness narratives.

Decisions by those involved with sports—and corresponding social media posts, news releases, interviews, videos, and related actions—became an integral part of the broader societal narrative of Covid-19. Because reactions to this disease came to hold significant economic, societal, cultural, and even political consequence, every emergent public step by athletes, league officials, teams, etc., suffered intense scrutiny by fans, politicians, and observers analogous to some of the more controversial prior public positions of athletes. Harvey (2017, p. 17) explained that "[t]he twenty-first century has found a radical increase in athlete activism.... However, commercial incentives still dissuade political activism among athletes." In taking a stand (or a knee), athletes necessarily balance elevating their respective voices for a cause with also representing a team or league that might not agree with individual athlete perspectives and/or angering a fan base. For example, Kaepernick's protest of police brutality by taking a knee as the U.S. national anthem played prior to a football game essentially cost him a career in the NFL (see related research by Anderson, 2020; Rugg, 2020; Towler et al., 2020). In the case of Covid-19, the ways in which members of the sports community responded to the pandemic mattered greatly—not just for the health and wellness of athletes or the economic survival of teams but also to the fans who witnessed the struggle of sports to juggle multiple concerns as strikingly similar to their own journeys through this unexpected and unprecedented season.

The Case of Covid-19

Following Gobert's Covid-19 diagnosis, sports skidded to a stop—much like the rest of the world. In Indiana, the beloved high school basketball tournament halted midround, leaving the state without a new champion for the first time in 109 years (Neddenriep, 2020). Neddenriep reported Covenant Christian head coach Scott Flatt's response: "I thought, 'Man, it's Indiana. We're going to get this thing in.' I was kind of in denial, hoping beyond hope" (para. 14).

March Madness—described by ESPN News as "one of the biggest

events in American sports, a basketball marathon of buzzer-beaters, upsets and thrills involving 68 teams"—never even released brackets in 2020 (https://www.espn.com/mens-college-basketball/story/_/id/28893285/ncaa-tournaments-canceled-coronavirus, para. 16). The NCAA decision to cancel the 82-year-old, high-profile collegiate athletic tournament (as well as all spring collegiate sports) stunned student-athletes left to wonder about what might have been. Emma Wolfe, a senior at Indiana Tech, commented during an interview with a local paper that "[h]aving a social media post end your season, especially end your career as a senior, instead of being on that hardwood floor, instead of having sweat dripping down your face and having that moment hit you.... The unanswered questions, it's not what we planned for. It's just surreal" (Sinn, 2020, para. 4). Baylor men's basketball coach Scott Drew admitted that "I'm overwhelmingly disappointed that our team won't have the opportunity to finish what was arguably the best season in program history.... To have that opportunity abruptly taken away by something out of our control is devastating for our team, coaches and fans" ("NCAA tournaments canceled over coronavirus," 2020, para. 29).

As fans and student-athletes well know, moments matter during March Madness. With no NCAA tournament basketball games played, we missed the thrill of last-minute swishes through the basket to win a close game and the annual emergence of "insta-celebrities," such as Loyola Chicago's 102-year-old chaplain, Sister Jean. "Cinderella" (a nickname for teams not seeded highly but that upset more top-ranked opponents during the tournament) never graced the dance floor. Coworkers lost the opportunity to gain bragging rights over tournament bracket competitions, and CBS and affiliated stations substituted reruns from prior tournaments and sporting events for the highly anticipated live action. Gyms sat still and silent, eerily empty at a time when they usually spring to life with players on the court and fans in the stands. However, as South Carolina women's basketball coach Dawn Staley reflected philosophically, "Sports is a big part of our lives, but just one part of how we are connected to each other. We need to step back and think about the larger good served by canceling events that put people at risk" (Powell, 2020, para. 5).

Such events included professional sports, which also screeched to an unprecedented stop on March 12, 2020, with the National Basketball League (NBA), National Hockey League (NHL), Major League Soccer (MLS), and Major League Baseball (MLB) all abruptly pausing play. Aschburner (2020) reported Dallas Mavericks owner Mark Cuban's initial response to the news: "It's not really about basketball or money.... This thing is just exploding to the point where all of a sudden, players

2. Through the Window of Sports 43

and owners alike, you think about your family. You want to really make sure you're doing this the right way. Because now it's much more personal."

National Hockey League Commissioner Gary Bettman referenced the inevitable possibility of NHL players contracting the disease in his statement that read in part:

> The NHL has been attempting to follow the mandates of health experts and local authorities, while preparing for any possible developments without taking premature or unnecessary measures. However, following last night's news that an NBA player has tested positive for coronavirus—and given that our leagues share so many facilities and locker rooms and it now seems likely that some member of the NHL community would test positive at some point—it is no longer appropriate to try to continue to play games at this time. We will continue to monitor all the appropriate medical advice, and we will encourage our players and other members of the NHL community to take all reasonable precautions—including by self-quarantine, where appropriate. Our goal is to resume play as soon as it is appropriate and prudent, so that we will be able to complete the season and award the Stanley Cup. Until then, we thank NHL fans for your patience and hope you stay healthy [https://www.nhl.com/news/nhl-coronavirus-to-provide-update-on-concerns/c-316131734].

Don Garber, commissioner of the Major League Soccer, followed suit with a similar announcement on the same day:

> Our clubs were united today in the decision to temporarily suspend our season—based on the advice and guidance from the Centers for Disease Control and Prevention (CDC), Public Health Agency of Canada (PHAC), and other public health authorities, and in the best interest of our fans, players, officials and employees. We'd like to thank our fans for their continued support during this challenging time [McCarriston, 2020, para. 3].

With the NCAA, NBA, MSL, and NHL swiftly suspending their respective seasons, given the positive case in the NBA, Major League Baseball also changed course on March 12 (after previously indicating intentions to play games as scheduled) by canceling spring training games and pushing the start of the regular season back by a few weeks (Perry et al., 2020). Ultimately, the MLB season began on July 23, 2020, instead of as originally scheduled on March 26 (Feinsand, 2020).

By the end of March 2020, Japan and the International Olympic Committee made the anguishing decision to postpone the 2020 Olympics (Garcia-Hodges et al., 2020; Wade, 2020), dashing the dreams of Olympians worldwide who had trained for competitions (Reichels, 2020) that would have happened under normal circumstances. According to Garcia-Hodges et al., the postponement constituted "the first major disruption to the Olympics since World War II, when the 1944 Summer Olympics, were canceled" (para. 11).

Reuters Staff (2020, para. 4) reported that "[a]thletes, national associations and sporting federations from around the world reacted with sadness, relief and mainly goodwill to the postponement of the Tokyo 2020 Olympic Games on Tuesday because of the coronavirus pandemic." As Andrew Parsons, International Paralympic Committee president, affirmed, "The health and well-being of human life must always be our number one priority and staging a sport event of any kind during this pandemic is simply not possible. Sport is not the most important thing right now, preserving human life is" (Reuters Staff, para. 5).

Despite the generally universal cautious approach by the leagues and teams near the beginning of the pandemic, the desire for a return to normal, juxtaposed with realizations about the realities of Covid-19, muddied responses in the ensuing months by administrators, coaches, players, and fans. Those mixed messages became part of shifting, fluid public conversations about relative risk of the disease, especially as individuals in the United States quickly grew more divided in their perspectives about the virus and increasingly discontented with the state of their lives amid pandemic-related restrictions and cancellations.

Even those who took the virus seriously wanted to protect public health while, at the same time, yearning for live sporting events to be back on some mediated platform (JWB3 Media Insights, 2020; Tamir, 2021). Indeed, according to JWB3 Media Insight's survey of consumers, "the majority of respondents made it clear that sporting events are looked upon as being as essential to their daily lives, as say, going out to a bar, a restaurant, or even shopping at the mall" (p. 1). The study also found that "[n]early two-thirds (62%) of Americans agree that sports on TV is an important step for the country returning 'back to normal,'" a statistic that grew to 78 percent for "avid sports fans" (p. 1). According to Joe Brown, a principal with JWB3 Media Insights, "As this study shows, fans agree that sports returning will make them happier and will bring families and communities closer together…. Returning to competition can be a real sign of strength in the face of a crisis" ("Study shows fans missing sports," 2020, para. 2)

Yearning for "Normal"

In those weeks when sports stood still, the collective gaze turned even more to the actions (or inaction) of leagues, teams, and players as devoted fans lacked new games to watch on TV while confined to home during quarantine. Although devastating for players and spectators alike, the unanticipated cancellations of personally important and financially lucrative sporting events underscored initially that Covid-19 should be taken seriously. For example, Alfons Hormann, president of the German Olympic Sports Confederation, asserted that the postponement of the 2020 Olympics "confirms to the world population that everything in sports is also being done to bring the global pandemic under control as best as possible and as soon as possible" (Reuters Staff, 2020, para. 17).

As Dahlberg (2020) noted, "sports become[s] even more important during a time of crisis. It's why baseball continued during World War II. It's why the NFL played two days after President John F. Kennedy was assassinated and why both Major League Baseball and the NFL rushed to get back on the field in the wake of the terrorist attacks of 9/11."

Yet, as the NBA, NCAA, and other leagues quickly realized, athletic events simply could not continue as planned during the pandemic, and, thus, sports could not be the same stabilizing, comforting source of reassurance to an increasingly frightened public as the industry had been during prior crises (see related work by Pederson et al., 2021). In those early days in March 2020, the perceived health risks to players (as well as for fans in the stands and others in their communities) outweighed the potential societal and economic benefits for decision-makers who opted to err on the side of caution and precaution (see Donnelly, 2020; Dove et al., 2020; Faghy et al., 2020; Hamilton et al., 2020; Harmon et al., 2020; Mann et al., 2020; Toresdahl & Asif, 2020). Mann et al. stressed:

> Public health centers on the recognition that *individual* athletes are situated in—and are integral parts *of*—wider communities that include other athletes, their multidisciplinary support teams, families and local/national/international societies. Flattening the curve of a pandemic depends on recognizing that a single athlete can be a vector for this communicable disease (and preventing that), but also that their role within their own complex social systems matters. Prevention here is bigger than *individual* athletes alone. Recognising, holding space for and negotiating athletes *as* community—as human beings who are part of this world rather than simply being commodities—has never been more important [p. 1071].

Yet, those prevention efforts illustrated and underscored the extent to which athletes and their teams are commodities. Fans certainly missed consuming the games, and the halt in action also stopped the usually lucrative flow of cash—no ticket sales, no media revenue, no paychecks for hourly employees who staff the concession stands or work game security, etc. ESPN News (2020, para. 15) reported that March Madness alone "generates almost a billion dollars in revenue each year for the NCAA and its hundreds of member universities and colleges, most coming from a television contract with CBS and Turner that pays the NCAA almost $800 million annually." Overall, the industry incurred "losses for the NCAA and the four major U.S. sports leagues" in the amount of "at least $14.1 billion so far" (Birnbaum, 2021, para. 4). That total does not include the financial hits to individuals who work at stadiums or in the sports industry as well as to universities that, for better or for worse, count on income from media packages and ticket sales to make athletic department payrolls (see Wertheim & Apstein, 2020).

Reckoning with Realities

As the days turned to weeks and weeks turned to months, and as the United States wrestled with an increasingly politicized pandemic, the world of sports (as with the rest of the world) sought to figure out a way to resume some semblance of what used to be "normal" while also mitigating individual health risks and protecting public health. Gobert's case illustrated the folly of assuming that professional athletes were immune to catching the virus or experiencing symptoms.

In the MLB, Julio Teherán (and some members of his family) became ill with the virus just before he was scheduled to leave for training camp (Digiovanna, 2020). Atlanta Braves first baseman (and the eventual 2021 National League MVP) Freddie Freeman's bout with Covid delayed his start to the 2020 season (Burns, 2020; Hall, 2021). On July 4, 2020, Freeman's wife, Chelsea, posted on Instagram that "Freddie has had body aches, headaches, chills and a fever. He is someone who rarely gets sick and this virus hit him like a ton of bricks" (https://www.instagram.com/p/CCPBWXUhcbf/?hl=en).

Legendary golfer Jack Nicklaus released a statement indicating that he and his wife had contracted Covid-19, but he recovered in time to attend the annual Memorial Tournament (which was delayed from its usual May date until July 2020) (Harrison, 2020). Race car driver Jimmie Johnson became "the first NASCAR driver to test positive [ending] … his streak of 663 consecutive Cup starts" (Marot, 2020, para. 4). He credited his wife's "diligence to do the right thing" by encouraging him to get tested after he experienced allergy-like symptoms (Associated Press, 2020d, para. 10). Otherwise, as Johnson—who was otherwise asymptomatic—told the Associated Press, "we'd be going on with life as normal, and who knows who we could have come in contact with and infected" (para. 10).

That threat of unintentionally spreading an unpredictable and life-threatening illness complicated getting athletes back on the court or field.

2. Through the Window of Sports

The sheer number of individuals involved in accomplishing a sporting event—players, coaches, trainers, staff, officials, media—multiplied the risk, not to mention the typical travel as teams compete in a usual season.

The NBA ultimately decided to continue its season after a four-month hiatus by bringing players into a protective "bubble" with no fans or outside contact at Walt Disney World. According to Zillgitt (2020), "[t]he NBA and the NBPA developed comprehensive health and safety protocols and pulled off an amazing feat. After 107 days, 172 games and thousands of COVID-19 tests at the Disney campus" (para. 7), the NBA bubble proved to be "a model for operating a safe and healthy environment that mitigated the spread of COVID-19 through daily testing, social distancing, mask-wearing and contact tracing" (para. 8) as well as no external contact with fans, family, or friends beyond the stakeholders involved in producing and playing the games.

However, even though the NBA proudly avoided a single positive case within the bubble (Zillgitt, 2020), some players contracted the virus before they could get to Disney. Russell Westbrook of the Washington Wizards tested positive for Covid-19 before eventually joining his team in Orlando (Deb, 2020). According to Deb, Westbrook encouraged fans to "[p]lease take this virus seriously. Be safe. Mask up" (para. 2). Mohammed Bamba's experience underscored why.

According to Umeri (2021, para. 6), "Bamba was diagnosed with the virus on June 11th, 2020, but tested negative before reporting to the bubble, where he played a total of 10 minutes. Nearly six months later, he still had not recovered." Umeri also described the health saga of Jayson Tatum, who plays for the Boston Celtics, reporting that "Tatum tested positive for the virus on January 9th [2021] and returned to the floor after missing more than two weeks later that month. Tatum detailed his struggles to feel 100 percent, saying: 'Just running up and down the court a few times, it's easier to get out of breath or tired a lot faster. I've noticed that since I've had COVID'" (para. 8).

WNBA player Asia Durr, a top pick in the 2019 WNBA draft, chronicled her journey as a Covid-19 "long-hauler" on her social media accounts. On July 7, 2020, she posted the following announcement on Instagram:

> After much thought and consultation with my doctors and the [New York] Liberty, I have decided not to play the 2020 WNBA season. After testing positive for COVID-19 on June 8, my battle with it has been complicated and arduous. As I continue to fight to fully recover, I had to make the difficult decision on a deadline to opt out as a Medical High Risk player. So much about this virus is unknown, and my heart is heavy, even as I make the decision that I know is best for my long term wellness.

Six months later, Durr updated viewers of HBO's *Real Sports with Bryant Gumbel* on her continuing fight to regain her health. According to Shapiro (2021a), "Durr, 23, discussed a litany of long-term COVID-19 symptoms on the show (para. 2).... She has lost 32 pounds since contracting COVID-19, and she has still not been cleared to play or practice" (para. 5). On January 27, 2021, Durr tweeted, "Thanks again everyone for the support. My hope is that in sharing my struggle, it will help others. PLEASE take COVID seriously folks. It's very real. Wear a mask! Protect each other. Young people, athletes, you too. We are not invincible."

These public testimonials worked to spotlight the dangers of the disease for all, not only older and less fit individuals. Yet, the overarching perception of invincibility—especially for big, strong athletes—impacted the tension between resuming normality and respecting the virus for both the sports industry, particularly, and individuals across the world, in general. For example, the WNBA did allow some players (such as Tina Charles from the Washington Mystics) to obtain a medical excuse that exempted them from playing in the 2020 season (Associated Press, 2021e). Elena Delle Donne, who suffers from post-treatment Lyme disease syndrome, was not so fortunate. She wrote that "I still wanted to play, but I was *scared*. I talked to my personal physician about what the league planned to do, and he felt that it was still too risky" (Delle Donne, 2020, para. 14). Given that the league denied her request for an exemption, she observed that "[w]hat I hear in their decision is that I'm a fool for believing my doctor. That I'm faking a disability. That I'm trying to 'get out' of work and still collect a paycheck" (para. 25).

Delle Donne (2020, July 15) acknowledged:

> I know that the decision I'm facing—risk my life or forfeit my paycheck—is far from a unique one. I know that millions of Americans right now, in situations that are much worse than my own, are facing similar decisions. And of course many are dealing with even worse than that: Millions more are out of work entirely. Many of them—especially Black and brown people, and especially Black and brown LGBTQ people—are dealing with food insecurity and homelessness. I want to express my deepest solidarity with them [para. 37].

The Washington Mystics quickly announced plans to pay Delle Donne in spite of the denied exemption, but as compensation for time to recover from back surgery rather than a Covid-excused leave (Gardner, 2020). However, this very public struggle of sports organizations and individual athletes with Covid-19 mirrored the near-constant tension felt by many nonathletes as well—grappling with realities and risks of the virus while at the same time thirsting for "normal"—financially, emotionally, socially, and culturally.

Affected athletes used Twitter and Instagram as virtual microphones, employing platforms afforded to them because of their celebrity status to call attention to the risk of Covid-19 amid institutional pressures to proceed anyway. According to Donnelly (2020, p. 38), "the voice of athletes ... has been aided by the increasing power of celebrity, by social media." Athletes wrestling with decisions about Covid-19 embraced that celebrity as empowerment to speak out even if their experiences ran counter to the positions of their respective team or league. (For a related example, consider Naomi Osaka's decision—shared via social media—to withdraw from the French Open after controversy about her decision not to participate in post-match press conferences; see Emba, 2021; Hill, 2021a; Torres, 2021.) As Hill argued, "top athletes are no longer willing to say silent about ... their own personal struggles.... They want the full scope of their humanity considered" (para. 10). Hill continued, "today's athletes aren't willing to put a happy face on their trauma just so the rest of us can be blissfully entertained" (para. 20). By extension, the illness and work narratives of prominent athletes, especially during the pandemic, functioned as examples and inspiration for nonathletes who struggled with similar conundrums as they also navigated risk and negotiated what they considered to be safe and fair employment conditions.

Kicking a Political and Cultural Football

During the summer of 2020, speculation about the status of U.S. college football surged (right along with a dramatic July spike in Covid-19 cases across the southern United States; see, e.g., Allen, 2020; Dodd, 2020; Gleeson, 2020; Leitch, 2020; McGraw, 2020; Witz, 2020). By July, the United States had been dealing with the pandemic for five long months. Professional sports had (finally) resumed but managed to do so with very restrictive conditions and expensive frequent Covid-19 testing. Should the experiment be stretched to a collegiate sports environment at a time when many universities offered only online instruction to their students due to safety concerns? What about liability of putting student-athletes in close, competitive spaces during a global pandemic? What gets lost if the players don't take the field? How do player perspectives factor into the equation?

COLLEGE FOOTBALL AS "ESSENTIAL"

Even the ways in which the controversy got covered in the media underscored the divisiveness not only in terms of college football but more generally regarding the state of responses to the pandemic. As

Allen (2020) astutely asserted, "This sets up a football season of unusual importance in understanding whether we can live with the coronavirus or must significantly alter our way of life until it's eradicated."

Dodd (2020) referred to the debate as "befuddling" and quoted the team doctor for the University of Washington: "We are in the middle of a pandemic, our country is one of the worst controlled on the planet.... We have more deaths than any country. We have cases surging all over the place. We haven't done what we needed to do to play fall sports" (para. 6). Yet, as Dodd acknowledged, "it's not over, this battle. Not by a long shot. In fact, it's getting worse and more intense" (para. 9). That intensity emerged for multiple reasons, but Allen's assertion hinted at a primary one—college football constitutes a "way of life" for devoted fans who didn't want to sacrifice that part of 2020 too.

According to a 2019 report by the National Football Foundation, college football ranked as the second most popular sport (topped only by the National Football League), with, in 2018, 47 million individuals attending games in person, 163 million watching regular season games on television, and 56 percent of U.S. adults claiming to be college football fans (https://footballfoundation.org/news/2019/6/11/2018-19_Attendance_Release.aspx). McGraw (2020) argued:

> About 150 million Americans watch college football on TV every season. The demographics tend to be a little richer and a little more suburban than average, but the audience is well-balanced in terms of race and gender. For TV networks, the viewing figures for college football are a dream that few other sports can rival. That's why the question of whether college football will be played this fall is symbolic in both the political and cultural sense [para. 6].

With the many sacrifices that Americans endured throughout the pandemic, the desire to not miss out on a cherished fall tradition makes sense. (As an Oklahoma football fan, personally, I didn't really want to skip a season of watching my Sooners on the field either, but that's easy to say from the comfort of my own couch.) Yet, extending from McGraw, the belief that college football should not be canceled due to Covid-19 also implied a prioritizing of personal preferences and allegiances over public health as well as the wellness of student-athletes—a position fueled by President Trump and echoed by his own fans (see Leitch, 2020; Smith & Alexander, 2020). As McGraw noted, "whether or not football games are on TV and bars are open is more important to many voters than fatality rates.... [A populist position] appeals to the part of voters who want what is best for themselves, even if it comes at the expense of the health of the community" (para. 24). A year without college football would also be costly to universities and to the student-athletes, given loss of significant income for the schools and exposure for the athletes who hoped to perhaps go pro (Witz, 2020).

Assessing the Risk

With significant potential societal, economic, and political impact at stake, league officials, coaches, players, and even politicians angled the issue of risk—what do we stand to lose if we just go ahead and play? Proponents of this perspective posited that Covid-19 really didn't present a threat to the student-athletes or the community. President Trump advocated repeatedly—through interviews, tweets, and speeches—for the return of college sports, and, in one interview, Trump claimed that "[t]he (virus) attacks old people very viciously. These football players are very young, strong people, physically.... I mean they're physically in extraordinary shape. So they're not going to have a problem (with the virus)" (Gleeson, 2020, para. 4).

In contrast, sports columnist Sally Jenkins (2020) contended that "[t]he only responsible choice, amid so many unknowns, is to take a collective knee and defer while campuses gauge the impact of reopening" (para. 2). However, she acknowledged the existence of some "folks who have never shown much inclination to put anybody's health above wins and losses.... Notre Dame once sent a student videographer to his death up a lift tower in 50-mph winds just to film a football practice. You can see the same sensibility at work in this pandemic—from office seekers as well as profit seekers" (para. 3).

The Big Ten conference initially canceled the entire fall 2020 sports season, referencing "too much uncertainty regarding potential medical risks to allow our student-athletes to compete this fall" (Giambalvo, 2020, para. 4; see also Purves, 2020). However, the conference soon caved to political/economic/fan pressure, reversed its position, and joined other conferences in allowing football—the big moneymaker for the Power 5—to proceed, as scheduled. President Trump heralded the reversal, tweeting that "[c]ollege football is an enormous part of fall Saturdays for millions of Americans, and it is coming back, thanks in no small part to the leadership of President Trump" (see Smith & Alexander, 2020, para. 8). (As Smith and Alexander noted in their article, Big Ten officials disputed Trump's claim of influencing the conference's decision.)

As leagues, teams, media, and even the president of the United States debated costs, benefits, risks, and realities of launching the 2020 college football season, what about the student-athletes who would be training in close quarters and competing in a contact sport at a time when people were supposed to stay six feet apart? How could they voice concerns and preferences, given the implicit power relationship of depending on the university for their scholarships (for related work, please see Frederick et al., 2017; Kluch, 2020; Staurowsky, 2014).

To be sure, some players supported moving forward with the season, albeit with conditions. Spearheaded by Clemon University quarterback Trevor Lawrence, around a dozen players started the #WeWantToPlay hashtag to encourage a return to play with safeguards (Kercheval & Sallee, 2020; Leitch, 2020). In a tweet that trended on Twitter, the players asserted that "[w]e want to play football this season. Establish universal health & safety procedures and protocols to protect college athletes against COVID-19 among all conferences across the NCAA. Give players the opportunity to opt out and respect their decision. Guarantee eligibility whether a player chooses to play the season or not" (Kercheval & Sallee, 2020, para. 4).

Even though the 2020 college football season ensued, it did so without consistency in terms of protection for players or approaches by teams and conferences. To my knowledge, no Division 1 college football player or coach died from Covid-19. However, Blinder et al. reported on December 11, 2020, that "[a]t least 6,629 people who play and work in athletic departments that compete in college football's premier leagues have contracted the virus ... (para. 2) [based on responses from] just 78 of the 130 universities in the National Collegiate Athletic Association's Football Bowl Subdivision" (para. 3). (Other schools declined to provide information.) According to Blinder et al., "The ranks of the infected have included some of the most prominent figures in college athletics. In football, Nick Saban of Alabama and Ryan Day of Ohio State tested positive" (para. 19). Lawrence, the eventual top pick in the 2021 NFL draft, did too (Hale, 2020). Although Lawrence experienced only "mild symptoms," according to his Instagram post on October 29, others were not so fortunate. Dellenger (2020) noted that "more college football players are revealing publicly their battle with COVID-19, and though none of them have died or been hospitalized long term, they have grown sick. At least 800 college football players have tested positive for the virus.... The actual number is likely much higher" (para. 4).

In a statement via Twitter on August 23, 2020, about his struggles with Covid-19, Arizona University receiver Jaden Mitchell pointed to the problem with reclaiming "normal" when the virus continues to loom as a threat. Mitchell emphasized that "[t]his virus is no joke. I lost 14 pounds and am still working on gaining it back and reconditioning myself.... The fact of the matter is that if this virus gets a hold of you and you experience symptoms, it will have a great impact on you."

Concluding Thoughts...

Perhaps no time in recent memory had "normal" seemed so elusive as during Covid-19. Sports provided the public, especially in the United States, with a collective, mediated window into what nonathletes were also experiencing—denial (and then grudging acceptance) that some unknown disease had made its way to us ... frustration that we had to give up or amend what we had originally planned to do ... fear that our own bodies or finances or future could be impacted ... anger that we couldn't flip a switch for life go back to pre-pandemic normal. Responses of athletes, teams, and leagues to Covid-19 through social media, public statements, and actions informed attentive fans about the physical impacts of the disease as well as the corresponding ones that also affected the rest of us as we tried to grapple with the myriad layers of the pandemic on our lives—physical, cultural, societal, economic, and political.

As I prepare to send this book to press, that saga continues.... Athletes eventually made their way to Tokyo for the "2020 Olympics" in the summer of 2021, with extremely few spectators amid health concerns as Covid continued to spike in Japan (see Keown, 2021; Murakami et al., 2021; Yamaguchi, 2021; https://www.reuters.com/world/asia-pacific/coronavirus-incidents-tokyo-olympics-2021-07-15/). Conversely, the 2021 NCAA football seasons premiered to packed stands in spite of the delta variant surge, with widely varying protocols for players and staff in terms of testing, quarantining, and encouraging vaccines (Levenson, 2021; Russo, 2021; Thamel, 2021). Although Levenson acknowledged that a few schools required fans to be vaccinated before entering the arena, he reported:

> College football and its crowd traditions are back to their full glory like they were in 2019, before Covid-19 restrictions sharply limited fan attendance in 2020. Some of the country's biggest powerhouses—including Georgia, Alabama, Ohio State and Oklahoma, to name a few—are hosting games to full capacity on Saturday. And fans who attend these games won't have to prove their vaccination status, won't be required to social distance and won't have to wear masks in their seats. The return of college football and its unique cultures, which began in earnest last week, are a source of communal bonding for sports fans, yet they also represent a source of anxiety for others [para. 2–4].

Earlier in this chapter, I suggested that sports have traditionally provided a sort of social comfort for us—as long as the game continues, we will too. Fittingly, that the game could not simply continue as originally scheduled also served an invaluable societal function during the pandemic too. If big, strong athletes could even be affected and if games had to be paused for an indefinite time, sports sent the message that Covid-19 should be taken seriously, at least in the first few months of the pandemic. However, the saga of sports during Covid-19 underscored the complexity of reconciling the quest for normal amid the realities of the disease.

CHAPTER 3

Fandom as Key to Politicization of Covid-19

Supporters created a Facebook group for Harris County Texas Judge Lina Hildago in 2020. Although the page is private, it could be found by anyone and included this description:

> Our elected Harris County Judge Lina Hildago has been under constant attack for attempting to keep the public safe during the COVID crisis. Racial slurs and hateful communications have been ongoing against Judge Hildago for a necessary "stay at home order" and "mask order" in order to keep people safe.... This page will represent our support for an intelligent and strong woman who was elected by the people.

Named the 2020 "Favorite Female Local Politician" by *OutSmart Magazine* (Zavaleta, 2020) and selected as a speaker at the 2020 Democratic National Convention (Svitek, 2020), the then-29-year-old judge prompted local, state, and national responses to her leadership during the Covid-19 health crisis, ranging from accolades and flowers to the threat of jail by Texas governor Abbott (O'Rourke, 2020). As O'Rourke noted, "this was Hidalgo's first experience leading in a national disaster that had the potential to affect all of the nearly 5 million people in her jurisdiction" (para. 6). Snyder (2020, para. 10) reported that "[a] Harris County official told me that after each of Hidalgo's public announcements, the volume of calls to the county switchboard is so great that extra staff is required to answer them. Many of the calls are not friendly: 'I've never seen this level of vitriol and hate,' the official said."

Indeed, this first pandemic in the era of social media has been marked by often strong reactions to public official policies and messages, with enthusiastic fans of their respective approaches endorsing practices and expressing appreciation (and angry opponents who fight to counter and change those same guidelines). With a death toll that has surpassed five million people in the world and cases again on the rise as of November 2021 (https://www.worldometers.info/

coronavirus/coronavirus-death-toll/), responses to public health initiatives (and to even previously little-known public officials) continue to be consequential for mitigating the spread of this disease.

This chapter explores how the orientation toward U.S. public officials as objects of fandom (or, indeed, the focus of anti-fandom) worked to fuel divergent, competing interpretive communities of fans (those who embraced a more science-based approach and those who disputed the necessity of adhering to prevalent public health recommendations) as well as to frame the two emergent master public health narratives in the United States. As both public officials and citizens sought to make sense of this disease, they implicitly co-constructed core features of the disease and preferred responses to it. In short, the enactment of Covid-19 through the lens of fandom proved consequential for interpretations of and reactions to it. In this chapter, I begin by discussing the ways in which fandom took a central role in the politicalization of Covid-19 in the United States. I then describe two features that served as the foundation for determining which of the competing narratives "rang more true" for those seeking to know what to think about this novel coronavirus (see W. Fisher, 1984)—which public officials became deemed as more trustworthy, and which could be counted as the "real" experts? I conclude this chapter by delving into the consequential nature of anti-fandom for orientations to Covid-19, bitterly and powerfully dividing communities and even families in the United States.

Fandom as Fuel for Politicalization

Of course, the complicated saga of the Covid-19 pandemic encompassed many diverse, complex, and interrelated issues and challenges. However, the social construction of public officials, especially in the United States, as objects of fandom provided a lens through which citizens responded to health recommendations and how the various levels of officials (local, state, national) treated the actions and utterances of each other.

Celebrity politics isn't new (see, e.g., Dean, 2017; Harvey, 2017; Wheeler, 2013; Wright, 2020). Wheeler recounted that "Teddy Roosevelt's politics owed much to the theatrics of vaudeville, which emphasized his 'larger-than-life' characteristics" (p. 39). Wheeler also observed that, after his performance in the 1960 presidential debates, "for the 70 million viewers who had watched the debates, Kennedy had developed a 'star quality' which coincided with the positive message of the 'New Frontier'" (p. 41). According to Wheeler, "both Kennedy's and Franklin

D. Roosevelt's presidencies would be noted for their cross-fertilization of the politics of fame with the marked increase of celebrity endorsements" (p. 41).

However, social media has amplified the treatment of political figures as not only celebrities but also objects of fandom to be supported by communities of like-minded fans, intensifying commitments (see related arguments by Harvey, 2017; Hinck, 2019; Wright, 2020). As Dean (2017, p. 409) explained, "fandom is now an established feature of contemporary politics." Sandvoss (2013, para. 3) argued:

> As fandom has become an increasingly ubiquitous mode of media consumption driven by ever greater access to and choice between different media texts are fueled by both media deregulation and media convergence in the digital age, these same forces have also eroded the boundaries between spheres of political and popular communication. Reflecting the shared platforms—television, magazines, the internet—through which both popular and political texts are accessed and commented on, contemporary political leaders are often represented and read in ways not dissimilar to celebrities drawn from the world of show business.

Unlike John Kennedy, Teddy Roosevelt, Franklin D. Roosevelt, and Ronald Reagan (a former movie star turned president), Trump's presidency unfolded in the postmodern era as he actively "broke the fourth wall" through near-constant tweets and calls to Fox News (see related work by Stelter, 2020). The hyper-mediated, politically charged environment since Trump's election in 2016 has energized fan cultures, not only regarding Mr. Trump but also myriad public officials from diverse political perspectives who find themselves attempting to share center stage.

In late March of 2020, a meme circulated on social media: "You wanted a reality show host as President, well now you're on *Survivor*" (Mandese, 2020, para. 2). As Mandese commented, "that's what we have folks, and he reminds us of it all the time, boasting about the TV 'ratings' of his national health crisis press conferences" (para. 5; see related article by Poniewozik, 2020, July 21).

Ouellette and Murray (2009, p. 7) argued that, "[a]lthough reality TV whets our desire for the authentic, much of our engagement with such texts paradoxically hinges on our awareness that what we are watching is constructed and contains 'fictional' elements." Further, they contended that "[m]ore and more programs rely on the willingness of 'ordinary' people to live their lives in front of the television cameras" (p. 9). With President Donald J. Trump, we had the successful businessman who bolstered his fame by stints on *Lifestyles of the Rich and Famous* and, of course, *The Apprentice*. He cultivated fans as an avid "base" of voters and Twitter followers, from his ride down the escalator, along the campaign trail, and into the White House, complete with "made for reality TV" moments such as the release of the *Access Hollywood* tape (see, e.g., Biressi, 2020; McDonnell & Wheeler, 2019; Ott, 2017).

The increasingly interactive and participatory nature of social media fosters dialogue between (and parasocial experiences with) not only political figures and supporters but also others in their circles of influence or interpretive communities (see related arguments by Meyrowitz, 1985). As I discussed in Chapter 1, the illusion of intimacy and interpersonal connections has intensified fan investments in the objects of their fandom as well as the positions that they embrace and promote (see, e.g., Horton & Wahl, 1956; Meyrowitz, 1985). Moreover, fans join with others in those interpretive communities of political celebrities and media personalities who share and spread related views. According to Sandvoss (2013, para. 33), "political fans are clearly motivated by an initial set of values and beliefs, but also develop an affective attachment to political parties and politicians."

Especially in the political realm, adherence to one set of beliefs, values, and convictions necessitates the rejection of other beliefs, values, and convictions. Endorsing a candidate means opposing his opponent. Again, as individuals participate more in the process and take it upon themselves to "like" information or "share" or "retweet" posts, that investment ties them even more to the object of their fandom—and, by extension, not the other person and that person's ideals, convictions, or positions. As Penney (2017, p. 417) asserted, "supporters take it upon themselves to build these culturally grounded associations by emulating patterns of effusive hero worship (and ridicule of perceived enemies) that are familiar in online fan communities." Sandvoss (2013, para. 49) explained that "[a]nti-fans, in contrast, demonstrate high levels of commitment to following and the object of their dislike, with which they are highly emotionally engaged." Sandvoss asserted:

> However, while the impact of political fandom on polarization and disengagement thus appears to vary from fan culture to fan culture depending on the dominant value systems of such fan cultures, there is a second consequence of political fandom for democratic processes that is more immediate and that even the more participatory fan cultures are unable to escape. In building and maintaining identification and affective attachment to a given party or politician, political enthusiasm utilizes the "interpretive fair" of digital media environments.... Political brands as fan objects, thus, are realized through practices of media consumption and selection [p. 105].

Ott (2017, p. 65) concurred, noting that "[i]n short, people across the political spectrum (the right and the left) are being fed a steady diet of what they want to hear. The result is the creation of ideological silos, powerful echo chambers of misinformation." As Kim and Kreps (2020) asserted regarding Covid-19, "Especially when messages disseminated through diverse communication channels are politicized, individuals' information-seeking behaviors become more likely to transform into information sharing only with the members of a homogenous group, which endangered efforts to prevent and control the COVID-19 pandemic" (p. 8).

Perhaps never have such mediated silos been so consequential as during the Covid-19 pandemic. As I finish this book, this contemporary hyper-mediated, contextual situation continues to serve as a powerful undercurrent for orientations to the Covid-19 pandemic. As I will discuss later in this chapter, then-president Trump set the tone early, interjecting uncertainty, hesitancy, and anti-science rhetoric into initial Covid-19 messaging—messaging that ended up splitting into two competing ideologically driven master narratives about the virus, fueled by public officials who became objects of deeply loyal and zealous mediated and fan communities.

As Dean (2017, p. 410) noted, "Scholars of celebrity politics have identified a now well-established phenomenon whereby media celebrities seek to leverage their celebrity status—including mobilizing their fan base—to push particular political claims." Lamerichs et al. (2018, para. 20) agreed that "today's politicians can easily construct and share their own framings of current issues on social media.... Trump himself is a perfect example of this behavior. His use of Twitter is functional, aimed at creating a specific, timely image of him and specific political events." According to Dean, "In this context, a celebrity's fan base—or at least a section of it—can become politicised when the celebrity-fan object takes up a particular political position" (p. 410).

As I will detail throughout the remainder of this chapter, early efforts to encourage a unified public approach by "flattening the curve" got derailed and fragmented as opposing fan communities embraced divergent perspectives that got spread like the wildfires that burned during part of the pandemic. Although Stanfill (2020, p. 127) acknowledged that "connecting fandom to broader social and electoral politics is less common," in this case, I will argue that fandom clearly contributed to the politicalization of Covid-19 by respective fan communities. Specifically, that politicalization stemmed from a near-perfect storm of general societal uncertainties about implications of this novel coronavirus, coupled with a dynamic leader who had amassed a devoted fan base (and who was seeking reelection during that very year) *and* an almost equally dedicated fan base with strong opposition already to that same leader. Thus, nearly from the very outset, competing fan communities (fans of President Trump, anti-fans of President Trump, fans of science, anti-fans of science) clashed, with catastrophic consequences for human life and long-term residual effects on the U.S. economy and culture.

Van Zoonen (2004, p. 48) asserted that "[i]n the context of politics, feelings of 'enthusiasm' (all is well) and 'anxiety' (something is wrong) are particularly relevant, because they produce the cognitive state of mind that enables the acquisition of information, the analysis of the situation, the assessment of alternatives and development of new routines." As I explain, the sorting out of "all is well" or "something is wrong" in terms of accepting and then spreading perspectives about Covid-19 extended powerfully from orientations to public officials as objects of fandom and responses by their respective fan communities. Collectively, those fans co-constructed what constituted "viable" explanations and "legitimate" options. It all came down to the voices that fan communities deemed to be trustworthy and credible as public officials, media personalities, and a host of other celebrities trotted out their own experts to support their version of "truth." In 2017, Penney cautioned:

> while the participatory culture framework is generally optimistic about the democratizing potential of interactive digital technologies and their uses by impassioned fan communities and other "grassroots intermediaries," this body of work has begun to acknowledge a range of negative social consequences that may result from a more open-ended and unrestricted communication environment [p. 407].

Amid the massive chaos of messaging in the public sphere, especially through social media, the co-determination of which people to trust, who should be counted on as "expert," and how to best proceed in social life amid a once-in-a-century pandemic extended from their respective interpretive, fan-like communities.

Deep Divides and Strong Alliances

During the second wave of the Covid-19 pandemic in the United States, Wisconsin governor Tony Evers asserted that "'[w]e're in a crisis right now and need to immediately change our behavior to save lives.... There's no other way to put it, we are overwhelmed'" (Bacon & Stucka, 2020, para. 9). However, perhaps one of the problems throughout the pandemic has been the starkly different "ways of putting it," especially by varied U.S. public officials. Each public statement, press conference, social media post, and response to other public figures contributed to not only that person's public presentation of self (see related work by Goffman, 1959), but those actions also worked to shape master narratives about Covid-19 and framed the ways in which their fans came to understand it as well. Especially early in the pandemic, fans drew lines as they responded to certain public officials as "trustworthy" or "expert."

Trustworthiness

Just as the pandemic swept through the United States in waves, the understanding of and orientation to it by both public officials and citizens evolved too. In the early days of the pandemic, two governors, in particular, captured considerable attention for earning the trust of their respective constituencies (see related work by Martin & Burns, 2020; Reisman, 2020; Villegas, 2020) by being highly dependable and relatable. Both routinely referenced their own families, embraced a paternal persona in shepherding citizens of their respective states in a calm and steady manner, and took to the airwaves daily as they offered information and reassurance to the sometimes millions who watched the live broadcasts. In so doing, they became quite the objects of fandom by individuals across the country who felt that they could count on them to lead the way through a very scary and uncertain time. Ohio governor Mike DeWine (and then Ohio Public Health Director Dr. Amy Acton) approached the virus by focusing on scientific facts, setting aside politics or political implications, and demonstrating empathy during daily press conferences. Then-New York governor Andrew Cuomo also met every day with New Yorkers, speaking frankly with them as "family" during daily briefings.

#WineWithDeWine

Amid considerable uncertainty and disruption to regular schedules, in March 2020, one event became routine for many Ohioans— Governor DeWine's daily press conferences about Covid-19 (see, e.g., Villegas, 2020). Along with Dr. Acton, DeWine provided "no-nonsense, high-fact" briefings (Witte & Zezima, 2020, para. 8) that also included folksy features, such as the "tie of the day" (usually representing an Ohio college or team) and a fun virtual tribute at the end (a performance by a band or choir, photos of masks or children in white coats, etc.). The press conference typically included an overview by DeWine (with any updates on closings or openings), a Covid-19 statistics update by Acton, and economic-based information from Lieutenant Governor Jon

Husted. Phrases such as "flatten the curve," "we're all in this together, Ohio," "wear a mask," and, one of Acton's favorites, "not all heroes wear capes. Mine wears a white coat" (Ryan, 2020, para. 4). Acknowledging a 30 percent increase over prior ratings for the same time slot, Lagatta (2020, para. 2) noted, "The daily afternoon news conferences in which DeWine and Acton share the latest information on the rapidly changing landscape regarding the coronavirus has led to a significant spike in ratings for area broadcast television stations, not to mention a drinking game for isolated locals tuning in."

One of my friends—a mom of four—confided that she reserved time each day to listen on her phone in her car—the one place where she could get some peace and quiet, given that her kids were all home and in her house. Others joked that "it must be 5 p.m. somewhere" so they poured a glass of wine (at 2 p.m. local time) while watching the press conference. Indeed, thousands joined the "Wine with DeWine" Facebook page, with the motto "Keep on drinking; we're going to be here awhile." Lagatta (2020, para. 9) reported that others connected "on Twitter with the hashtags #WineWithDeWine and #SnackinWithActon." According to Lagatta, some even started "a drinking game for isolated locals tuning in ... prompting them to take a sip when, for instance, they hear the phrase 'flatten the curve' or when Acton removes or puts on her glasses" (para. 10).

Beyond the amusement of drinking games, fun merchandise for sale on the internet with DeWine and Acton's phrases and images, and a sense of community with others who were all at home in quarantine as well, DeWine's and Acton's respective approaches to the crisis received widespread praise for their commitment to science-based facts and seemingly genuine, heartfelt concern for their fellow Ohioans (see Allard, 2020; Martin & Burns, 2020; Quinn, 2020; Witte & Zezima, 2020). According to Witte and Zezima, "The governor's ahead-of-the-curve response has won raves from public health experts and from politicians of both parties, who say DeWine's reliance on medical advice and his unwillingness to put a sheet on the crisis' damaging impact stands out" (para. 9).

As Quinn (2020, para. 1) reported, "Ohio seems to be having a lovefest with its governor, Mike DeWine, and its health director, Dr. Amy Acton, based on a new poll and what people are telling Cleveland.com." One of the poll's respondents replied, "Looking at the medical side of this nightmare and putting politics aside, Ohio's governor has shown from the beginning that he is the head of the family of Ohio" (para. 5). According to Quinn, another person wrote that "[o]ur Governor has shown to all of us that he truly cares and isn't afraid to make bold moves whether or not his choices are looked highly upon by his political party. Because of this brave courageous man, Ohio should come out of this medically better than many of the states. He has become the man that everyone is watching and following" (para. 6).

Arguably, though, a major factor in Governor DeWine's early success with the pandemic stemmed not only from his decisiveness but also his compassionate counterpart—Dr. Amy Acton. Dr. Acton attracted national attention for the ways in which she explained medical information and advocated for action. In a column for the *New Yorker*, P. Williams (2020) reported on some of the expressions of fandom that Acton inspired:

> A singer performed an Amy Acton tribute song on YouTube ("I trust you completely"; "You look so fine in your long white coat"). The National Bobblehead Hall of Fame and Museum unveiled an Amy Acton figure. Little girls dressed up like Acton and staged living-room press conferences. On Facebook, a fan page accrued more than a hundred and thirty thousand members. An Ohio nurse told an NBC affiliate, "I actually cry pretty much every time I watch her, because she's very inspiring." At a presser, Acton, after reading one child's thank-you letter aloud, said that as a public servant it was her "*job* to do this for you" [para. 14].

Acton participated in a CNN special, "The ABCs of Covid-19," with *Sesame Street* characters in June 2020 (Richardson, 2020), and she sparked a *New York Times* analysis of her briefings. According to Allard (2020, para. 4–5), the analysis concluded that "[t]he big three themes in Acton's delivery ... have been 'empowerment,' 'brutal honesty,' and 'vulnerability.' Acton does not *order* residents to follow state guidelines. She makes them feel like they should, like doing so is *heroic*.... Even saying 'I don't know' ... can be calming when so many leaders are unwilling to admit uncertainty."

The Cuyahoga County Board of Health Commissioner Terry Allan commented in an online article that "[s]he actually tells the truth. She says, 'This is going to be hard, this is going to be difficult, there will be more cases, there will be deaths. This will be heartbreaking, but we can get through this'.... She makes us feel like we have a shared responsibility to take care of this" (Ryan, 2020, para. 24). According to Ryan, one fan even uploaded a Twitter post on March 17, 2020, confiding that "I think I would follow Dr. Amy Acton off a cliff at this point" (para. 4). As Yost (2020, para. 7–8) asserted, "Acton instantly became a female role model for many and a trusted voice for most Ohioans.... The results are clear. Most Ohioans listened to Acton. That's why Ohio's rate of cases and deaths are nearly half that of neighboring Michigan and Pennsylvania, which reacted more slowly."

As the pandemic ensued, though, not everyone continued to feel the same way, for reasons that we outline in the next few sections. Within only a few months of the pandemic's onset in Ohio, Acton received threats, and she decided to resign in June 2020 (Ludlow, 2020; Rosenberg, 2020; Yost, 2020). In response, "[m]ore than 1,000 Ohio residents signed and submitted a digital 'thank you' card [that read] 'Thank you for your steady and effective leadership of Ohio's public health response to COVID-19. Your public health orders have saved countless lives, and I appreciate the work you have done on behalf of all Ohio residents'" (C. Anderson, 2020, para. 1–2). I signed the card, and I later received an email from the sponsoring "Red, Wine, & Blue" fan group, updating that number to "more than 20,000 people—from almost every county in Ohio—signed our thank you card to Dr. Amy Acton." Yet, Yost argued:

> Acton brought out the best in us, and regrettably, the worst, as best described by House Minority Leader Emilia Sykes, D-Akron. "Having an abusive legislature constantly introducing and passing bills to curb her power in the middle of a pandemic had to have been difficult to withstand. Having anti-Semitic insults being hurled at her by elected officials and protesters camped out on her family's lawn must have been upsetting. Having an entire Economic Recovery Task Force created to undermine and criticize the well-informed and best-intentioned actions she was taking to save lives had to have been insulting" [para. 10–11].

Governor DeWine also faced lawsuits and criticism from some citizens and lawmakers as well as an impeachment challenge ("ABC6/Fox28 poll," 2020; Balmert, 2020; Campbell, 2020). According to Cillizza (2020), "DeWine's handling of the ongoing coronavirus pandemic, which has won him plaudits from coast to coast, has so angered a part of the Republican base in his state that a trio of lawmakers from his own party have decided to try and do something about it" (para. 7). The editorial staff at the *Toledo Blade* commented that "[p]roving that no good deed goes unpunished, Ohio Gov. Mike DeWine—among the most highly praised leaders during the coronavirus pandemic—is being targeted for impeachment" ("Impeachment is foolishness," 2020, August 30). However, as Ingles and Kasler (2020, para. 7) reported, "legislative leaders quickly shot down the proposal to impeach DeWine." One DeWine proponent observed:

> Okay, let me get this straight: Florida opens up too early and the COVID-19 rate jumps, so it has to back down; same with Texas. Georgia's governor prevents localities from requiring masks, the COVID-19 rate jumps, so he backs down. Ohio's GOP governor listens to medical professionals and shuts the state down early on. Ohio does pretty well, but under pressure from the

extreme right Governor DeWine backs away from requiring masks as he opens the state. The COVID-19 rate jumps. So DeWine returns to rationality and requires masks. The COVID-19 rate drops. And our governor deserves to be impeached? [Balmert, 2020, comments].

Governor DeWine responded to the impeachment possibility with "[i]f that's how they want to spend their time I'd just say to them, have at it" (Troy & Skalka, 2020, para. 2), to which another fan asserted, "[g]ood, strong words, Governor Mike! You continue to handle all of this well, even without the great-smart Dr. Acton by your side. Stay strong and continue doing the right things for the people of Ohio!" (Troy & Skalka, 2020, comments).

Indeed, the loyalty to both DeWine and Acton continued well into fall 2020. According to an approval poll released on September 25, 2020, "public support for DeWine and his response to the coronavirus (COVID-19) pandemic remains strong," with a 72 percent approval rating ("Most Ohioans approve," 2020). However, amid increasing political pressure from others in his own party, legal limitations that Ohio legislators placed on his authority, and the absence of Acton by his side, DeWine's pandemic leadership faded, disappointing some who embraced his initial approach (see, e.g., Borchardt, 2021; Decker, 2021).

For her part, Acton's fans continue to post articles and resources in the Facebook groups that bear her name, and they carry her torch by advocating for wearing masks, distancing, and taking the virus seriously. As Witte (2020, para. 4) argued, "To her legions of fans, she's a hero whose aggressive action as Ohio health director has saved lives, and whose calm, clear and compassionate style is a national model for how leaders should be communicating amid an unparalleled public health crisis." One reader commented on Witte's article, noting that "Dr Actin is an Ohio hero. She bases her decisions on the best science, takes the time to educate, and always delivers her recommendations with empathy. I salute Governor Dewine for selecting and standing by her" (comments). Another asserted that "Amy Acton is a calm voice of reason and sanity, promoting health science and common sense in the face of belligerence and proud ignorance. When at long last this coronavirus threat has passed, I sincerely hope our next authentic U.S. president invites her to the White House and proclaims her an American hero" (Witte, 2020, comments).

The "Luv Gov"

As he closed each of his press conference (on over 100 consecutive days, including weekends and holidays throughout the pandemic),

New York governor Andrew Cuomo referenced the same slide—"New Yorkers are Tough, Smart, United, Disciplined, and Loving" (see, e.g., Cuomo, 2020, dedication). The "loving" part of his slogan became just as important as fighting for resources. He committed to "just the facts, ma'am" (as he liked to say), inspiring independent-thinking New Yorkers to comply with rigid regulations and pleading with citizens to stay the course with mitigation measures (see, e.g., Jong-Fast, 2020; McBain, 2020; Spector, 2020). McBain asserted that "Cuomo's handling of the pandemic has not only underlined his fundamental competence, his honesty, acumen and calm authority thrown into sharper relief by Trump's blustering ineffectualness. It has also revealed a softer side and a new relatability. Cuomo never inspired much public love or affection—until now" (para. 6).

Jong-Fast (2020, para. 4) insisted that she really hadn't been a Cuomo fan before, "[b]ut what a difference a pandemic makes. All of a sudden, I love Governor Cuomo, his soothing Queens accent, his stories about his dad Mario ... and his 88 year old mother Matilda. And then there's Andrew the dad, embarrassing his kids with stories of their upbringing after his divorce when he was a single father." As B. Smith (2020, para. 6) added, "He has publicly worried over his daughters and his 88 year old mother."

Given this transparency and reflexivity about the governor's own family, Dowd (2020a, para. 1–2) reflected that "[i]t's no wonder that watching Andrew Cuomo's daily briefings can make some people crave Chianti and meatballs. Besides coolly explaining the facts in this terrifying and stultifying plague season, the governor of New York evokes the feeling of a big Italian family dinner table." In fact, he often helped viewers to feel as though they were invited to pull up a chair. One Sunday morning, he talked about plans to make pasta sauce after the briefing for Sunday dinner with his daughters (who were quarantining with him) as well as his daughter Mariah's boyfriend. As Shepherd and Armus (2020) reported, Cuomo then casually launched into advice for other dads, as though he and the viewers were just sitting around chatting about parenting. According to Shepherd and Armus, Cuomo asserted that "[t]he answer on what you think of the boyfriend is always, 'I like the boyfriend.' ... Otherwise it triggers NDS. NDS is natural defiance syndrome ... and then they like the boyfriend more because he is opposed by the father. So the answer has to be 'I like the boyfriend'" (para. 4).

Apparently, Cuomo really did like this boyfriend at the time, and Cuomo fans appreciated this moment at the briefing. As one physician (who happened to be tuning in for the press conference) tweeted,

"Cuomo talking about his daughter's boyfriend and his weekly Italian family dinner of spaghetti and meatballs during his daily governor's #COVID19 update is the most normal thing that I've seen on TV in weeks" (Shepherd & Armus, 2020, para. 12).

Cuomo's banter with brother Chris, who happened to be a CNN anchor, on the latter's prime-time show fueled not only the governor's popularity but also fostered further connections with viewers (see Aiello, 2020; Bricker, 2020; Contreras, 2020; Pat, 2020; Schnurr, 2022; Spector, 2020). As Contreras noted, "In recent weeks, the two brothers have become a beloved pair for Americans watching TV at home. Their funny rapport and candid nature with one another has injected a sense of humanity into the news, something that viewers enjoy seeing amid reports of the coronavirus" (para. 2). Bricker claimed:

> Their banter, the kind only two brothers can share no matter how old they are, often went viral, and in a way almost served as the peanut butter that masks the taste of medicine for your dog; the vital updates about the coronavirus were being made more palatable by Andrew and Chris' affectionate ribbing. Serious talking points about the pandemic were interrupted by jabs about Andrew's tired appearance or Chris' love for the gym [para. 20].

According to Dowd (2020, para. 4), at least for the press conferences, Andrew Cuomo acknowledged "this is as much of a social crisis as a health crisis." With candor and compassion, Dowd contended that "the governor has become a sort of national shrink, talking us through our fear, our loss, and our growing stir-craziness" (para. 12). Jong-Fast (2020) reflected:

> As the pandemic rages, and my city is decimated and I watch the empty streets from my window, I'm comforted by Andrew Cuomo's 11 a.m. press conferences, which both the local news and national networks are showing. It's nice to know that someone is governing, that someone is keeping track of the hospital beds and the ventilators and the masks, and keeping pressure on the federal government.... There's something nice about having someone in government whom you can actually trust [para. 14, 16].

Indeed, for his most devoted fans, Governor Cuomo's daily press briefings provided familiarity, stability, and reassurance that helped instill trust that he had their best interests at heart and would fight to protect them. In response to Dowd's (2020a) *New York Times* column, one reader commented:

> I've been watching Cuomo's briefings almost daily with great attention. To me, he doesn't come across as anything out of the ordinary or super human. He comes across as anyone's dad who is trying to do what is best for his family and that is exactly the point. He is smart, but not overly bookish. He is

common sense wise, but not condescending. It doesn't take a genius to figure out what needs to be [done] in a situation like this. It takes a solid understanding of the gravity of the problem and the practical knowhow of how to solve it and that is exactly the point. Politicians don't act like this. In public, they don't act like they are someone's dad. Everything they say is measured for maximum political benefit. Your dad is more interested in keeping you safe than scoring votes from the family. Your dad doesn't play politics with your safety and that is exactly the point. Trump, on the other hand, is all about scoring points. He is all about the politics of Trump. He surrounds himself with people who are most concerned with promoting his grandiosity. Cuomo's daughters are most concerned with helping their father succeed in protecting New Yorkers. The difference couldn't be more striking and that is exactly the point. We will beat this virus with the guidance of people like Cuomo, in spite of the errors of the ego driven Trump. Every kid should have a dad like Andrew Cuomo. That's what America needs now and that is exactly the point [comments].

Another fan also commented on that same article, noting "I just want to praise the guy. I want to praise his father, too. Whatever it was that made Mario such a decent human being, Andrew got it. These are the kind of people we need to lead us. I trust what he says, and I would do what he asks me to do. That's the leadership that we need right now" (comments).

As with Governor DeWine and Dr. Acton, support for Governor Cuomo certainly was not universal at the time. As Berman (2020, para. 3) recounted, "In contrast to other prominent state and local leaders, Cuomo's initial response to the coronavirus outbreak was slow and mistake-filled." Gold and Robinson (2020, para. 2) went further, asserting that "Cuomo should be one of the most loathed officials in American right now." For example, as Vielkind et al. (2020, para. 6) claimed, "[m]illions of people continued to pack commuter trains and subways in the five-day span between Mr. de Blasio's 'shelter in place' guidance and Mr. Cuomo's eventual shutdown order." Nonetheless, as Berman argued, "the governor's buoyant image has been a study in the power of public communication to overshadow policy failures: Cuomo's detailed, candid, and often weirdly funny daily briefings became appointment television for New Yorkers stuck in their homes and for a national cable audience transfixed by a leader who, unlike Trump, was tackling the crisis head-on" (para. 3).

Of course, although Cuomo navigated initial concerns about the rapidity of his response and handling of nursing homes during the pandemic, just under a year and a half from the time when he achieved rave reviews as a governor, he abruptly resigned amid allegations of sexual harassment and considerable corresponding cooling of some former fans (see, e.g., Ferré-Sadurní & Goodman, 2021; Flood, 2021; Jong-Fast, 2021). Indeed, Ferré-Sadurní and Goodman referred to the extraordinary turn of events as an "astonishing reversal of fortune for one of the nation's best-known leaders" (para. 1). For example, Jong-Fast, one of the individuals who praised Cuomo's reassuring press conferences, joined with those who called for his resignation:

> My [original] take was the subject of some ridicule from various smart people back then but here's the thing about back then: I was really really really scared. I was convinced I would die of coronavirus (para. 4).... And at a time when Trump was holding daily briefings with no information at all, just his madman ravings as doctors and others stood by, somebody projecting decency and competence seemed appealing to me and to tens of millions of others who tuned in. (para. 6)... And a better take would have been to see the ways, more obvious in hindsight but not hidden then, that Cuomo mismanaged the crisis here, by delaying an urgently [sic] shutdown *because* his rival Mayor Bill de Blasio had called for one and, most damning, by forcing nursing homes to accept COVID patients from hospitals and then fighting for nearly a year to cover up the death count tied to that decision [para. 8].

Summary

As I wrote this book, perhaps the most riveting (and challenging) piece—other than the fact that the pandemic has ensued for now nearly two years—has been the fluidity of this dynamic public construction of both public participants and the virus itself. DeWine, Acton, and Cuomo emerged quickly like bright shooting stars, providing powerful illuminations of comfort and clarity during an otherwise dark time. For those early months as individuals dealt with the trauma of Covid-19— images of stacked body bags, health care providers in hazmat suits, empty streets, and lengthy food lines, among others—their voices resonated with millions and mattered greatly in mitigating the spread of the virus in their respective states. During those moments that seemed to linger at the time but in retrospect passed like a flash, they cultivated their respective fan bases that beloved them and, perhaps more important, trusted them about issues that could, quite literally, save their lives—the need to "stay safe at home" and then to engage in social distancing and wearing a mask—before the advent of vaccines.

Although three of the more visible public figures during this crisis, Mike DeWine, Amy Acton, and Andrew Cuomo represent thousands of state and local officials who sat in front of a television camera or behind a computer keyboard and sought to provide guidance and reassurance to their anxious constituents (and who attained fan-like gratitude as well as, often, scorn from those who disagreed with their approach). For the reasons noted above, messages from DeWine, Acton, and Cuomo particularly resonated as observers oriented to them as likeable, concerned, relatable, but, most important, trustworthy—someone to give the best information and advice that they had when they obtained it. Indeed, the ways in which these public figures spoke of certain details, referenced sources, and recommended actions worked reflexively to position other professionals as "the experts."

Expertise

In his book, Andrew Cuomo (2020) commented that "'[u]nfortunately, every expert [regarding Covid-19] had a different position on the 'facts'" (p. 40). Truly, in fairness to the World Health Organization and the U.S. Centers for Disease Control and Prevention and other national and international public health organizations, Covid-19 comprised a novel coronavirus that no one had encountered before. Indeed, with a plethora of questions and much speculation about how the virus got transmitted (e.g., on surfaces or through the air) or how to prevent its spread from the very start (e.g., masks or no masks), I found myself nodding as I read Cuomo's observation about the challenges of navigating such conflicting information.

Yet, the occurrence of such a major health event certainly was not unprecedented in world history, as evidenced by the 1918 Spanish flu (see, e.g., Barry, 2018; Crosby, 2003), or necessarily even unanticipated by contemporary leaders. According to Mosk (2020, para. 1), "In the summer of 2005, President George W. Bush was on vacation at his ranch in Crawford, Texas, when he began flipping through an advance reading copy of a new book about the 1918 flu pandemic. He couldn't put it down." The book was an early edition of Barry's *The Great Influenza*. Mosk reported that Bush became "obsessed" (para. 12) with preplanning for a possible pandemic, resulting in significant national preparations:

> In a November 2005 speech at the National Institutes of Health, Bush laid out proposals in granular detail—describing with stunning prescience how a pandemic in the United States would unfold. Among those in the audience was Dr. Anthony Fauci, the leader of the current crisis response, who was then and still is now the director of the National Institute of Allergy and Infectious Diseases [para. 14].

Although other public officials established trustworthiness and credibility in the United States over the 10 months, perhaps no one else became more visible and revered as "the expert" than Dr. Anthony Fauci, director of the National Institute of Allergy and Infectious

Diseases (see related work by Ceccarelli, 2020). As Ceccarelli wrote in her analysis of Fauci "as rhetorically savvy scientist citizen" (p. 239), "the ethos Fauci constructs for himself in multiple public interviews is the expert as truth teller, consistent, patient, and prudent" (p. 241).

As I noted in the beginning of this book, in the early days of the pandemic, actress Julia Roberts participated in the "#PassTheMic" campaign (A. Fernández, 2020; Wanshel, 2020). She gushed that "there are very few experts of anything in the world and you truly have emerged as a personal hero for me" (A. Fernández, para. 5).

Roberts isn't alone in her fandom of Fauci. One of the Facebook groups in his honor achieved over 154,000 fans. He was selected as a 2020 Robert F. Kennedy Human Rights Ripple of Hope Award laureate (A. Kim, 2020), and the National Italian American Foundation paid tribute to Fauci with a star-studded tribute gala as well as newly established "Fauci Fellowships" "to support research in infectious diseases in recognition of Dr. Fauci's contributions to humanity and the medical and scientific community" (Wulderk, 2020, para. 6). The Washington Nationals selected Fauci to throw the first pitch of the new baseball season, noting "'Dr. Fauci has been a true champion for our country during the Covid-19 pandemic and throughout his distinguished career, so it is only fitting that we honor him as we kick off the 2020 season and defend our World Series Championship title,' the team said in a statement" (Treisman, 2020, para. 4; see also Bailey, 2020). Afterward, his commemorative baseball card "shattered an all-time sales record run for the company [Topps NOW] in selling 51,512 cards in the span of just 24 hours" (Concha, 2020, para. 1; see also West, 2020).

Further, as "Fauci emerged as an at times reluctant—and polarizing—media star ... [his] emails show that he was inundated with correspondence from colleagues, hospital administrators, foreign governments and random strangers—about 1,000 messages a day, he says at one point—writing to seek his advice, solicit his help or simply offer encouragement" (Paletta & Abutaleb, 2021, para. 6). Based on an analysis of Fauci's emails (secured through a Freedom of Information Act request by the *Washington Post*), Paletta and Abutaleb reported that, "[i]n the early days of the pandemic, everyone, it seemed, wanted a piece of Fauci. Numerous organizations wrote to offer awards and honorariums" (para. 21), and others invited Fauci for a variety of high-profile speaking engagements and collaborations. One endeavor involved production of a documentary in which filmmakers followed Fauci as he responded to the pandemic. Disney+ released *Fauci*, a documentary produced by National Geographic, in August 2021 (https://films.

nationalgeographic.com/fauci; for a trailer, please see https://www.youtube.com/watch?v=NBEau86jZjI).

Yet, as Fauci sought the national microphone over the course of the pandemic to promote staying home and then wearing masks, maintaining distance, washing hands, and the vaccine, then-president Trump coveted his popularity and chose to muffle Fauci's message by initially blocking his testimony before Congress (Pramuk, 2020) and implicitly and explicitly undermining his expertise (Leibovich, 2020). As to the former, Trump sought to schedule his own pitch at Yankee Stadium, an idea quickly tabled (Rogers & Weiland, 2020) and complained about his own comparative popularity (Chapman, 2020; Crowley, 2020; Nazaryan, 2020; see related article by Parker et al., 2020). Crowley reported that "President Trump devolved into self-pity during a White House coronavirus briefing on Tuesday, lamenting that his approval ratings were lower than those of two top government medical experts (para. 1).... 'They're highly thought of—but nobody likes me'" (para. 3).

In early June of 2020, at the start of the "summer surge" in cases, Sciutto and LeBlanc (2020) noted that Trump had not spoken with Fauci in two weeks. Over a month later, in July 2020, Senior reported "that the Trump White House waged a highly unusual campaign last week to undermine [Fauci's] credibility" (para. 3). Rogers (2020, para. 1) reported that "Fauci hit back on Wednesday [July 25, 2020], calling recent efforts to discredit him 'bizarre' and a hindrance to the government's ability to communicate information about the coronavirus pandemic."

Nearly one year later, Fauci continued to battle to retain his credibility and affirm his expertise (see France-Presse, 2021; Massie, 2021). On June 16, 2021, France-Presse wrote that "[s]everal Republican lawmakers, eager to blame a US government official for the response to the coronavirus pandemic, introduced a bill Tuesday to fire Anthony Fauci, the face of American efforts to combat COVID-19" (para. 1). However, according to Massie, Fauci "says he puts 'very little weight in the craziness of condemning me' after he became a target for right-wing critics" (para. 1).

Yet, as I detail in the next section, the dispute over Fauci's expertise became a central point for both fans (and anti-fans) of the two competing Covid-19 master narratives. Those who affirmed a traditional scientific narrative that echoed official public health recommendations hailed Fauci as an expert; whereas, those who embraced a narrative that took a more skeptical perspective of both Covid-19 and those official public health recommendations positioned Fauci as an enemy.

Implications of Fandom and Anti-Fandom for Covid-19 Master Narratives

Notably, the relationship between President Trump and his team of medical advisers began as hesitant but not overtly adversarial (see Woodward, 2020). However, as I detail now, the failure of national-level leadership to remain on the same page led not only to confusing, inconsistent messaging but also to fractured, competing narratives driven by the fan communities that embraced them. Reflexively, national (and, to some extent, state and local) messaging in the United States got shaped by fandom as well. Thus, I suggest that the story of what came to be splintered narratives did not emerge in a clear, simple, linear manner, but rather in a messy, convoluted, and cyclical one instead. In the remainder of this chapter, I document the ways in which fandom (and anti-fandom) in terms of public officials influenced the splitting of one dominant public health narrative into two as well as the implications for public health.

Evolution of Competing Covid-19 Public Health Narratives

As I've argued throughout this book, our interpretive communities provide a lens through which we make interpretations. For a president of the United States, certainly, daily briefings and advisers provide not only information but also guidance for assessing risks and making decisions (see related websites for more information: https://www.intelligence.gov/publics-daily-brief/presidents-daily-brief; http://electioncollege.com/cabinet-presidents-official-advisors/). Of course, presidents choose many of their advisers who help them with policy choices, and, obviously, they come into the role (and any subsequent decision-making) with the background of prior relationships and professional and educational experiences. We can't turn off what we have experienced or ignore what has impacted us or opportunities that await us.

Public materials help us to gain a sense of the lens through which Donald Trump envisioned and handled Covid-19 from the outset—a best-selling book by a family member (https://www.dw.com/en/mary-trumps-book-about-the-president-a-bestseller/a-54211526), investigative reporting by a host of reporters, as well as Trump's personal tweets and actions. Based on a series of interviews with then-president Trump, Bob Woodward reported in his book that "[t]he president maintained his upbeat rhetoric in the early weeks of the virus had been deliberate. 'I wanted to always play it down,' Trump told me... 'I still like playing it down, because I don't want to create a panic'" (p. 286).

In her book, Mary Trump (2020) contended that Trump's approach might have extended more from a more personal motivation. She argued that "Donald's initial response to COVID-19 underscores his need to minimize negativity at all costs. Fear—the equivalent of weakness in our family—is as unacceptable to him now as it was when he was three years old" (p. 207). She theorized that "Donald didn't drag his feet in December 2019, in January, in February, in March because of his narcissism; he did it because of his fear of appearing weak or failing to project the message that everything was 'great,' 'beautiful,' and 'perfect'" (pp. 207–208). Mary Trump argued that "[a]cknowledging the victims of COVID-19 would be to associate himself with their weakness, a trait his father taught him to despise" (p. 210).

Whatever the reason, Donald Trump's public utterances did, indeed, minimize the threat of Covid-19 (see, e.g., Blake & Rieger, 2020; Coppins, 2020; Parker & Rucker, 2020; Paz, 2020; Woodward, 2020), echoing concurrent voices on Fox News. Stelter (2020) argued that Trump's fandom of Fox News, coupled with pressure on the network by fans to produce pro-Trump programming, worked to both reiterate Trump's hesitant, skeptical, dismissive tone about the virus as well as to fuel it. According to Stelter, "my reporting indicates that he was lulled into complacency by Fox's downplaying of the disease" (p. 25). Moreover, Stelter claimed, "Day by day, tweet by tweet, the country came to grips with the fact that presidential statements—which used to really mean something—were now just the misinformed and misspelled rants of an elderly Fox fan" (p. 112).

In his book *Hoax: Donald Trump, Fox News, and the Dangerous Distortion of Truth*, Stelter (2020) documented both Trump's fandom of Fox News as well as his frequent contributions to it. Trump routinely called in to various shows on the network, such as *Fox & Friends* and *Hannity*. Stelter asserted that "Trump and Hannity brought out the worst in one another. Trump programmed Hannity's show, and Hannity produced Trump's presidency. Hannity fed misinformation to Trump, and Trump fed it right back to Hannity" (p. 6). Stelter observed that "it is impossible to know how much an individual's choices are influenced by the TV hosts they trust. But it is readily apparent that Fox failed its viewers at key moments during the pandemic" (p. 13) [and] "it is obvious that Fox's fingerprints were all over the government's response" (p. 14).

Parker and Rucker (2020, para. 5) reported that "[p]eople close to Trump . . . say the president's inability to wholly address the crisis is due to his almost pathological unwillingness to admit error; a positive feedback loop of overly rosy assessments and data from advisors and Fox News; and a penchant for magical thinking that prevented him from fully engaging with the pandemic." Blake and Rieger (2020) asserted that "President Trump gambled very early and often on the idea that the coronavirus outbreak wouldn't turn out to be nearly as severe as some health officials warned it could get. The thrust of Trump's statements about the virus has been almost relentlessly optimistic" (para. 1–2).

In their summary of the "201 times that Trump has downplayed the coronavirus threat" (title), Blake and Rieger (2020) referenced Trump assurances such as "'[i]t's going to disappear. One day, it's like a miracle, it will disappear'" (para. 22), and "'[w]e're doing very well and we've done a fantastic job'" (para. 32). Paz (2020) also compiled a list of Trump's statements that turned out not to be factual at the time, such as "'[c]oronavirus numbers are looking MUCH better, going down almost everywhere,' and cases are 'coming way down'" (para. 10).

Indeed, Trump shared his perspectives of and responses to Covid-19 with a massive audience, not only in terms of nearly 89 million Twitter followers before Twitter suspended the account (https://www.tweetbinder.com/blog/trump-twitter/) but also those who tuned in for his own near-daily press conferences in March and April of 2020—virtual and physical pulpits for dispensing his equivocal position on the virus to viewers who often clung to his every word. At one point, Trump attained "an average audience of 8.5 million on cable news, roughly the viewership of the season finale of 'The Bachelor.' And the numbers are continuing to rise.... On Monday [March 23], nearly 12.2 million people watched Mr. Trump's briefing on CNN, Fox News and MSNBC" (Grynbaum, 2020, para. 2–3).

From January to October 2020, Trump juxtaposed his positive take on Covid-19 with more cautionary input from medical advisers (including Fauci; see McGraw & Oprysko, 2020; Woodward, 2020). On March 11, 2020, Coppins described Trump's handling of Covid-19 from late January through early March:

> As with so much of the president's messaging, this narrative began with tossed-off tweets and impromptu public statements. But in recent days as U.S. health officials have raised growing concerns about the outbreak, Trump's efforts to play down the pandemic have been amplified by the same multi-platform propaganda apparatus he's relying on for reelection in November. From the White House communications office to the MAGA meme warriors of Instagram, from the prime-time partisans on Fox News to the Trump campaign's Facebook feed, the overarching message has been the same: *Pay no attention to the fake-news fearmongering about the coronavirus. It's all political hype. Things are going great* [para. 2].

Fluid, ever-evolving understanding of Covid-19 exacerbated such speculation, introducing possible reason for doubt as recommendations about risks and remedies shifted amid emergent information. For example, in one of his interviews with Woodward (2020), Trump commented that "[w]ell you know Fauci got it wrong.... Fauci said no problem in late February" (p. 315). However, as Woodward then explained, "Trump was partially correct. Fauci had said on the *Today* show, 'Right now the risk is still low, but this could change'" (p. 315). In response to those who challenged his expertise nearly a year later, Fauci noted:

> The people who are giving the ad hominems are saying, "Ah, Fauci misled us. First he said no masks, then he said masks." Well, let me give you a flash. That's the way science works. You work with the data you have at the time (para. 3).... It was not a change because I felt like flip-flopping. It was a change because the evidence changed, the data changed. It isn't a question of being wrong. It's a question of going with the data as you have, and being humble enough and flexible enough to change with that data [Massie, 2021, para. 5–6].

After cases grew in early March 2020, Trump acknowledged that something had to be done. According to Woodward, "If we can follow the guidelines for 15 days, [advisors] said, and close everything down, perhaps we can start to 'flatten the curve'.... Trump finally said, let's try it for 15 days.... That day at the briefing, Trump said, 'This is a very contagious virus. It's incredible. But it's something that we have tremendous control over'" (p. 281). Woodward continued, noting that "Fauci and Birx returned ... right at the end of the 15 days. They needed to extend the time of the shutdown and advocated for another 30 days to 'slow the spread'.... Trump turned to Fauci and Birx. 'You guys feel really strongly about this?' 'Mr. President,' they said, 'we really do need to do it.' 'Okay, we'll go with it,' Trump said. 'I hope you guys are right'" (p. 296).

Although medical advisers attained agreement from Trump on the initial 15-day stay-at-home order, the subsequent 30-day one quickly fell apart as he engaged in actions that undermined and contradicted his very executive order and public health team (Shear et al., 2020a; Woodward, 2020). Woodward wrote:

> On April 17, in the middle of what was supposed to be the 30-day extension of the "15 Days to Slow the Spread," Trump tweeted "Liberate Minnesota," "Liberate Michigan," and "Liberate Virginia," expressing support for a subversion of his own guidelines. Fauci's jaw dropped. He asked his colleagues, What was going on? The answer was obvious. The Finest Hours were over. The White House and Trump were laser-determined to open up the country [p. 353].

The narrative grew further fragmented as Trump interjected ideas and options inconsistent with his own public health advisers. For example, daily public briefings with members of the Covid Task Force abruptly became much less frequent following Trump's on-air musing about the possibility of injecting bleach to mitigate the virus during one live broadcast—a question that he quickly reframed as "sarcastic" (see Baker & Haberman, 2020; Chiu et al., 2020; McGraw & Stein, 2021; Poniewozik, 2020; Reston, 2020).

Baker and Haberman reported that the "offhand comment ... sent public health agencies scrambling to warn the public not to try such an approach because it could be fatal" (para. 14). Jacobs (2020, para. 3) noted that "some scientists fear Mr. Trump's remarks could breathe life into a fringe movement that embraces the medicinal powers of a powerful industrial bleach known as chlorine dioxide." Jacobs provided the example of one person who latched onto the possibility on Twitter: "'Do you realise how freaking cheap and easy it would be to mass produce chlorine dioxide for 100,000's of people?' Jordan Sather, a follower of the pro–Trump QAnon conspiracy theory, wrote on Twitter. 'We could wipe out COVID quick!'" (para. 8).

Trump's reluctance to wear a mask—something that had, by then, been advocated by the CDC and NIH—coupled with speculation about the potential of substances (such as hydroxychloroquine) that had not yet been subjected to clinical trials about medical efficacy regarding Covid-19 as well as inconsistent public and private statements by unofficial advisers and members of his administration, fostered more confusion—was the virus a threat or not? Was it "just a flu"? What do we have on hand to treat it? Does mask-wearing help or hurt? (e.g., Andrews & Paquette, 2020; Cathey, 2020; Farr, 2020; Frenkel & Alba, 2020; Lerman et al., 2020; Madhani et al., 2020; Robins-Early et al., 2020; Rucker et al., 2020; Sullivan, 2020; Weise & Weintraub, 2020). Madhani et al. pointed to "a chasm ... between the president and the experts. The result: daily delivery of a mixed message to the public at a moment when coherence is most needed" (para. 2). Even cabinet members became spreaders of inaccurate information (Kessler, 2020), and Trump's Chief of Staff Mark Meadows "repeatedly questioned the scientific consensus that wearing masks helps contain the spread of the novel coronavirus ... and admonish[ed] [Dr. Fauci] to 'stay on message' ... and not opine on restrictions or make policy in the media" (Rucker et al., para. 3).

Yet, the "on message" kept shifting, from outright denial to resigned acceptance (and shifting back and forth). From "it's going to disappear like a miracle" in February, the directive from the White House became "learn to live with it" in July of 2020 (C.E. Lee et al., 2020, para. 1; see also Mathis-Lilley, 2020). Amid the rising death toll and official recommendations about social distancing and mask-wearing, Trump heralded crowded rallies where most attendees disregarded such advice (see Astor & Weiland, 2020; Burnett et al., 2020; Tollefson, 2020). The White House ceremony to celebrate Supreme Court Justice nominee Amy Coney Barrett (with little mask-wearing or social distancing) became a Washington super-spreader event, resulting in several cases (Rucker et al., 2020; Voght, 2020). Wilentz (2020) asserted:

> Trump's cavalier conduct in the face of the coronavirus pandemic has shown that he imagines himself to be not only above the rules but above science itself, above knowledge, above medicine, immunology, and epidemiology. Trump has known since February that COVID-19 is a serious disease. Nonetheless, he and his staff have gone about their business publicly as if there were no pandemic (para. 2).... Perhaps he didn't really believe that the virus could touch him. Perhaps Trump thought the pandemic was only for other people, suckers, and losers [para. 4].

Shortly thereafter, President Trump tweeted that "[t]onight, @FLOTUS and I tested positive for COVID-19. We will begin our quarantine and recovery process immediately. We will get through this TOGETHER!" (https://twitter.com/realDonaldTrump/status/1311892190680014849; see also Baker & Hagerman, 2020b; Besser, 2020; Dawsey & Itkowitz, 2020; Rucker et al., 2020; Voght, 2020).

Yet, precisely because of the myriad mixed messages, inaccurate information, and inconsistent actions, some even wondered if the president and first lady were truly ill with Covid-19 (Applebaum, 2020; Guynn, 2020a; Lyall & Epstein, 2020; Pinsker, 2020). Of course, the news turned out to be true (Baker & Hagerman, 2020b; Besser, 2020; Dawsey & Itkowitz, 2020; Dowd, 2020b; A. Fisher, 2020; Karni & Haberman, 2020).

At the time, some hoped that Trump's personal experience with the disease might serve as a "wake-up call to us all" (Besser, 2020, para. 12; see also Kristof, 2020) or that "perhaps the president and his supporters will at last take the pandemic seriously and engage in very simple and easy preventative measures" (A. Fisher, 2020, para. 17). Slavitt (2020, para. 7) concurred, noting that "[t]he president, First Lady, and first family have an enormous opportunity ahead of them. They can use this moment the same way British Prime Minister Boris Johnson did. By telling the country they must take this more seriously, by wearing masks everywhere they go." Yet, if anything, the saga seemed to embolden a visibly weakened Trump to double down and not change course at all (see Jackson et al., 2020; Lee et al., 2020; Miller et al., 2020; Pinsker, 2020; Tapp, 2020; Treene, 2020).

His fans expected nothing less. One person commented on social media that "[h]aving worked for Trump personally years ago, it was made clear to me in those occasions that he is not an idiot. I believe that he knows this is a farce and a hoax.... Trump will take the hydroxychloroquine, he will be 'cured' and the masses will know it via an official press conference'" (Guynn, 2020b, para. 7). Scheyder and Brown (2020, para. 10–11) affirmed that "[s]ome Republicans said the diagnosis could actually help the president. 'Trump will prove to the American people that you can survive COVID,' said Cathy Lukasko, auxiliary chair of the Trumbull County, Ohio, Republican Party."

After then-president Trump returned from Walter Reed Medical Center, he hobbled up the stairs and stood on the balcony, striving to affirm an image of strength even while struggling to breathe (S. Kim, 2020). That moment—some nine months into the pandemic—symbolized both Trump's undermining of Covid-19 as well as his fierce determination to carry on in spite of it. It also exemplified Trump's commitment to rhetorically constructing the illusion of "all is well here" for his fans who joined him in opposing any suggestion to the contrary. That oppositional approach worked to politicize Covid-19 and to polarize those who embraced divergent perspectives of it, making clear that "those not with us are against us."

That approach, one shared by conservative media outlets (Graber, 2020; Moser, 2020; Stelter, 2020) and other Republican public officials (Crump, 2020; Kessler, 2020; Shepherd, 2020; Sollenberger, 2020; Woolson et al., 2020), contextualized how Trump's followers on Twitter and those who aligned with his perspectives came to construct Covid-19 as a "hoax," "just like the flu," "only impacting the elderly," etc. (see, for example, Applebaum, 2020; Coppins, 2020; Gross, 2020). Radio talk show host Rush Limbaugh, whose show "was syndicated to 600 stations and regularly attracted 15 million listeners before his death from cancer in February [2021]" (McEvoy, 2020, para. 8), led "the parade of Covid-19 denial and deflection with a quote that would echo through the right-wing chamber for months to come: 'The coronavirus is the common cold, folks'" (Moser, para. 36). Moser argued:

> More aggressively than anyone with a larger audience, even the president, Limbaugh turned Covid-19 into a culture war, a partisan litmus test.... Mask wearing was a "symbol of fear," he preached from the start; taking precautions against the virus was downright unpatriotic. "This isn't who we are, folks, this cowering and fearful and almost giving up in the face of this enemy, Covid-19," Limbaugh declared.... Pay no heed to Dr. Anthony Fauci, that known "Hillary Clinton sympathizer" working to "get rid of Donald Trump." Don't go around looking like a "mask-wearing freak." Instead, gird yourself for battle [para. 37–38].

As Bump (2021a, para. 12) asserted, Limbaugh's "unapologetic toxicity was often amusing to his supporters and generally reviled by his opponents, a polarization that helped fuel attention and popularity."

Coppins (2020, para. 7) pointed to another implicitly divisive tactic, explaining that "Trump supporters have been warned incessantly not to trust mainstream journalistic coverage of the issue.... When White House Press Secretary Stephanie Grisham appeared on *Fox & Friends*, she condemned the media for using the virus 'as a tool to politicize and to scare people.'" Stelter (2020, p. 294) concurred:

> As the number of cases ballooned ... Fox's overarching storyline was set: The damn Democrats were unfairly using the virus as a cudgel against Trump.... This "coronavirus is being weaponized" message whipped all around right-wing media, from Rush Limbaugh's radio show to Donald Trump Jr.'s Twitter feed and back to Fox & Friends and Hannity.... At a rally in North Charleston, South Carolina, Trump ripped into the Democrats and said, "This is their new hoax."

In those first few days after getting out of the hospital, instead of using his example to encourage caution, Trump continued to make upbeat tweets, heralding the success of the expensive and experimental therapeutics that he had the privilege to receive and minimizing the threat of the virus (Haberman & Thomas, 2020; Miller et al., 2020). Haberman and Thomas reported that "President Trump claimed on Wednesday that catching the coronavirus was 'a blessing from God' and portrayed as a miracle cure the unproven therapeutic drug he was given after testing positive last week for the virus.... Mr. Trump said he planned to make the [experimental and unapproved] antibody cocktail ... free to anyone who needs it" (para. 1–2).

Moreover, according to Miller et al., "Even as the White House has become a ghost complex this week because of the disease, Trump pushed out video of South Dakota Gov. Kristi Noem speaking of her decision to resist COVID-19 restrictions in her state" (2020, para. 12). As Slavitt (2020, para. 8) bemoaned, "Trump has always had the power to depoliticize the pandemic, yet he's chosen to politicize it and add to our divisions at every turn."

Through his words and actions, Trump sowed seeds of distrust regarding the traditional scientific process of determining treatment efficacy and prevention methods within his community of supporters, including voters, media representatives, and other politicians. However, not only did his fans come to believe the narrative that Covid-19 did not comprise a worse threat than other possible risks (such as the flu, hurting the economy, jeopardizing personal freedoms and choice). Trump's rhetoric motivated them to adamantly counter the more pro-science narrative that Covid-19 constitutes a risk to be taken seriously—meriting preventative measures such as wearing a mask, engaging in distancing, and getting vaccinated—and that possible treatments should be vetted per scientific studies. The deeply polarizing discourse compelled both sides to dig heels firmly in the sand as these opposing fan-based, interpretive communities reaffirmed their respective positions through what they shared on social media; commented on the radio, television, and floor of Congress; and even threatened violence.

Trump's determination to minimize the risk of Covid-19 and to stress that the "cure cannot be worse than the problem itself" (Haberman & Sanger, 2020, para. 2) motivated fans to oppose proponents of official public health recommendations. For example, early in the pandemic, Michigan governor Gretchen Whitmer "called out the Trump administration for failing to help Michigan and other states get tests and protective equipment—and Trump responded by insulting her. Soon Michigan became one of the most visible sites of conservative protests against social distancing rules—protests encouraged by Trump's tweets" (North, 2020, para. 4). In October of 2020, Whitmer became the target of a kidnapping plot. Just after law enforcement disclosed the plot, Segers (2020) reported:

> During a rally in Lansing, Michigan, on Tuesday, Mr. Trump blasted Whitmer for imposing stay-at-home orders earlier in the year due to the coronavirus pandemic [which, for at least a short time, coincided with Trump's own stay at home orders at the national level]. When the president first mentioned the Michigan governor's name, the crowd began chanting, "lock her up." Mr. Trump responded, "'I don't comment on that because every time, if I make just even a little bit of a nod, they say, 'the president led them on.' Now, I don't have to lead you on." Mr. Trump also said of the alleged plot against Whitmer, "Maybe it was a problem, maybe it wasn't" (para. 3). Whitmer drew a direct link between Mr. Trump's words and the threats she received (para. 4).... [Whitmer] said that "I think that the mob mentality that has been stoked, the fear that has been exploited, the anger that has been incited, is real and it has real impacts" [para. 7].

Anthony Fauci also experienced the wrath of that "mob mentality," forcing him to obtain protective services (Diamond, 2020; Place, 2021; Stein, 2020). In April 2020, Diamond reported that "[s]ome of Trump's most zealous far-right supporters have targeted Fauci online, arguing that he's worked to undermine Trump by publicly disagreeing with the president, and have begun spreading conspiracy theories about Fauci's role" (para. 8). According to Stein (para. 1–2), "Dr. Anthony Fauci said Wednesday that he has received death threats and his daughters have been harassed as a result of his high-profile statements about the coronavirus pandemic. 'Getting death threats for me and my family and harassing my daughters to the point where I have to get security is just, I mean, it's amazing.'"

In addition to having to hire personal security, Fauci had to deal with some other public officials, such as U.S. Senator Rand Paul, who "accused Fauci of promoting 'undue fear' and said, 'We shouldn't presume that a group of experts somehow knows what's best for everyone. We just need more optimism'" (Henderson, 2020, para. 5). According to Goldmacher (2021), Florida governor Ron DeSantis has even "sold merchandise saying 'Don't Fauci My Florida'" (para. 12).

Public officials who supported Fauci faced criticism of their own. Trump's attempt to squelch Fauci's visibility prompted prominent Republicans Dick and Liz Cheney to issue support for mask-wearing and Fauci's expertise (Fandos, 2020; Hunt, 2020). A Republican representative from Wyoming, Liz Cheney tweeted that "Dr. Fauci is one of the finest public servants we have ever had. He is not a partisan. His only interest is in saving lives. We need his expertise and his judgement to defeat this virus. All Americans should be thanking him. Every day" (Hunt, para. 3). Yet, as Hunt also reported, Cheney's support of Fauci got treated as lack of support for Trump.

Madhani et al. (2020, para. 12) explained that "the medical experts on the White House coronavirus task force [during the Trump administration] ... walked a tightrope. They [pressed] ... to deliver the best science to the public while trying to avoid appearing to directly contradict Trump—in hopes of maintaining influence in the decision-making process." However, as the pandemic ensued, those efforts became more and more difficult, both for his medical advisers as well as other public officials around the country.

For example, in June 2020, "President Donald Trump told the Wall Street Journal that he believes some Americans are wearing masks during the coronavirus pandemic not to protect others but simply to show that they disapprove of him" (Sheth, 2020, para. 5). In July 2020, "the White House released a document listing the number of times Fauci had been wrong in his predictions about Covid-19" (Woodward, 2020, p. 379). Sun and Dawsey (2020) reported that the White House pressured the CDC to adjust its public health recommendations, and Alba (2020) noted that the CDC director had expressed concerns about an adviser added to the staff in August 2020 who was "arming Trump with misleading data about a range of issues, including questioning the efficacy of masks, whether young people are susceptible to the virus and the potential benefits of herd immunity" (para. 2). Meanwhile, the U.S. surgeon general during the Trump administration, Dr. Jerome Adams,

3. Fandom as Key to Politicization of Covid-19   83

urged others to "do what the president, with rare exceptions, does not do: follow public health guidance and wear a mask. 'I'm pleading with your viewers, I'm begging you: Please understand that we are not trying to take away your freedoms when we say wear a face covering'" (Stolberg & Weiland, 2020, para. 5–6; see also D.K. Li, 2020).

Health advisers such as Anthony Fauci and Deborah Birx faced the challenge of sharing (or correcting) information while also trying to avoid upsetting Trump (Baig, 2020; Bellware et al., 2020; Tillett, 2021). Parsley (2021, para. 17–18) reported:

> In an interview with CBS earlier this year, Birx, now retired, suggested her role in the White House limited her work as a public health advocate. "When you have a pandemic where you're relying on every American to change their behavior, communication is absolutely key, and so every time a statement was made by a political leader that wasn't consistent with public health needs, that derailed our response," she said then. "It is also why I went out on the road, because I wasn't censored on the road."

After the two appeared in a post–Trump presidency, 2021 CNN documentary, Trump fired back and "attacked Anthony Fauci and Deborah Birx, his administration's top coronavirus advisers, in a highly personal—and at times inaccurate—statement released after the two criticized the administration for its response to the pandemic" (Din, 2021, para. 1).

Yet, as I mentioned in the Introduction, the muddling of the narratives stemmed not only from mixed messages through tweets or extemporaneous comments at a podium or actions inconsistent with standard public health recommendations. The House Select Subcommittee on the Coronavirus Crisis revealed documentation in November 2021 that the Trump White House actively intervened in CDC efforts to communicate with the public about Covid-19:

> The emails and transcripts detail how in the early days of 2020 Trump and his allies in the White House blocked media briefings and interviews with CDC officials, attempted to alter public safety guidance normally cleared by the agency and instructed agency officials to destroy evidence that might be construed as political interference.
>
> The documents further underscore how Trump appointees tried to undermine the work of scientists and career staff at the CDC to control the administration's messaging on the spread of the virus and the dangers of transmission and infection [Banco, 2021, para. 4–5].

Viglione (2021) reported that the committee "released a report documenting 47 instances in which government scientists had been sidelined or their recommendations altered" (para. 2). For example, in addition to hushing experts, according to Viglione, the Trump administration "attempted to meddle with a mainstay of the American public-health community: a weekly, peer-reviewed report that's meant to facilitate the rapid release of epidemiological data" (para. 13) and "leaned heavily on Food and Drug Administration (FDA) commissioner Stephen Hahn to issue an Emergency Use Authorization (EUA) for the treatment despite a lack of solid evidence that it helps people" (para. 16). Such actions constrained communication from federal agencies and very likely contributed to confusion, uncertainty, and, by extension, openness to varied "facts" and perspectives.

Implications of Polarized Public Health Narratives

Fauci, Birx, and others who affirmed public health recommendations could not overcome the rallying cry for Trump fans who strongly opposed those who dared to claim otherwise (see Henderson, 2020; O'Kane, 2020; Pinsker, 2020; Porter, 2020). Some lawmakers—such as GOP U.S. Senator Thom Tillis and U.S. Representative Louie Gohmert— gave voice to conspiracy theories filled with misinformation about Covid-19 or simply disregarded guidelines themselves (see Crump, 2020; Elfrink, 2020; Sollenberger, 2020; Sonmez et al., 2020). Local and state officials who aligned themselves with Trump followed suit, disputing the risk of Covid-19 through social media posts, personal actions, and public policy choices (see Serwer, 2021). Texas and Florida became Covid battlegrounds as some mayors sought to institute Covid mitigation mandates while their respective governor made policies to the contrary (see Serwer, 2021; Wootson et al., 2020). According to Wootson Jr. et al., "As the virus spread out of control in Florida, decision-making became increasingly shaped by politics and divorced from scientific evidence, according to interviews with 64 current and former state and administration officials, health administrators, epidemiologists, political operatives, and hospital executives" (para. 4).

Those decisions contributed to sharply contrasting public health narratives, influencing individual choices and costing lives. Former Republican presidential candidate Herman Cain "became an emblem of Trump-supporting, mask-defiant science skeptics, openly if not aggressively disdainful of public health officials who warned Americans to avoid large crowds, cover their faces and do as much as possible to limit contact with others" (Peters, 2020, para. 2). Sadly, Cain became yet another casualty of Covid-19 (see Peters, 2020; Wagner et al., 2020).

On June 20, 2020, then-president Trump held a rally in Tulsa, an event legal in the state of Oklahoma even though inconsistent with the

3. Fandom as Key to Politicization of Covid-19

CDC recommendations for social distancing at the time (see Williams & Gregorian, 2020). According to Steaklin and Rubin (2020), "While the Trump campaign conducted temperature checks and handed out masks and hand sanitizer in Tulsa, social distancing was not enforced, and most rallygoers did not wear masks inside the arena" (para 14), including Cain, who "was photographed inside the arena not wearing a mask" (para. 16). Cain tested positive for Covid after attending the rally. According to Karl (2021, para. 32), "Days after testing positive, Cain was hospitalized. A month later, on July 30, Cain died from complications of the coronavirus. The news devastated Trump campaign staff. Many felt like they were to blame for his death."

Former New Jersey governor Chris Christie, a Republican and one-time close ally of then-president Trump, acknowledged that he almost paid too high of a price for not remaining vigilant against the virus (Bash & Stracqualursi, 2020; Christie, 2020). In his op-ed article, Christie admitted that he had been careful about Covid-19 but "let my guard down and left my mask off. I mistook the bubble of security around the president for a viral safe zone. I was wrong. There is no safe zone for this virus" (para. 1). Christie continued, pushing back against the politicalization of Covid-19 and, especially, mask-wearing. Christie asserted that "[o]ne of the worst aspects of America's divided politics is the polarization of something as practical as a mask. It's not a partisan or cultural symbol, not a sign of weakness or virtue" (para. 4). Moreover, he called out the ramifications of inconsistent messaging from leaders. According to Christie, "When Americans are given proper and consistent information, they will overwhelmingly make good health choices, including the wearing of masks. But that doesn't work if partisan media and public officials send mixed messages" (para. 5).

Although admirable that Christie owned his mistake and encouraged others not to do the same, I'm not sure that his disclosure moved the needle on perceptions of mask-wearing by those who support (or supported) former President Trump. I don't know that a Twitter post by Liz Cheney of her dad, Dick Cheney, with the caption "Dick Cheney says WEAR A MASK" (Niemietz, 2020) shifted deeply set perspectives either. Yet, soon after Donald Trump wore a mask for the first time in public, "[t]hree out of four survey respondents, including 58% of Republicans, said they strongly or somewhat favor requiring Americans to wear face masks in public" (Grzeszczak, 2020, para. 2).

Some Republican-led states shifted gears when approaches such as reopening the economy too soon or not requiring masks resulted in case spikes and increased deaths and ICU bed occupancy (see Achenbach & Brulliard, 2020; Goldmacher, 2021; Hawkins & Iati, 2020; Marcotte,

2020; Stanley-Becker, 2020; Stanley-Becker & Witte, 2020). A year later, "[m]ost top Republicans, including every Republican governor, have been vaccinated and have encouraged others to do so. But most have also stopped short of supporting inoculation requirements" (Goldmacher, 2021, para. 8). As Serwer (2021) noted, in Texas, "San Antonio Mayor Ron Nirenberg and Bexar County Judge Nelson Wolff held a press conference urging residents to get vaccinated" (para. 3); [whereas] "Republican elected leaders fear the wrath of the GOP primary electorate more than they fear thousands of residents of their states dying of COVID-19" (para. 7).

Indeed, even though President Trump launched the successful "Operation Warp Speed" to produce vaccinations (Gillom, 2020)—something that should have been a significant cause for celebration and promotion by his administration—he elected to quietly get the vaccine off-camera prior to leaving the White House instead of using his platform to advocate for vaccinations as did several other governors and public officials (Calvin, 2021; Haberman, 2021; see also related article by Lange, 2021). By March 2021, when Trump finally did admit that he had taken the vaccine before leaving the White House (Halon, 2021), the damage was done (Dastagir, 2021).

Dastagir (2021) explained by referencing the work of Dominic Packer, author of *The Power of Us*. According to Dastagir, Packer asserted that "when a leader builds an identity around the narrative of 'us versus them,' they are pressured to stay in the bounds of 'us,' and find it difficult to veer into the territory of 'them'" (para. 5). In the case of the Covid-19 vaccine, consenting to vaccination could amount to not only going against the prevalent discourse in their interpretive community; it could mean joining the ranks of those whom they oppose.

Discussion

When Jonathan Swan interviewed President Trump on August 3, 2020, he noted, "I've gone to your rallies. I've talked to your people. They love you. They listen to you. They listen to every word you say … so when they hear you say, everything's under control, don't worry about masks…. It's giving them a false sense of security." President Trump responded, arguing, "Yeah. Under the circumstances right now, I think it's under control…. They are dying. That's true. And *it is what it is*" ("Donald Trump interview," 2020, 6:58, emphasis added; see also Bump, 2020b; Rupar, 2020). Tollefson (2020, para. 1) described some of those people whom Swan referenced:

People packed in by the thousands, many dressed in red, white and blue and carrying signs reading "Four more years" and "Make America Great Again." They came out during a global pandemic to make a statement, and that's precisely why they assembled shoulder-to-shoulder without masks in a windowless warehouse, creating an ideal environment for the coronavirus to spread.

However, those who have witnessed the horrors of Covid-19 firsthand joined Dr. Fauci and other public officials who wanted to foreground science and safeguards, eager (perhaps desperate) to find a way for messages about mask-wearing, distancing, and vaccinations to resonate with fans of Trump and others who have convinced them otherwise (Lopcz, 2020; Wong, 2020; see related article by Baltz, 2020; Martin & Burns, 2020). For example, in response to Trump's now-deleted tweet that he and the first lady had tested positive for coronavirus, one person replied, "Maybe you'll issue a FEDERAL MASK MANDATE Now." Another person responded to that post with "HOW MANY F***ING TIMES DO PEOPLE HAVE TO SAY THIS! IT'S ON THE BOXES IT'S IN MEDICAL JOURNALS! MASKS DO NOT PROTECT YOU FROM GETTING THE CORONAVIRUS" (https://twitter.com/realDonaldTrump/tatus/1311892190680014849).

Notably, I couldn't find a single time when former President Trump cited medical journals to dispute the efficacy of masks. However, both his behaviors and his hesitant questioning about them established enough doubt for fans to accept more extreme positions. On August 12, 2020, for instance, Trump made the following comment: "My administration has a different approach: We have urged Americans to wear masks, and I emphasized this is a patriotic thing to do. Maybe they're great, and maybe they're just good. Maybe they're not so good" (Victor et al., 2020, para. 9).

On October 5, 2020, Trump tweeted what Goodykoontz (2020) dubbed "the single most irresponsible thing ever posted on social media" (para. 4). At 11:37 a.m., after receiving treatment for Covid-19, Trump made the following post on Twitter: "'I will be leaving the great Walter Reed Medical Center today at 6:30 p.m. Feeling really good! **Don't be afraid of Covid. Don't let it dominate your life**. We have developed, under the Trump Administration, really great drugs and knowledge. I feel better than I did 20 years ago'" (Goodykoontz, para. 1, emphasis added). Trump's Twitter account has been permanently suspended (https://blog.twitter.com/en_us/topics/company/2020/suspension) so I'm uncertain of the eventual response to the October 5, 2020, tweet. However, Goodykoontz snapped a screen shot of it before publishing his article at 2:11 p.m., not even three hours from the time that Trump posted it. The tweet had already garnered 55,600 retweets and over 206,000 likes.

Importantly, the tweet did not only get a strong reaction from Trump's fans but also from those who vehemently disagreed. In her article, Wong invited family members who lost a loved one due to Covid-19 to express reactions to Trump's tweet. One family member commented that "I'm sickened by the president's constant dismissal of the reality of COVID and the consequences of portraying COVID as harmless. When I last spoke to my brother [who died of Covid-related complications] … he pleaded with me to let people know 'COVID isn't a joke. It's not a hoax'" (Wong, para. 20). As another shared, "He [Trump] lied to people, and that's why my stepdad is dead" (Wong, para. 30). Renwick (2020, para. 10–11) reported:

> Tsion Firew, an emergency room doctor in New York … said the president's tweets were not only offensive—they were also dangerous. "He rushed to try to normalize" the virus, she said, even as it was clear to medical professionals that he was struggling to breathe when he appeared in public on Monday. "So he is trying to downplay it while he's still suffering from the disease—and he's not out of the woods."

As I write the conclusion of this chapter, the story of Covid-19 remains incomplete. A new variant has been detected (Alfonso III & Vogt, 2021), and cases are starting to spike again in some areas (https://www.healthline.com/health-news/here-are-the-states-where-covid-19-is-increasing-2), even though individuals in the United States now have convenient, free access to three effective Covid-19 vaccinations (https://www.hhs.gov/coronavirus/covid-19-vaccines/distribution/index.html). Exhausted health care workers fight to save (mostly unvaccinated) patients who could likely have avoided serious illness had they agreed to be vaccinated (see, e.g., Rafiquddin, 2021), and officials at the local, state, and national levels continue to navigate mitigation efforts amid persistent doubt that a public health problem even exists—doubt planted by some who must continue to deal with the ongoing fallout.

Chapter 4

Celebrity Contributions to Public Narratives About Covid-19

Standup comedian Laurie Kilmartin had traveled the sad road of watching a parent die before. She responded to her father's battle with (and death from) cancer with comedic wit, even creating a comedy special (*45 Jokes About My Dead Dad*) and writing a book, *Dead People Suck: A Guide for Survivors of the Newly Departed* (Kilmartin, 2018; see also http://www.kilmartin.com/bio.html). No stranger, then, to confiding otherwise private moments with audiences, Kilmartin took to Twitter and Instagram as she narrated her mom's death from Covid-19 (Babayan, 2020; Del Rosario, 2020; Shah, 2020). As Babayan noted, "Kilmartin tweeted daily during the last days of her mother's life, sharing with her 100,000 followers the strange, painful, and sometimes comical details of remotely looking after a dying family member in the middle of a pandemic" (para. 2).

She revealed the shock of learning that her otherwise healthy 82-year-old mom had contracted this potentially life-threatening illness. On June 18, 2020, Kilmartin tweeted that "I cannot believe how fast this happened. My COVID-free Mom entered a skilled nursing facility on Monday, to get strong enough to go to the bathroom by herself (I was 100% on board with this goal, as you can imagine)" (https://twitter.com/anylaurie16/status/1273511538926600194?ref_src=twsrc%5Etfw%7Ctwcamp%5Etweetembed%7Ctwterm%5E1273511538926600194%7Ctwgr%5E%7Ctwcon%5Es1_&ref_url=https%3A%2F%2Fwww.distractify.com%2Fp%2Flaurie-kilmartin-live-tweets-moms-death-covid). On June 13, 2020, she tweeted, "Thank you for sending love to my mom but really it's my dead dad who needs your thoughts and prayers. I'm sure he thought he'd get a few more years to himself" (https://twitter.com/anylaurie16/status/1271658991702077446?ref_src=twsrc%5Etf

w%7Ctwcamp%5Etweetembed%7Ctwterm%5E1271658991702077446%7Ctwgr%5E%7Ctwcon%5Es1_&ref_url=https%3A%2F%2Fwww.latimes.com%2Flifestyle%2Fstory%2F2020-06-18%2Fcomedian-laurie-kilmarten-live-tweets-her-mothers-death).

She chronicled the indignities of relying on technology to "be with" a hospitalized family member during the pandemic (Shah, 2020). She tweeted on June 14, 2020, that the "[n]urse is stroking mom's hair, which I would be doing if I were there" (https://twitter.com/anylaurie16/status/1272267730243248129). According to Shah, "Many of the tweets read like diary entries, underscoring the unnatural ways people are forced to connect and communicate with their loved ones in hospitals right now, when coronavirus means visitations can be restricted" (para. 7).

Kilmartin's mom passed away on June 18, 2020, and the comedian again invoked humor, noting on Twitter that "[m]y sister and I are both heartbroken that mom's last words to us were complaints about the nursing home and not about our appearance" (https://twitter.com/anylaurie16/status/1273618043285823489?ref_src=twsrc%5Etfw%7Ctwcamp%5Etweetembed%7Ctwterm%5E1273618043285823489%7Ctwgr%5E%7Ctwcon%5Es1_&ref_url=https%3A%2F%2Fwww.hollywoodreporter.com%2Fnews%2Fgeneral-news%2Fconan-writer-laurie-kilmartin-tweets-mom-covid-19-death-1302622%2F). A few weeks later, she incorporated her mom's death into a commentary on those who align with President Trump's approach to Covid: "I was just notified that since my mom was a Trump supporter who died from COVID, her death has been ruled a suicide" (https://twitter.com/anylaurie16/status/1277033337823977472?ref_src=twsrc%5Etfw%7Ctwcamp%5Etweetembed%7Ctwterm%5E1277033337823977472%7Ctwgr%5E%7Ctwcon%5Es1_&ref_url=https%3A%2F%2Fwww.hollywoodreporter.com%2Fnews%2Fgeneral-news%2Fconan-writer-laurie-kilmartin-tweets-mom-covid-19-death-1302622%2F). During the ordeal, Kilmartin responded to a tweet by an anti-masker with "Aubrey, my mom is dying of COVID, I'm watching it on Facetime. The palliative care team says her bed will be ready for you in 12–24 hours. See you then!" (https://twitter.com/anylaurie16/status/1273091927592759297). She updated that post on June 18 with "UPDATE: The bed's available" after her mom passed away.

A longtime writer for *Conan* on TBS, Kilmartin later appeared on camera with Conan O'Brien and spoke with him about the loss of her mom and her desire to raise awareness of how "strange and surreal and awful" that this experience had been (https://www.youtube.com/watch?v=IhS4FXIOTI8). (The YouTube video of the July 8, 2020,

Kilmartin-Conan interview has garnered over 124,000 views thus far.) During the interview, Conan acknowledged the outpouring of support expressed for Kilmartin on social media. As Shah (2020) noted, "Thousands of people responded with messages of support and sympathy as they accompanied her journey through the loss" (para. 1). Shah explained that "Kilmartin's tweets allowed people to bear witness to the suffering, a small window into the grief that blankets the country. They serve as a reminder of the humanity and the incalculable loss behind each death" (para. 28).

In Chapter 2, I described the ways in which athletes (and the sports industry) contributed to public conversations about Covid-19. I don't believe that the story of how Covid-19 unfolded in the United States could be told without including those narratives from the world of sports. Moreover, as I discussed in Chapter 3, the construction of public officials as objects of fandoms became consequential for the two competing master narratives that emerged regarding Covid-19.

However, as I detail in this chapter, celebrities from a host of spheres powerfully shaped and perpetuated those emergent Covid-19 public health narratives in the United States, drawing in millions of fans. Their behaviors and posts permeated a plethora of crowded platforms, which, in turn, got shared or retweeted by their fans, who also impacted an even broader network of interpretive communities. Speaking out from their vistas in the worlds of sports, music, theater, film, television, media, etc., and engaging their various platforms and audiences, celebrities elevated awareness about the disease, provided support in myriad forms, and, in some cases, engaged politically—all actions that implicitly captivated public attention and contributed to what individuals had available on an array of mediated platforms to consider as they formed their own perspectives about Covid-19.

As I discussed earlier, not all in the public spotlight echoed public health messages as advocated by the CDC, either in words or actions, contributing to the controversy and confusion of the pandemic (see, e.g., Harven, 2021; Perez, 2020; Stelter, 2020). Instead, some fueled a powerful counternarrative that swayed perceptions about the pandemic, medical practitioners, and public health (see, e.g., Bella, 2021; Darcy, 2020; Ecarma, 2021; Farhi, 2021; Rosenwald, 2021; Stelter, 2020).

Others just confused the matter through what they did or posted online. Madonna posted a video that Instagram eventually pulled for being "false information" (Andrews, 2020). The Kardashians jetted off to a remote island getaway for a birthday celebration while Covid cases continued to rise back home, something that Kim Kardashian acknowledged was "out of reach" for most (Aquilina, 2020, para. 5). According to Aquilina, "The tweets received a torrent of criticism online, with many users—the vast majority of whom lack access to private islands—accusing Kardashian of being out of touch and tone-deaf" (para. 8). As Sanders (2020) wrote, "Wealthy people are quick to say 'we're all in this together,' but the truth is, we aren't. They don't have to worry about losing their jobs like others; they don't have to sleep on the streets like those who don't have a home. They're protected" (para. 3).

Actress Vanessa Hudgens just didn't quite seem to grasp the situation either (Blomeley, 2021; Harven, 2021). In a now deleted Instagram post, Hudgens commented, "It's a virus, I get it. Like, I respect it. But at the same time, like, even if everybody gets it, people are gonna die, which is terrible but, like, inevitable?" (Ali, 2020, para. 10). Hudgens later attempted to walk back her comments in a March 20, 2020, tweet, noting in part that "I realize my words were insensitive and not at all appropriate for the situation our country and the world are in now. This has been a huge wake-up call about the significance my words have, now more than ever" (https://twitter.com/Vanessa Hudgens/status/1240014528366043136?ref_src=twsrc%5Etfw%7 Ctwcamp%5Etweetembed%7Ctwterm%5E1240014528366043136 %7Ctwgr%5E%7Ctwcon%5Es1_&ref_url=https%3A%2F%2Fwww. oprahdaily.com%2Fentertainment%2Fa31737673%2Fvanessa-hudgens-coronavirus-video-apology-reaction%2F).

As my co-authors and I concluded in a previous project on celebrity health narratives, celebrity words (and actions) can, indeed, hold incredible significance for public health messaging (Beck et al., 2015). According to Beck et al., three primary features of these narratives involve using public presence (a) to raise awareness about an illness or physical condition, (b) to provide various forms of support, and (c) to engage in related advocacy by referencing personal health challenges or concerns. Covid-19 affected millions at once, including prominent individuals who, unlike those who suffered from prior pandemics, described their personal (and otherwise private) journeys with the disease with fans or "followers" on social media as well as through subsequent media coverage of their respective sagas on social media. As one early study pertaining to Covid-19 messaging affirmed, "celebrity health exemplars can exert a greater influence on public risk perceptions than exemplars featuring noncelebrities" (E.L. Cohen, 2020, para. 1; see also Gillmor et al., 2021; Kaminski et al., 2021; Lai, 2021; Lookadoo et al., 2021; Myrick & Willoughby, 2021)

4. Celebrity Contributions to Public Narratives 93

Raising Awareness

From the outset of the pandemic, celebrities employed mediated platforms to describe their symptoms (or loss) and, in so doing, testified that the virus was real and encouraged others to stay safe. As I mentioned earlier in the book, actor Tom Hanks and actress Rita Wilson made headlines for revealing that they were hospitalized for Covid-19 in Australia and, with that revelation, drew dramatic and immediate attention to this novel coronavirus (Shafer, 2021). Other celebrities subsequently followed by documenting their own respective journeys with Covid-19, including some who spotlighted the plight of "long-haulers," individuals who continue to battle Covid-19 for months after first contracting the disease.

Stay Safe—It's Real

As I mentioned in Chapter 1, celebrity posts on social media and through other forms of media perform relational work, fostering a sense of intimacy and immediacy between celebrities and their respective "followers" as well as nurturing para-social relationships. Notably, celebrities choose what they want to disclose about their health, activities, families, etc.—nothing requires them to provide details about what could be kept as private to others in the public sphere. Yet, with the ease of social media and prevalence of other mediated platforms that cater to the "inquiring minds who want to know," celebrities often choose to update fans with both the mundane and the consequential, such as an engagement or a positive Covid-19 test, as well as their losses. For example, CNN's Fareed Zakaria had covered the pandemic since its onset, but, when Covid cases spiked in India in the spring of 2021, the coverage became deeply personal and painful as he elected to reveal his mother's death as part of his broadcast (Pitofsky, 2021). Zakaria concluded his April 11, 2021, episode of *Fareed Zakaria GPS* on CNN by noting that "[w]e are approaching 3 million COVID deaths worldwide, and people have often pointed out that behind these statistics are individual human beings. This week, my mother, Fatima Zakaria, became one of those statistics" (https://twitter.com/FareedZakaria/status/138 1323508052004865?ref_src=twsrc%5Etfw%7Ctwcamp%5Etweetembed %7Ctwterm%5E1381323508052004865%7Ctwgr%5E%7Ctwcon%5 Es1_&ref_url=https%3A%2F%2Fthehill.com%2Fmedia%2F547783-fareed-zakaria-pays-tribute-to-his-mother-after-she-died-of-covid-19-complications). Zakaria highlighted his mother's accomplishments and sacrifices before emotionally acknowledging that "I feel that sorrow of distance this week because, thanks to the pandemic, I was not able to see my mother for the last time nor bury her. Which is why I thought I might take this opportunity and say goodbye Ma. I love you."

By sharing their stories, celebrities employed their public platforms to personalize the statistics for those who watch their performances, listen to their music, and follow them on social media. As individuals, such as Zakaria, revealed, often in a raw way, loss and suffering through Covid-19, they raised awareness in riveting, powerful ways, especially for fans who care deeply about them.

Camila Banus

On December 28, 2020, Camila Banus, an actress on *Days of Our Lives*, went live on Instagram for just over 14 minutes. She welcomed fans who tuned in with personal greetings and then confided that "I was traveling, as you guys know, in Florida. I got engaged, which is super-amazing, and was heading back on the 25th and I was not feeling right. So I went and I got myself a COVID test yesterday, and your girl tested positive" (https://www.instagram.com/tv/CJW7SD6pp4p/?hl=en). In a very conversational tone, she described her symptoms and reassured those who were watching that she felt "pretty chilling" about what she was experiencing. She thanked fans by their usernames for all of the "great information" that they were posting in the comments as she spoke and encouraged them to send emails with their own tips and descriptions of their respective Covid journeys. She concluded with "wash your hands. Wear a mask. Be safe." Although Banus interacted very personally and directly with fans who posted comments during her chat and even said "love ya" to some and called them by name, the Instagram video garnered far more wide-reaching attention, achieving over 42,000 views since as well as reference in popular press articles about her disclosure (Bowe, 2020; Fairman, 2020; Mason, 2020).

However, making the choice to confide personal details about health experiences—as well as to post images that display behaviors associated with health and wellness, such as wearing a mask or not—implicitly draws "followers" into the narrative as they now "co-own" previously private health information (see related arguments by Petronio, 2010). Banus invited participation in her own health narrative both by asking questions of fans during her video chat and urging them to keep messaging her with suggestions. However, as Mason (2020) reported, when "some fans questioned her decision to travel over the holidays ... she wasn't having it" (para. 1–2) According to Mason, "In an Instastory that she labelled 'for all the idiots talking negativity,' Gabi's portrayer [Banus] said, 'Let me nip this in the bud really quick. I posted my life on Instagram because I wanted to post it. There will be no negative talk on my page, or you will be blocked'" (para. 3). However, as Mason also noted, "[o]nce Banus had that out of the way, she addressed 'those of you who have said really nice things, supportive things, giving me ideas and recommendations.' To those folks, she said, 'I love you, I support you, and I appreciate you'" (para. 4).

Peter Thomas

Peter Thomas (from the television series *Real Housewives of Atlanta*) posted on Instagram on August 3, 2020, that "Covid got me" (https://www.instagram.com/p/CDZPIM7J17y/; see also M. Marr, 2020). Thomas recorded a video—that has attracted over 198,000 views—revealing that "I'm in bed now for the last eight days" with "excruciating [abdominal] pain" and imploring followers to "wear your masks, wear gloves, practice social distancing." Thomas emphasized that "I'm celebrating I'm still alive" and that "I want you guys to take this extremely serious because it's no joke. I can't wait for this s—t to be over."

Although the post prompted many supportive responses, one follower commented that "I hope and pray that you get better but I hope that you have learned your lesson because all your posts I have seen that you have not worn a mask now is hitting home please wear a mask let all your employees wear a mask." Notably, in his video, Thomas suggested that taking his mask off for selfies with adoring fans could have been how he contracted the disease—photos that likely made their way on the internet as those same fans posted and tagged Thomas. Just as Thomas spoke to fans directly through his bed via video, his mask-less face in those selfies also implicitly sent a message to those who follow him on social media about his position on mask-wearing.

Anna Camp

Anna Camp, an actress who starred in *Pitch Perfect*, also admitted to not wearing a mask (but only once) and linked that mistake to catching the virus. She posted the following Instagram message on July 21, 2020:

> Hi friends.... I felt it was my responsibility to share that I ended up getting Covid-19. I have since tested negative, but I was extremely sick for over three weeks and still have lingering symptoms. I was incredibly safe. I wore a mask. I used hand sanitizer. One time, when the world was starting to open up, I decided to forgo wearing my mask in public. One. Time. And I ended up getting it. I believe it may have been because of that one time. People are saying it's like having the flu, but I've had the flu, and this is absolutely

not that. The panic of contracting a virus that is basically untreatable and is so new that no one knows the long term irreparable damage it does to your immune system is unbelievably stressful. Completely losing my sense of smell and taste without knowing when or even if they will return is extremely disorienting. I'm only smelling about 30 percent of how I used to now. Other persistent symptoms are (a month later) dizziness, extreme fatigue, impacted sinuses, upset stomach, nausea, vomiting, and fever. I'm lucky. Because I didn't die. But people are. Please wear ur mask. It can happen any time. And it can happen to anyone. Even that one time you feel safe. We can all make a difference. Wearing a mask is saving lives. Thank you to everyone who reached out to check on me during this scary time. Please be safe out there. Let's all do our part and wear a mask. I don't want any of you to go through what I did. Even though it's a little thing, it can have a huge impact, and it's so incredibly easy do do♥♥ [https://www.instagram.com/p/CC6f8rcAnY8/].

Like Thomas, Camp expressed gratitude for surviving while specifying stressful and challenging symptoms, and she encouraged mask-wearing as a vital way for followers to protect themselves. Through her post (which has been liked by nearly 110,000 individuals thus far), she implored readers to "all do our part and wear a mask" because "I don't want any of you to go through what I did." In so doing, she articulated a personal appeal, advocating for mask-wearing out of concern for those who follow her. As one follower responded, "I love your post. Thank you for sharing about your experience and the importance of wearing a mask. I'm so glad you are getting better."

Judi Evans

Judi Evans, an Emmy-winning actress who has starred on multiple daytime dramas, stressed the insidious nature of Covid during an interview with *Extra* from her hospital bed on June 10, 2020 (https://www.youtube.com/watch?v=-oV_UBYD4iM), a video that has been watched by nearly 39,000 to date on YouTube. Evans also gave interviews from her hospital room on *Good Morning America* and *Inside Edition* as well as released a statement through her publicist.

Notably, Evans did not go to the hospital because she already had Covid; instead, she contracted the virus while in the hospital recovering from a horseback riding accident, "which resulted in several broken ribs, fractured leg injuries, two chipped vertebra and a broken collarbone" (Rico, 2020, para. 2). She doesn't know exactly how she caught the virus. However, in the *Extra* interview, she recalled several times when she had to sit in a waiting room or be transported through the hospital for tests—all without a mask. Citing the statement by Evans's publicist, Rico reported that "the 55-year-old began experiencing 'mild

4. Celebrity Contributions to Public Narratives 97

symptoms,' including fever, aches, a cough ... [and] almost had both her legs amputated on two separate occasions due to 'COVID blood clots'" (para. 4).

When asked about the advice that she would give to those who were watching, Evans responded emotionally and passionately:

> It is so easy to pass so, if you can stay home, stay home. I know it's hard. Protect yourself. Protect the people you love. Wear a mask. Stay six feet apart. Listen to the experts, please. It's not a hoax. I was in a Covid ward, and there were people dying all the time. You know, it's frightening. It happens fast. Please just care about your fellow man, your fellow family members [https://www.youtube.com/watch?v=-oV_UBYD4iM].

Danny Burstein

In two deeply personal guest columns in the *Hollywood Reporter*, Broadway actor Danny Burstein, a seven-time Tony nominee, also underscored the stark reality that anyone can contract Covid. In a preface to Burstein's first column, editor David Rooney (2020) wrote that "Burstein is one of several members of the 'Moulin Rouge!' company, including co-star Aaron Tveit, struck by COVID-19" (para. 3). According to Paulson (2021), "At least 25 members of the 'Moulin Rouge!' company wound up infected, making this the hardest hit show on Broadway" (para. 5). As Rooney noted, Burstein "became severely ill in the days following the March 12 Broadway shutdown and was hospitalized as his condition worsened to an alarming degree" (para. 3).

On April 13, 2020, Burstein revealed how "I had a day where I had trouble breathing several times and thought it might be my time. I just kept calming myself down every time it seemed dire. Strength through stillness, I kept telling myself, lengthening the back of my neck as I did. It was very isolating and scary" (2020a, para. 13). He was released from the hospital after six days, but some symptoms lingered for months. In a follow-up guest column on August 10, 2020, Burstein confided that "[w]hile my symptoms have dissipated for the most part, they also remain in subtle and, on some days, not so subtle ways. I can suffer terrible exhaustion. I've had swelling in my hands and feet. I had a few weeks where I had short-term memory loss" (2020b, para. 1). Later in that column, he reflected that "I keep thinking that if the people who believe this is all a hoax could experience just one hour in a COVID ward, their minds would change immediately" (2020b, para. 9). Burstein continued, "I was coughing up blood in my ER isolation room and still didn't want to believe my life was in danger. But when my nurse came to break the news to me that I had tested positive for coronavirus and then immediately followed with, 'By the way, are you an organ donor?' I sobered up fairly quickly" (2020b, para. 9).

Melissa Joan Hart

Over a year later, the delta variant sparked a fourth wave of the pandemic in the United States, leading to even more patients in hospitals engaging in their own sobering and often devastating conversations and realizations. However, for those who chose to take one of the three vaccines that had been given emergency-use authorizations by the Food and Drug Administration, CDC and FDA messaging implied that life could return to somewhat normal (Hawkins & Pietsch, 2021; Huang, 2021), including relaxing pandemic restrictions regarding travel (Rabin, 2021) and getting children back in school (https://www.healthline.com/health-news/kids-and-covid-19-vaccines-what-does-this-mean-for-the-new-school-year).

On August 15, 2021, Melissa Joan Hart (an actress who played the title role in *Sabrina the Teenage Witch*) posted photos on social media from her family's trip to Walt Disney World for her 1.6 million followers on Instagram and 1.8 million followers on Facebook. However, just three days later, she uploaded a two-minute video on Facebook and Instagram, explaining that the joy from her family's end-of-the-summer trip had transitioned to fear and anger because of her breakthrough Covid case (when someone tests positive in spite of being vaccinated) (C. Murphy, 2021; White, 2021). Hart confided:

> Hey, um, like I never do videos, but I really felt like this was important how I'm feeling and what's going on with me and my family. (clears throat). I got, I got Covid. I am vaccinated. I got Covid, and it's bad. Um, it's way in my chest, and it's hard to breathe. Um. One of my kids I think has it so far. I'm praying that the other ones are okay. I'm mad. I'm really mad. Cause we tried. And we took precautions, and we cut our exposure by a lot, but we got a little lazy, and around this country, we got lazy. I'm really mad that my kids didn't have to wear masks in school. I'm pretty sure that's where this came from. And I thinking about now.... My little one luckily wore his mask every day "Mom, I wore my mask," and I was so thankful, and now if he ends up getting it, I'll tell him that he's a superhero to those in his classroom because he protected his teacher and his classmates from it. And, um, I just really hope that my husband and the others don't get it because if someone has to be taken to the hospital, I can't go with them, and um, just scared and sad and disappointed in myself and some of our leaders and a lot of people including myself, and I just wish that I'd done better so I'm asking you guys to do better to protect yourselves and your families. Protect your kids. Stay vigilant and stay safe [https://www.instagram.com/tv/CSuyivyFZQa/?hl=en].

The video—which has been watched by over 858,000 viewers thus far on Instagram as well as several thousand on Facebook—garnered nearly 11,000 comments to date. Some praised her for raising awareness about the risk that continued just over 18 months after the onset of the pandemic. One person commented, "Thank you for using your platform to share!!! Prayers that you get better soon and also that nobody else gets it!!!" Another remarked that "[d]oing this broadcast may help save a life. God bless you!" Still another stated that "I feel so much for you and your family! Keep speaking your truth and know that you are supported and loved by your fans.... We need reminders of vigilance. Best wishes to you and your family."

However, some comments went further, commiserating with Hart about her feelings, echoing her statement about the "need to do better" and referencing the confusing messaging during this part of the pandemic. One person advised her to "first off, just relax, don't stress and take care of yourself and your babies. Thank you for this video and your openness to always share—good or bad. We all need to do better whether we are vaccinated or not. I hurt for you but I'm thankful you shared. It may just save other people and families. You are loved and you and your entire family are in my prayers." A fellow mom noted "that was rough to watch. It's hard being a mom. I was vaccinated and got sloppy. I got covid and barely had any symptoms. However, the fact that I could've given the virus to my children who don't have the option to be vaccinated was a mommy fail moment. It's hard." Another wrote that "I'm the same as u!! I got Covid and had my vaccinations also. I cried for days thinking I could of gave it to my 83 year old mom. I'm mad that we were told we didn't need our mask anymore. I hope it's not too bad for you." Still another pointed to the inconsistent public messaging about masks, stating, "Don't beat yourself up, Melissa. Those of us who were vaccinated and were told we could go out unmasked and then all of a sudden that changed. I know you were at Disney and I live here in Orlando. The numbers are high. Stay strong. Praying you feel well soon and that no one else gets ill."

Long-Haulers

By disclosing personal journeys with Covid-19, celebrities raised awareness and accomplished the important work of testifying to the existence of a virus that had been politicized but very much existed as a real threat to anyone. As they described their personal vulnerability to this disease, they revealed that it could happen to people who are prominent, famous, and purportedly "careful." Their frank and intimate disclosures, especially with "followers" on social media, brought attention to the gravity of symptoms and the risk of contracting an unpredictable and frightening new disease.

On March 31, 2020, CNN anchor Chris Cuomo revealed that he "wanted to be a cautionary tale" (Li & Arkin, 2020, para. 4). He confided that he had been diagnosed with Covid-19 but that he was going to keep on broadcasting remotely from his basement (Chappell, 2020). However, months after his initial diagnosis, Cuomo continued to talk about his own ongoing struggles with Covid-related symptoms on his nightly CNN broadcast as well as in interviews such as one with *Inside Edition* on July 15, 2020 (https://www.youtube.com/watch?v=utFi8leu8hY). Cuomo also used his show as a platform for Covid "long-haulers" like himself. On March 10, 2021, nearly a year after Cuomo began his own journey with Covid, he spotlighted the saga of one family who still suffered symptoms after 365 days (Holcombe & Waldrop, 2021).

These instances in which a case of Covid does not resolve in the typical time frame of 10 days to two weeks have also drawn the attention of the medical community. On February 23, 2021, just over a year after the first Covid-19 case in the United States, Dr. Francis Collins, director of the National Institutes of Health (NIH), announced:

> a major new NIH initiative to identify the causes and ultimately the means of prevention and treatment of individuals who have been sickened by COVID-19, but don't recover fully over a period of a few weeks. Large numbers of patients who have been infected with SARS-CoV-2 continue to experience a constellation of symptoms long past the time that they've recovered from the initial stages of COVID-19 illness. Often referred to as "Long COVID," these symptoms, which can include fatigue, shortness of breath, "brain fog," sleep disorders, fevers, gastrointestinal symptoms, anxiety, and depression, can persist for months and can range from mild to incapacitating [para. 1].

According to M. Fernandez (2021), "The NIH allocated about $470 million for the project spanning 100 researchers and 30 institutions in the U.S." (para. 5). Dr. Collins noted that "[w]e know some people have had their lives completely upended by the major long-term effects of COVID-19.... These studies will aim to determine the cause and find much-needed answers to prevent this often-debilitating condition and help those who suffer move toward recovery" (National Institutes of Health, 2021, para. 3).

Alyssa Milano

One of Cuomo's guests on August 7, 2020, Alyssa Milano (an actress whose credits include television shows such as *Charmed* and *Who's the Boss?*) updated her Instagram followers about her battle with Covid on August 6, 2020, along with a photo of herself in a breathing mask:

4. Celebrity Contributions to Public Narratives   101

> This was me on April 2 after being sick for 2 weeks. I had never been this kind of sick. Everything hurt. Loss of smell. It felt like an elephant was sitting on my chest. I couldn't breathe. I couldn't keep food in me. I lost 9 pounds in 2 weeks. I was confused. Low grade fever. And the headaches were horrible. I basically had every Covid symptom. At the very end of march I took two covid19 tests and both were negative. I also took a covid antibody test (the finger prick test) after I was feeling a bit better. NEGATIVE. After living the last 4 months with lingering symptoms like, vertigo, stomach abnormalities, irregular periods, heart palpitations, shortness of breath, zero short term memory, and general malaise, I went and got an antibody test from a blood draw (not the finger prick) from a lab. I am POSITIVE for covid antibodies. I had Covid19. I just want you to be aware that our testing system is flawed and we don't know the real numbers. I also want you to know, this illness is [not] a hoax. I thought I was dying. It felt like dying. I will be donating my plasma with hopes that I might save a life. Please take care of yourselves. Please wash your hands and wear a mask and social distance. I don't want anyone to feel the way I felt. Be well. I love you all (well, maybe not the trolls. Just the kind people.) ♥ [https://www.instagram.com/p/CDhQ43NgPO2/].

Followers expressed support, including Milano's friend, actress Reese Witherspoon, who commented, "Oh babe. I'm sorry you were so sick but thank you for helping educate us. We need to learn more."

In a subsequent Instagram post on August 8, 2020 (that has been viewed nearly two million times), Milano posted a video, demonstrating significant hair loss by simply brushing it. She wrote, ""#longhauler. Thought I'd show you what #Covid19 does to your hair. Please take this seriously. #WearADamnMask #LongHauler" (https://www.instagram.com/p/CDroDxYAdzx/).

Months later, Milano reported progress but still not complete recovery (Mazziotto, 2021). According to Mazziotto, "[f]ourteen months after she got COVID-19, Alyssa Milano is still dealing with long-haul symptoms" (para. 1). Mazziotto explained that Milano still experiences "shortness of breath, heart palpitations, brain fog, exhaustion" (para. 5). Milano sighed that "I'm done with fighting it, so I've kind of just almost surrendered to the idea that this might be how I feel now for the rest of my life" (Mazziotto, 2021, para. 6).

Emma Samms

Actress Emma Samms (an actress whose credits include roles on *Dynasty* and *General Hospital*) won't concede defeat by Covid yet, noting, "I'm not going to allow myself to worry about the possibility of being like this forever" (Finan, 2021b, para. 11). However, during her over yearlong battle with Covid-19 symptoms, some days likely felt like forever (see also Natale, 2021). According to Finan, "A year after contracting

COVID, the actress continues to suffer from symptoms, including shortness of breath, and she battles fatigue so debilitating that getting out of bed can be a challenge" (2021a, para. 2). In her interview with Finan for *People*, Samms explained that "[o]n a good day, I feel like there's a small dog sitting on my chest.... On a bad day, it feels like an elephant. It's so hard for me to catch my breath, to feel enough oxygen is in me. And that horrible sensation is constant" (Finan, 2021a, para. 5).

In spite of (or, perhaps, because of) her prominence, Samms initially experienced difficulty in convincing her doctors that she continued to suffer from exhaustion due to her illness from Covid. "They looked at me, an actress of a certain age, like 'Yeah, right.' ... But I'm not a histrionic person. You find yourself getting defensive. I had to convince them that there's nothing psychosomatic about what I'm going through" (Finan, 2021a, para. 7). Sharing her story with various media outlets has been powerful in raising awareness about the saga of long Covid. Additionally, as I describe in the next section, like several other celebrities, she has worked to provide resources for finding solutions (Finan, 2021b; Natale, 2021; Silver, 2021).

A Little Help from Our "Friends"

One of the most intriguing and impactful features of the pandemic has been the intense engagement of prominent individuals who confide personal accounts and perspectives as well as try to help in some way. Public accounts of private battles with Covid underscored that anyone could be vulnerable. If Tom Hanks, "regularly referred to as 'America's Dad'" (Freeman, 2020b, para. 14), could contract Covid, everyone was vulnerable. As Freeman (2020b, para. 1) noted, "On *The Daily Show*, Trevor Noah said: 'It's almost like coronavirus chose Tom Hanks just to send a message to the rest of us.' Like prison rules: 'If I can get Hanks, I can get to anyone.'"

A year later, Hanks and Wilson were back in the news, remembering their experience with Covid-19, expressing gratitude for their survival, and noting that they had donated plasma for research and planned to get the vaccine as soon as possible (Weisholtz, 2021). Wilson even donated money from a remix of a song to MusiCares Covid-19 Relief Fund (Freeman, 2020a). In so doing, Wilson, Hanks, and several other celebrities provided important resources during a time in which the medical community needed additional support for research and supplies and so many individuals who had lost jobs (and even homes) needed food, cash, and strategies for recovering from the virus.

Fundraising Support

With other former *Dynasty* cast members, Emma Samms hosted a 40th-anniversary reunion via Zoom, with proceeds from ticket sales donated to long Covid research ("Emma Samms on GH status," 2021). The lead researcher for the project that benefited from the funds, Dr. David Arnold, commented, "To have the support of someone like Emma who knows exactly what long Covid sufferers go through every day means so much to us working on the study. With the support of Emma and the Dynasty reunion, we're working to understand why this happens and if there are any therapies to help people" ("Dynasty cast reuniting," 2021, para. 15–16).

Samms and the former *Dynasty* cast members were certainly not alone in employing their celebrity status and connections with devoted fans to raise much-needed funds to help communities stricken by the disease as well as to encourage research. Athletes Tiger Woods, Peyton Manning, Phil Mickelson, and Tom Brady raised over $20 million for Covid-19 relief efforts during a benefit golf outing (Harig, 2020). Katy Perry and Adam Lambert headlined a show to benefit the LGBTQ+ community (Wallis, 2020), "Can't Cancel Pride," that raised $4 million to support members of the LBGTQ+ community who had been affected by Covid-19 (https://www.iheartmedia.com/press/pg-and-iheartmedia-announce-show-lineup-cant-cancel-pride-june-4-benefit-lgbtq-community). In November 2020, celebrities, including Billy Crystal, Oprah Winfrey, Stevie Wonder, and Gloria Estefan, united for "Nurse Heroes Live!," "a Thanksgiving concert benefiting nurses and their loved ones amid the ongoing coronavirus pandemic" (Pitofsky, 2020, para. 1).

According to Vlessing (2020, para. 1), "Canadian artists like Celine Dion, Shania Twain, and Michael Buble [teamed] up [for] their own star-studded broadcast event in Canada to support food banks and hospital workers battling the novel coronavirus," with the "Stronger Together, Tous Ensemble" production. According to Vlessing, other performers included Bryan Adams, Sarah McLachlan, Howie Mandel, Will Arnett, Russell Peters, Jason Priestley, Margaret Atwood, Justin Bieber, Mike Myers, Ryan Reynolds, Avril Lavigne, Kiefer Sutherland, David Foster, Robbie Robertson, Dan Levy, and Eugene Levy.

Nersessian (2020) reported that the "national salute to front-line workers combating COVID-19" (para. 1) generated more than $8 million for Food Banks Canada. Food Banks Canada responded enthusiastically, tweeting "Canada, you're amazing. The @foodbankscanada website has crashed under the weight of your generosity. Remember you can still donate after the show—please keep trying" (France-Presse, 2020, para. 10). Nersessian noted:

> According to the non-profit organization, it's among the largest amounts ever raised as a result of a charitable television special in Canada, as well as the most raised through a text-to-donate channel in Canada in such a short period: more than $1.6 million over a four-day span. The money raised [provided] immediate support as food banks respond to the coronavirus crisis [para. 2].

The need to support food banks could not have been more critical. An April 1, 2020, press release by Feeding America quoted its CEO, Claire Babineaux-Fontenot: "The people we serve and the charitable food system in the United States are facing a 'perfect storm,' with surges in demand, declines in food donations and volunteers, and disruptions to normal operating procedures, as a result of the COVID-19 crisis" (https://www.feedingamerica.org/about-us/press-room/feeding-america-food-bank-network-projects-14-billion-shortfall-due-covid-19, para. 3). Feeding America produced a stewardship report in July 2020, reporting that the organization "provided 1.3 billion meals between March 1 and mid–June, an astonishing 40% more than the same period last year" (p. 12).

Special shows by the casts of *All My Children*, *Parks and Recreation*, and *Guiding Light* sought to encourage donations, with Feeding America as a beneficiary (Eades, 2020; Goldberg, 2020; Yang, 2020; https://www.soapoperadigest.com/content/virtual-guiding-light-reunion-to-benefit-feeding-america/). Rick Springfield recorded a new song, "The Wall Will Fall," with a music video featuring celebrity friends, that rose to number one on the iTunes Rock Chart, and he donated all proceeds to Feeding America as well (Clifford, 2020; https://cashboxcanada.ca/features-music/rick-springfield-vance-degeneres-wall-will-fall-raises-fund-feeding-america/3965; https://www.rockcellarmagazine.com/rick-springfield-the-wall-will-fall-vance-degeneres-covid-19-feeding-america/).

Comedian and actress Tina Fey hosted "Rise Up New York," a "star-studded" virtual fundraising event in collaboration with nonprofit organization Robin Hood, that raised $115 million for New Yorkers (Blistein, 2020; Chan, 2020; Martinez, 2020). Performers included Barbra Streisand, Billy Joel, Sting, Lin-Manuel Miranda, Idina Menzel, Jimmy Fallon, and Jon Bon Jovi. According to Chan, "'We care about our neighbors, and that's why we want to help.' New York native and acting legend Robert De Niro kicked off Robin Hood and iHeartMedia's *Rise Up New York!* telethon on Monday (May 11) with that simple reasoning about why the benefit show was happening" (para. 1).

4. Celebrity Contributions to Public Narratives 105

Of course, the stars who shined on "Rise Up New York" and other prominent Covid-19 fundraisers were not just regular, ordinary "neighbors" appealing to other regular, ordinary neighbors to chip in for the greater good—they had considerably more financial security than others who suffered greatly due to disrupted income. Sanders (2020) argued that "celebrities and wealthy people ... can donate millions of dollars and still wouldn't have to worry about whether they could afford to eat dinner. And yet, they continue to ask regular people, who don't have a great surplus of wealth and need every penny they have right now, to donate" (para. 4). As Giorgis (2020) explained, much of celebrity fundraising during the pandemic "reveal[ed] a dysfunction that unites celebrity culture and American individualism writ large.... The nation's wealthiest citizens are offloading responsibility for public health and economic survival onto the shoulders of the people most affected by the crisis" (para. 4).

Another successful venture took a different approach. Early in the pandemic, performers combined for "One World: Together at Home," a benefit concert broadcast on multiple platforms in the United States and Canada ("One World: Together at Home," 2020), with the goal of raising money for the World Health Organization's Covid relief efforts. In addition to Lady Gaga, who took a lead role in the concert, other artists included:

> Alanis Morissette, Andrea Bocelli, Billie Eilish, Billie Joe Armstrong of Green Day, Burna Boy, Chris Martin, David Beckham, Eddie Vedder, Elton John, FINNEAS, Idris and Sabrina Elba, J Balvin, John Legend, Kacey Musgraves, Keith Urban, Kerry Washington, Lang Lang, Lizzo, Maluma, Paul McCartney, Priyanka Chopra Jonas, Shah Rukh Khan, and Stevie Wonder ["One World: Together at Home," 2020, para. 15].

Hugh Evans, CEO of Global Citizens, stated that "[a]s we honor and support the heroic efforts of community health workers, *One World: Together at Home* aims to serve as a source of unity and encouragement in the global fight to end COVID-19.... The global live-cast will celebrate those who risk their own health to safeguard everyone else's" (One World: Together at Home, 2020, para. 14). Significantly, according to Giorgis (2020), this initiative "found a way to give something to the public without simply requesting a donation in return" (para. 10). Giorgis reported that "[n]oting that first responders and medical workers deserve more than just thanks, [host Stephen] Colbert instructed 'everyone at home to take out their wallets—and then put them away. We aren't asking for money tonight.' [Fellow host Jimmy] Kimmel added that the event had already raised more than $50 million for the World Health Organization" (para. 10).

A year later, May (2021) reported that the broadcast raised $127.9 million, with "55.1 million [going to] ... the World Health Organization's COVID-19 Solidarity Response Fund and $72.8 million to local and regional responders" (para. 3). For its part, according to May, the WHO provided "PPE, medical teams, and emergency assistance to over 162 countries" (para. 4) with its $55.1 million.

Financial Support

Individual celebrities also certainly contributed more than their time, talent, and visibility. They also helped to address issues of food insecurity and gaps in support for health care workers and facilities through monetary and physical donations.

Chef and talk show host Rachael Ray focused on pandemic-related food insecurity. Through two charitable organizations that she sponsors—the Rachael Ray Foundation and the Yum-o! Foundation—Ray gave $4 million, with the "overall goal ... to support American families affected during the Covid-19 crisis with assistance for two-legged and four-legged family members" (Gallagher, 2020, para. 5)

In a March 17, 2020, Instagram video, Seattle Seahawks quarterback Russell Wilson posted that "[t]he world needs us ALL. Unprecedented times. @Ciara & I are supporting our community in Seattle by donating 1 million meals with Seattle @FoodLifeLine bit.ly/38VdUuB Rally & support your local food bank. @Feeding America." According to Kasabian (2020), NBA star Stephen Curry and his wife also committed to donating one million meals to their local food bank. Kasabian also reported that "Houston Texans defensive end J.J. Watt and Chicago Red Stars forward Kealia Ohai donated $350,000 to the Houston Food Bank, and New Orleans Pelicans forward Zion Williamson and Milwaukee Bucks forward Giannis Antetokounmpo donated $100,000 apiece to workers at their respective home arenas" (para. 6).

Singer Jon Bon Jovi and his wife, Dorothea, took a very hands-on approach to providing food through their nonprofit foundation, Jon Bon Jovi Soul Foundation. In a *People* magazine interview, Jon commented that "[f]or the first two months [of the pandemic], five days a week I was washing dishes at the Red Bank, N.J., Soul Kitchen. Then in light of what happened with COVID, we realized the need for a food bank." Dorothea explained that "[w]ithin a three-week span we had our first delivery to the pantries [in East Hampton], and we've delivered I don't know how many tens of thousands of meals. I can now operate an electric pallet.... Jon's good at the hand jack" (Nelson, 2020, p. 34).

Actress and talk show host Drew Barrymore partnered with

McCormick Spice for a virtual Taco Tuesday on May 19, 2020. According to a press release, the event "celebrate[d] the power of food to bring the community together over shared stories and conversation while supporting one another" and resulted in "a $1 million donation to No Kid Hungry to ensure children have reliable access to food during this ongoing pandemic" (https://www.prnewswire.com/news-releases/mccormick-and-drew-barrymore-partner-for-tacostogether-live-virtual-event-on-may-19th-and-1-million-donation-to-provide-hunger-relief-to-children-in-need-301060785.html). In her May 15, 2020, Instagram post (that has been viewed nearly 600,000 times to date), Barrymore called the partnership "'one of the most important things that I'm going to do in my life...' and asserted that [being part of] 'donating $1 million ... to the absolute right place and feeding kids who are not in school right now'" (https://www.instagram.com/p/CAOvob8jURX/?hl=en).

Beyond giving funds and food to combat food insecurity, celebrities also provided vital resources for first responders. In another celebrity-company partnership, Matthew McConaughey collaborated with Lincoln. The actor announced in a May 22, 2020, Instagram post that "[t]hanks to @Lincoln for donating 110 thousand masks ... hitting the road to get em to rural hospitals in need across Texas" (https://www.instagram.com/p/CAeCKY-AHfg/?hl=en). Inspired by her children, Sandra Bullock gave 6,000 KN95 masks to health care workers (Fernández, 2020). On April 28, 2020, actress Octavia Spencer announced her partnership with Miku to donate breathing monitors to medical facilities (https://www.instagram.com/p/B_h6EG_gtkg/?utm_source=ig_embed&ig_rid=1463d53f-c342-4fab-957b-763f99220292).

Ryan Seacrest donated $1 million, with "[t]hree-quarters of [the] donation ... to house and feed 200 first responders with the FDNY and EMTs in apartment housing in New York City" (Leonard & Boucher, 2020, para. 4). According to Leonard and Boucher, Seacrest explained that, "[a]fter seeing a news report about first responders sleeping in their cars in New York to avoid putting their loved ones at risk, I wanted to do something to help make sure these New Yorkers stay safe while they're away from their families busy taking care of ours" (para. 3).

After singer Pink and her young son contracted Covid-19, she commented on Instagram on April 3, 2020, that "[p]eople need to know that the illness affects the young and old, healthy and unhealthy, rich and poor, and we must make testing free and more widely accessible to protect our children, our families, our friends, and our communities." However, importantly, she also continued by committing financial resources to support public health efforts: "In an effect to support the healthcare professionals who are battling on the frontlines every day, I am donating $500,000 to the Temple University Emergency Fund in Philadelphia in honor of my mother.... Additionally, I am donating $500,000 to the City of Los Angeles Mayor's Emergency COVID-19 Crisis Fund" (https://www.instagram.com/p/B-il39tJ57d/?hl=en). Her post has been liked by 1,373,918 people to date.

Actress Charlize Theron shared her concern about domestic violence during the pandemic and specified how she personally planned to help. In her April 22, 2020, Instagram post, she argued that "[d]uring this unprecedented global crisis, we are being told to shelter in the safety of our homes—but what if our homes aren't safe? For the millions of women and children around the world sheltering with their abuser, home can be dangerous" (https://www.instagram.com/p/B_Sg0p-hQV4/?hl=en). In that same post, Theron stated:

> That's why in support of the global fight against domestic violence during the #covid19 crisis, @ctaop and I are joining forces with CARE and the Entertainment Industry Foundation in standing #TogetherForHer. My team is committing $1 million to COVID relief efforts, with $500,000 specifically designated towards our Together For Her campaign, supporting women against domestic violence through the provision of funds and resources to trusted domestic violence shelters around the world.

Even higher-stakes donations included Beyoncé, who contributed $6 million. According to a press release, "Beyoncé's BEYGOOD is supporting organizations that are on the ground 24/7, including United Memorial Center, Bread of Life, Matthew 25 and others, to address these dire needs in some of the hardest hit areas, providing basic necessities, including food, water, cleaning supplies, medicines, face masks, and personal hygiene items" (https://www.beyonce.com/beygood-offers-aid-during-covid19-pandemic). Jack Dorsey, then–CEO of Twitter and Square, contributed $1 billion to create a foundation with the goal of providing Covid relief until "we disarm this pandemic" (Isaac, 2020). Oprah Winfrey gave $12 million to assist those whose lives were disrupted because of Covid, noting that "[t]his thing is not going away. Even when the virus is gone, the devastation left by people not being able to work for months who were holding on paycheck to paycheck, who have used up their savings—people are going to be in need" (S. Brown, 2020, para. 5).

Emotional Support

That need certainly extended beyond tangible resources. Starting in mid–March of 2020, the emotional toll and stress of the global

4. Celebrity Contributions to Public Narratives

pandemic hit home as lockdowns and restrictions dramatically and abruptly disrupted life as it had been pre–Covid (see Italie, 2021; Lee, 2020; Schwartz et al., 2021; Trudon, 2021). Students missed months of school, playdates with friends, and familiar activities. Families missed special milestones, traditions, and celebrations. Friends missed face-to-face connections and conversations. As Italie described, Covid changed the ways that we lived and the ways in which millions died and loved ones mourned.

As the mom of four daughters, my heart went out to others who were much more affected than our family. I counted myself fortunate that my college-age daughter was only a junior so we wouldn't miss her graduation. We had been planning the graduation of our youngest from sixth grade, but, even though it had to be canceled in May 2020, we remained grateful that it was "only" sixth grade, not a "big" moment such as high school or college commencement or prom. We felt blessed that we didn't have to postpone or reimagine a wedding, and we even felt some relief that one of our relatives had passed away in 2019 when, mercifully, we had been able to hold a "proper" funeral.

However, as Italie (2021) observed, some turned lemons into lemonade by coming up with creative ways of connecting with others and even marking milestones. Some held Zoom playdates and binge-watching sessions, coordinated "drive-through" birthday parties, and played trivia on FaceTime. In this moment of social disruption and loss, celebrities also helped by treating us to often marvelous substitutes. As McNamara (2020, para. 6) explained, "There's a reason that entertainers from Bob Hope to Kathy Griffin have been dispatched to entertain the troops ... that David Letterman, the cast of 'Saturday Night Live' and Emmy's host Ellen DeGeneres all stepped forward amid the psychic cultural wreckage of the 9/11 attacks." McNamara continued, asserting that "[d]uring the COVID-19 pandemic, the entertainment industry, though hamstrung by the mandate for physical isolation, has done its level best to boost morale and provide moments that millions can share, separate but together, in real time" (para. 7).

SOME GOOD NEWS (SGN)

In his *Some Good News* (*SGN*) online show, John Krasinski, indeed, tried to highlight a bit of good news during a difficult season. In fact, the show's YouTube channel declared that it was "dedicated entirely to good news" (https://www.youtube.com/channel/UCOe_y6KKvS3PdIfb9q9pGug). According to Norcia (2020, para. 1), "For two months, John Krasinski looked on the bright side." McNamara (2020, para. 1) called Krasinski "an entertainment first responder who understood a pandemic-isolated world's need for connection and celebrity pixie dust and conjured the program to meet it." For example, in his *Hamilton* reunion episode, Krasinski asked a young girl, Aubrey, to be his guest via Zoom. Renau (2020, para. 5) detailed:

> Aubrey's family had tickets to see *Hamilton*, but the performance was cancelled due to the pandemic. Her mom tweeted that Aubrey decided to watch *Mary Poppins Returns* (starring Krasinski's wife, Emily Blunt) that night instead, figuring a movie that included Lin-Manuel Miranda was the closest she could get to *Hamilton*. Oh, was she wrong.

First, Krasinski introduced Aubrey to "Mary Poppins" herself when his wife joined him on his makeshift home set. The girl's jaw dropped. Yet, she wasn't completely starstruck as she subsequently disclosed that she watched *Mary Poppins Returns* in order to see Lin-Manuel Miranda because she couldn't go to *Hamilton*—and that she had seen only memes from *The Office* (Krasinski's show). Right on cue, Miranda joined the Zoom, and Krasinski shared his plans to fly Aubrey and her mom to see the show after Covid. Manuel replied that "I think that we can top that right now though," and, suddenly, original cast members from *Hamilton* populated the Zoom screen, each from their respective homes, singing the opening number from the hit Broadway play, *Alexander Hamilton* (https://www.youtube.com/watch?v=oiZ1hNZPRM). Aubrey could barely get a word out in stunned response. Millions got to enjoy her special treat too as they watched from their homes. (The YouTube video of this episode of *SGN* has been viewed nearly 14 million times.)

One fan commented on the *SGN* YouTube channel that "I love how John and Emily have no ego whatsoever, they connected this girl with her heroes and laughed at her not being very starstruck with them." Another commented that "THESE are examples of celebrities who do it RIGHT! I have so much respect for them using their fame & talent to bring joy to even the littlest big fans. And her face of utter shock was PRICELESS!!" Still another wrote, "Wow. Tears. You know there were some really kind acts during a crazy time that lifted our souls. Seeing this reminds me of our collective humanity." As one more fan posted, "This is exactly what I needed. Thank you for bringing so much joy in these difficult times. I am bawling my eyes out, but with happy tears. John, you are the BEST and Emily, you are AMAZING. Please keep it up and thank you from the bottom of my heart."

Commencement Celebrations

Just as Krasinski could not make *Hamilton* be open in its physical location on Broadway for little Aubrey, he couldn't conjure in-person

4. Celebrity Contributions to Public Narratives   111

commencements for those who planned to celebrate completion of a degree. However, in *SGN*'s fifth episode, he marked the occasion with a similarly special and memorable virtual alternative to traditional commencement ceremonies (https://www.youtube.com/watch?v=Iwe S2CPSnbI).

Viewed nearly four million times thus far, *SGN*'s graduation episode featured guest appearances by Steven Spielberg, Jon Stewart, Oprah Winfrey, and Malala Yousafzai as well as photos, videos, and Zoom participation by a host of individuals who were graduating as part of the Class of 2020. The show created a montage of excerpts from class speakers, and four grads got to engage in commencement conversations with the celebrities, who offered compelling and thoughtful advice and encouragement (https://www.youtube.com/watch?v=IweS2CPSnbI).

One fan commented that "[s]o many celebrities are spewing this 'we're all in this together' stuff right now, but with this show, I can tell that you mean it. You're not just SAYING we're all in this together, you're showing it by literally bringing such diverse people together. It's amazing." Another viewer expressed deep appreciation for how the show helped to celebrate her own accomplishments, noting, "I can't stop crying! I've missed not only 1, but now 2 graduations in my lifetime. It took me 30 years to finally finish my bachelor's degree and then Covid19 took this away. I've been so depressed and upset. This is so uplifting. I can't THANK you enough for this! Keep this going! THANK YOU, THANK YOU." Another viewer echoed that gratitude, sharing that "I cannot begin to say how much this has meant to us in the Class of 2020. As much as it's still sad to look at all the things we've missed, these episodes have taken a terrible situation and made it into something that can make us cry from happiness instead of sadness! Huge credit to your whole team, you guys are legends!"

Facebook and Instagram also co-hosted a live, star-studded, virtual graduation ceremony (Spangler, 2020; Walsh, 2020). According to Spangler, "The social giant announced more than 70 stars—including Selena Gomez, Cardi B, Usher, Matthew McConaughey and TikTok influencer Dixie D'Amelio ... [as well as] a commencement address from Oprah Winfrey and a performance by Miley Cyrus" (para. 2–3). IHeartMedia hosted a celebrity-filled podcast, "Speeches for the Class of 2020," with celebrity speakers including "Jimmy Fallon, Hillary Clinton, Eli Manning, Mellody Hobson, General Stan McChrystal, David Solomon, Abby Wambach, David Chang, Katie Couric, Mike Krzyzewski, Dr. Oz, Chelsea Handler ... and more" (Norris, 2020). YouTube offered "Dear Class of 2020," with special presentations by Barack and Michelle Obama, Condoleezza Rice, Lady Gaga, and BTS (Shaffer, 2020).

However, perhaps the capstone event to all of these virtual commencement festivities came with *Graduate Together: America Honors the High School Class of 2020* on May 16 (https://www.obama.org/updates/president-obamas-graduation-message-class-2020/), "a Peabody-nominated, one-hour primetime special that aired across ABC, CBS, Fox, and NBC, and streamed on multiple platforms, including Facebook, Instagram, PEOPLE, and YouTube" (https://www.eifoundation.org/programs/graduate-together-america-honors-the-high-school-class-of-2020/, para. 1). According to the Entertainment Industry Foundation, 20 million watched "this commercial-free broadcast [that] included a collection of commencement addresses, celebrity performances, and inspirational vignettes [and] featured a breakaway … offering hundreds of local affiliates the opportunity to celebrate the achievements and resilience of high school students in their local communities" (para. 2).

LeBron James took a key role in planning the event, including co-sponsoring it through his LeBron James Family Foundation (along with the Entertainment Industry Foundation and the XQ Institute). In a *People* article that promoted the event and invited submissions of inspirational student stories, James asserted, "While this won't be the graduation experience [these seniors] were supposed to get, we hope we can still give them something special.… Because they deserve it" (*People* Staff, 2020, para. 12).

Certainly, a commencement speech by Barack Obama (that was subsequently also published in the *Washington Post* and the *New York Times*) could certainly count as special (Obama, 2020; "Read the full transcript," 2020). In his remarks, Obama (2020) acknowledged the loss of a traditional commencement ceremony but encouraged grads to savor what remains:

> Even if we can't all gather in person, I want you to remember that a graduation ceremony doesn't celebrate just a moment in time. It's the culmination of all your years of learning—about the world and yourself. The friends and family who supported you every step of the way—they aren't celebrating a piece of paper.… You can see that love in all the amazing ways that families have come up with their own at-home graduations, from drive-by parades to handmade yard signs. The point is, don't let the lack of a big, crowded ceremony take anything away from what your graduation signifies.

The Locher Room

From massive events that brought millions together to smaller-scale efforts, celebrities stepped up to support fans, providing meaning-

4. Celebrity Contributions to Public Narratives 113

ful and often nostalgic programming completely free of charge. For example, Alan Locher, who worked in public relations for daytime dramas such as *As the World Turns* and *Guiding Light*, decided to launch *The Locher Room* during quarantine, with the goal of "bring[ing] smiles to TV fans around the country. I have worked in public relations in the TV industry for many years and I appreciate how enthusiastic TV fans are. I hope these reunions/chats make you smile" (https://podcasts.apple.com/us/podcast/the-locher-room/id1528187213). In an interview with *Soap Opera Digest*, Locher explained:

> I was looking at Instagram and seeing people doing these great Instagram Live interviews and thought, "Maybe I should do something. Tomorrow is AS THE WORLD TURN's anniversary, and maybe I'll call a few people and see if anyone's interested to cheer people up." There was just something that hit me with the anniversary and that everyone was home at the same time, and a lot of WORLD TURNS fans and GUIDING LIGHT fans hadn't seen these actors in 10 years at that time [because both shows had been cancelled nearly a decade earlier]. And Michael Park [ex–Jack, ATWT] was the first person I called, and he said, "Whatever you want," because he knew that the cast of *Dear Evan Hansen* had just done something on a streaming platform. He said, "Why don't you see if it's something we can do on a streaming platform so we can have more than just me?" And that's basically how it began. I just called people I knew because it was just easier, and then as daytime fans were finding the show, they were asking me to do other shows that I hadn't worked on. Here I was, I was home and the whole world was locked down, and I just kept producing more and more and it kept growing from there. I think it was the perfect timing in that everyone was in the same boat, many people were disconnected from their families because of what was happening in the world, and here they were, able to connect with their daytime families that they love ["The Locher Room marks 1st anniversary," 2021].

He streamed these reunion shows of former cast members from various daytime dramas live on Facebook as well as podcasts. He did so without charging viewers a penny, meaning that neither Locher nor the stars who appeared on his shows got paid by fans for their time and talents.

The number of views for his now-over 200 episodes ranges from a few hundred to more than 5,000. On April 1, 2021, *The Locher Room* celebrated its first anniversary, and one fan commented in the chat that "I'll never forget the first one—watched it three times now. Just so uplifting when we needed it most." Another fan responded in the chat to the 200th episode: "Thank YOU Alan!!! Congratulations to you and know that I'm forever thankful for you! Thank you for your hard work, for your sacrifices ... thank you for restoring ATWT and GL family filling a hole in my heart in such dark and trying times, thank you for inspiring us and sharing YOUR own stories." Still another one wrote: "Thank you Alan! You and your guests brought a lot of heart and a lot of smiles to so many, especially during the worst time in so many people's lives! Please know how much you are beloved and appreciated!!!"

Lucci Partnership with AARP

Susan Lucci, famous for her role as Erica Kane on *All My Children*, was one of Locher's guests. She also engaged in her own efforts to help others during the crisis with a focus on nursing homes. Lucci hosted a Coronavirus Tele-Town Hall. In a May 20, 2020, Instagram post, Lucci asked, "How can we support our loved ones in care facilities during the #coronavirus pandemic? Join me and @JoAnn Jenkins of @aarp for a special live Q&A event on May 21 at 1 p.m. ET, where I'll share my own family's caregiving experience" (https://www.instagram.com/p/CAaSVveFe-4/).

Lucci took on this initiative in honor of her mother, Jeanette Lucci, who was 103 at the time. (The elder Lucci passed away in June 2021, according to Dugan, 2021.) According to Aminosharei (2020), Lucci "partnered with AARP on its campaign to bring attention to the crisis American nursing homes are facing in the time of COVID-19" (para. 1). According to Aminosharei, the tele-town hall provided useful tips for those trying to assist loved ones, and, as Lucci noted, "I love that in addition to that practical aspect, they're also simply letting people know they're not alone. Especially in this time of COVID-19 isolation, that's a huge challenge that many, many people are feeling" (para. 7).

Informational Support

In addition to raising awareness, providing needed money and resources, and offering social support, some celebrities also engaged in dialogue with their fans about remedies for dealing with and recovering from the virus. For example, singer Bebe Rexha posted a 25-minute conversation with Dr. Ken Duckworth from the National Alliance on Mental Health on Instagram on May 5, 2020, with the goal of sharing tips about managing anxiety during the pandemic (Brar, 2020). Notably, Rexha brought in someone from the medical community to provide professional expertise, in addition to confiding her own struggles with mental health.

In other cases, although not medical professionals, celebrities confided "what worked for me" in a manner resembling friends exchanging tips. Perhaps most consequentially for some constituencies, others heralded possible remedies with mixed (and potentially deadly) results.

4. Celebrity Contributions to Public Narratives 115

OVER-THE-COUNTER STRATEGIES

In an April 15, 2020, Instagram post, Jennifer Wayne, a country singer, disclosed that "I've been struggling with whether or not to share, because to be honest it's kind of rocked me and I wasn't sure that putting it on a public platform was right for me." However, she opted to post the following advice:

> But as I've been telling people, I've had so many people reach out and say they have/had the virus and what did I do, what were my symptoms etc. So anyway, I am sharing this because I did contract Covid 19 (I'm assuming from the grocery store, it's the only place I've been?!) and I had some great advice from doctors and friends and family (@travelingwithfinn!) ... and this helped me kick this things ass. Everyone is different and each body's immune system fights it off in a different way, so I am definitely not saying I have any answers ... just wanted to share what I did in case it helps. I loaded up on Vitamin C, Vitamin D3, B complex; chaga mushrooms and ZINC! Lots of Zinc. I also drank more water and Gatorade than I ever have in my life. I wanted to flush that thing out of my system. Those vitamins and staying hydrated and rest were a lifesaver for me. I've read lots of articles about what to do as far as self isolation etc ... but not so many on what to do to combat it because there is so much unknown. But that seemed to really help me and I really felt I needed to share. Next up, donating my blood and plasma to help others. Sorry for the long post, and sending LOTS of love to all of you and hope you are staying healthy and safe! [https://www.instagram.com/p/B_AXzkrKYG/?utm_source=ig_embed].

Notably, Wayne cautioned that her strategy might not work for everyone. However, in outlining what worked for her, she implicitly offered a testimonial for the possible efficacy of approaching the symptoms as she did. Indeed, one follower commented that she should not "apologize for the long post especially if it helps people get over the virus and possibly saves their lives."

About three weeks after disclosing that she also had Covid-19, country singer and Tony-nominated actress Laura Bell Bundy posted an amusing TikTok video on Instagram on April 25, 2020, with the caption "Corona Choreo. Here are my symptoms of #coronavirus in a @tiktock dance! (Turn up sound) #coronachoreography #covid19 #symptoms" (https://www.instagram.com/p/B_IrZrDpi72/). The humorous display spotlighted symptoms such as chills, fever, lack of smell, etc., all set to lively music. One follower commented that "[t]his is the coolest thing I've seen surrounding this heavy and heartbreaking subject matter. Everything about COVID-19 is so dark and heavy, I love that you brought some light into it."

However, Bell Bundy treated the situation more seriously when she initially announced her diagnosis on March 25, 2020. Along with that announcement, she told followers that she was "[g]oing live on Instagram today at 1:30 p.m. to answer any questions you may have about my symptoms and how I'm taking care of myself. Please please stay home, take care of yourselves. God Bless." According to Davis (2020), "she continued to update her page as her symptoms continued to develop" (para. 1).

This interactive, transparent dynamic with those who follow her on social media fostered a friend-like intimacy, and, while, yes, Bell Bundy provided only one perspective amid a plethora of vistas being circulated about the virus, she actively promoted recommendations to her 79,000 followers. Her "No Corona" post remains as a button on her Instagram page well over a year later, with photos of recommended over-the-counter products in addition to a slide simply encouraging others to "HYDRATE." Bell Bundy noted that "[t]he reality is that the combination of the Western medicine which was my X-ray, my blood work, my EKG and my actual testing for COVID-19, with the combination with the Eastern which is the herbal ... was a perfectly harmonized situation" (Nichols, 2020, para. 10).

Much like some of his characters in blockbuster movies (such as *Moana*, *Tooth Fairy*, and *The Game Plan*), Dwayne "The Rock" Johnson combined "tough-guy" strength with sensitivity and humor as he told followers about his family's battle with Covid-19 in a YouTube video uploaded on his Instagram (https://www.youtube.com/watch?v=_gbRyapECUw; for related article, see Marcin, 2020)—a post that has garnered nearly 12 million views to date and that appeared on myriad news outlets as part of an Associated Press (2020f) story. Johnson began by noting that he "wanted to give you guys a helpful update on what I've been going through on my end for the past two, two and a half weeks now." Speaking very familiarly and conversationally, he confided that his entire family had tested positive for Covid-19, including his wife, Lauren, and their daughters, Jazzy and Tia (then ages two and four). He emphasized that "I can tell you that this has been one of the most challenging and difficult things we have ever had to endure as a family." He proceeded to explain that "[t]he reason why I feel like this is different [from other sorts of adversity that he had experienced previously] is because my number one priority is to always protect my family and protect my children, my loved ones." He quickly added, "By the way, I know I speak for all of you guys. It is our number one priority, all of you guys around the world. You always want to protect your families and your babies."

By framing his video as "a helpful update," Johnson presented his news as building upon what had been shared before and characterized

4. Celebrity Contributions to Public Narratives

disclosing such personal information as not unique. Further, he expressed a desire for the information to somehow be useful to those who watched. Johnson also made the rhetorical move of establishing "common ground" with his listeners (see K. Burke, 1950/1969), using the language of "our number one priority"—not just his priority. In so doing, he indicated not only an understanding of but also commonality with his listeners. As such, he positioned himself as qualified to "speak for all of you guys."

As with most of the other celebrities who disclosed a positive Covid-19 test result, in his September 2, 2020, Instagram video, Johnson stressed that his family had taken great care and, essentially, had been "on lockdown since March." However, they purportedly let their guard down one time around another family with whom they were close friends. He emphasized that "[w]e are counting our blessings.... We all have been hit by this thing.... We are well aware that it isn't always the case that you don't always get on the other end of Covid-19 stronger and healthier. Some of my best friends have lost their parents, their loved ones to this virus that is so relentless and unforgiving, and it is insidious."

In that same Instagram post, Johnson then shared tips about what had worked for him and his family (and hinting at what he wished that he would have done more), encouraging others to "stay disciplined. Boost your immune system. Commit to wellness. Wear your mask. Protect your family. Be strict about having people over to your house or gatherings. Stay positive. And care for your fellow human beings. Stay healthy, my friends" (https://www.instagram.com/tv/CEppiNRlpvs/?hl=en).

None of these celebrities presented themselves as medical professionals. They framed the disclosures as a response to questions and conversations with fans who were interacting with them. Nonetheless, they disclosed what had worked for them in responding to Covid-related symptoms. By sharing their tips, though, they implicitly endorsed practices and products that reduced discomfort and seemed to facilitate healing.

Anecdotal evidence indicates that some took tips and tried them. For example, one person responded to Alyssa Milano's post about her journey with Covid with the following post: "I happened to scroll [through] Instagram and see @debimazar used her inhaler and nebulizer. I was literally a day away from go[ing] to er. It saved me. Because that was beyond horrible."

Problematic Alternatives

However, less credible and even dangerous alternative remedies also gained traction with certain constituencies. When Donald Trump suggested that ingesting bleach could be useful in the treatment of Covid, some tried it, with adverse consequences (Reimann, 2020; Smith-Schoenwalder, 2020). As Cram et al. (2003) asserted, "[w]hile celebrity spokespersons have remarkable potential to transmit important medical information, one notable concern is the possibility for well-meaning public figures to use their influence to promote unproven or dangerous behaviors" (p. 1604).

Mike Lindell, CEO of My Pillow, encouraged those stricken with Covid (including President Trump and First Lady Melania Trump) to take oleandrin, touting it as a "miracle drug" (Dicker, 2020; H. Murphy, 2020). According to H. Murphy, "The unsubstantiated claims alarmed scientists. No studies have shown that oleandrin is safe or effective as a coronavirus treatment. It's unclear what dose the purported treatment would have, but ingesting even a tiny bit of the toxic shrub the compound comes from could kill you, experts say" (para. 4). In contrast, as Dicker reported, Lindell claimed that the drug was "100% effective" (para. 3).

Notably, nine months later, a preliminary study of oleandrin's efficacy and safety in combating Covid-19 suggested initial promise, but also notably, even at that point, scientists had tested the drug only on hamsters, not people (see Plante et al., 2021). Thus, even if medical researchers ultimately approve the drug for human consumption to address Covid-19, Lindell's promises of "100%" effectiveness and safety for people at a time when the drug had not undergone any kind of preliminary research or clinical trials was premature at best, especially for use by the then-president of the United States.

When conservative media personalities, such as Fox News's Laura Ingraham, promoted the use of ivermectin, a drug used to deworm horses, listeners embraced it as a legitimate solution (Blake, 2021), leading to at least one unsuccessful lawsuit in which a patient's family sued to force a hospital to provide it (Elfer, 2021). As Yee (2021, para. 2) reported, "the Centers for Disease Control and Prevention and the Food and Drug Administration have advised against using it for the prevention or treatment of COVID-19." Indeed, the FDA noted that it "has received multiple reports of patients who have required medical attention, including hospitalization, after self-medicating with ivermectin intended for livestock" (https://www.fda.gov/consumers/consumer-updates/why-you-should-not-use-ivermectin-treat-or-prevent-covid-19, para. 4).

In response, the FDA issued a stark and direct warning about the matter: "You are not a horse.... You are not a cow. Seriously, y'all. Stop it" (Pengelly, 2021, para. 2). However, as Yee (2021) noted, "Nevertheless, prescriptions in the U.S. have jumped from a pre-pandemic baseline of 3,600 per week to 88,000 per week in mid–August, according to the CDC" (para. 3).

Star Power as Platform for Mask and Vaccine Advocacy

As the pandemic ensued, as people grew weary and more divided, notions of what constituted "truth" or "good practice" blurred (Havey, 2020; Samore et al., 2021). Perhaps even more significantly, polarization driven by politicization planted a wedge between those who accepted the need to wear a mask and get a vaccine and those who starkly opposed both (see, e.g., Hardy et al., 2021; J.R. Lewis, 2020).

Mask-Wearing

When Bill Nye (the Science Guy) posted a science experiment on TikTok, discussing how different types of materials could be effective for mask use, (https://www.youtube.com/watch?v=A0UclAmrhVI) and which has attained nearly 400,000 views to date, one fan replied, "Thanks Bill for spreading this message, and explaining the importance of wearing a mask to the general public! You're awesome! Now we just need to make this a public service announcement on all US TV channels. Spread this video as far and wide as you can everyone!" Another posted that "[m]y childhood friendly neighborhood scientist never disappoints. Thanks bill bill bill bill!" A third fan asserted that it "[d]oesn't matter where you stand politically, we all grew up trusting Bill Nye."

However, as Lee Corso likes to say on ESPN's *College Game Day*, "not so fast, my friend." Although the comments on Bill Nye's YouTube link generally praise his pro-mask message, not all agreed. One viewer responded with "[I'd] rather not breathe in my own carbon dioxide and [i]nstead breathe fresh oxygen, but thanks Bill!" Another commented that "oh dang it I thought you were good but take this into consideration this is a free country and the government telling us what to do [is] not so free."

Yet, even amid some mixed reactions from followers on social media, mask advocates recognized the potential of star power to motivate mask use. Then-governor Andrew Cuomo (D–New York) invited a few celebrities to help with his "Mask Up America" campaign—a series of short, promotional videos featuring celebrities who encouraged mask-wearing. According to Trepany (2020), the PSAs featured "[Robert] De Niro, Kaitlyn Dever, Jamie Foxx, John Leguizamo, Anthony Mackie, Rosie Perez, and [Ellen] Pompeo" (para. 4).

In late June, fashion designer Tory Burch urged followers to "#WearaDamnMask" (Sanchez, 2020). On June 29, 2020, she posted on Instagram:

> I am sure you all are seeing what I am seeing, COVID 19 rates in the USA are rising at a truly scary rate. One thing I know for sure is that there's a very easy way each of us can help, and that's to #WearaDamnMask whenever we are in public. #WearaDamnMask because we want to protect ourselves and, even more importantly, we want to protect others #WearaDamnMask because clearly, the doctors and data say we are not going to beat this pandemic unless we each do our part to get rid of it #WearaDamnMask because is it not a political issue, it is an issue of saving lives #WearaDamnMask because it is the only way to keep our most vulnerable safe and the only way to get our economy back on track. I challenge @loganlaurice @mindykaling @kerrywashington @bradgoreski @ariannahuff @bagsnob @samiranasr @jasonbolden @gayleking @amygriffin @keeganmichaelkey @drsanjaygupta @perrip08 @jamietisch @marjoriegubelmann @jaredcohen81 to join me in getting this message out by posting a masked selfie and tagging others to do the same. And I invite every single one of you to help spread the word. Will you also post a masked selfie with #WearADamnMask and then tag as many people as you can? (Trust me, it takes a lot for me to post a selfie, this is urgent!) We are all in this together 🖤
> Tory xx [https://www.instagram.com/p/CCBq83egcZO/?igshid=10jjcjic00lhc].

Celebrities, including Jennifer Aniston, quickly accepted Burch's challenge, making their own selfies and encouraging fans to #WearADamnMask. On June 30, 2020, Aniston uploaded her own appeal on Instagram for her 38 million followers:

> I understand masks are inconvenient and uncomfortable. But don't you feel that it's worse that businesses are shutting down ... jobs are being lost ... health care workers are hitting absolute exhaustion. And so many lives have been taken by this virus because we aren't doing enough. I really do believe in the basic goodness of people so I know we can all do this 😊 BUT still, there are many people in our country refusing to take the necessary steps to flatten the curve, and keep each other safe. People seem worried about their "rights being taken away" by being asked to wear a mask. This simple and effective recommendation is being politicized at the expense of peoples' lives. And it really shouldn't be a debate. If you care about human life, please ... just #wearadamnmask 😊 and encourage those around you to do the same 🖤 [https://www.instagram.com/p/CCEvWDPjXc8/?hl=en].

Aniston's post achieved nearly seven million likes along with generally positive comments. However, the over 90,000 comments included negative ones as well. One person posted that "[m]asks are modern day slavery!!! Elite and rich are trying to control the masses with media with wrong information!!! Will pray one day you pray for the real GOD, not your satanic ways!!!" Another responded, "I hope people like you will be payed out for there part on these crimes against humanity! When Nuremberg 2 trails begin! Because they will!! Shame on you!!! You may not have kids yourself but dont be so heartless to other people's children that the government are killing with there bio weapons and masks!! You make me sick!!!!!"

In an article about celebrity mask advocacy, Allaire (2020) acknowledged other actors, such as Anne Hathaway, Patrick Dempsey, and Reese Witherspoon, who participated as well. Allaire asserted that Dempsey's post was especially refreshing, given a recent study that found men are less likely to wear masks, because they consider doing so is a "sign of weakness" (para. 6).

In August 2020, television writer William Lucas started another project to encourage mask use. The first post of the "Who Am I? Mask Challenge" on Twitter, uploaded on August 7, 2020, provided simple instructions: "#WhoAmIMaskChallenge #1 Why do you wear a mask? Share your face. Add your voice. Tag others. Instagram: @whoamimaskchallenge Facebook: @whoamimaskchallenge YouTube: #whoamimaskchallenge Twitter: @WhoAmIPSA" (https://twitter.com/whoamimaskpsa?lang=eng). Lucas brought together celebrities who agreed to promote mask-wearing by recording a short video and uploading it to social media and encouraging noncelebrities to do the same: "In a pandemic, I realized that stars aren't our heroes. Everyday people become the heroes, so the tagline became, 'Your voice could be the one that saves a life'" (J. Brown, 2021, para. 6).

As a new president entered the White House, Lucas linked his message to the new administration's appeal for mask-wearing. The April 17, 2021, Facebook post detailed:

> President Biden has asked all Americans to "mask up for my first 100 days." For the 550,000 lives lost to Covid-19, #WhoAmIMaskChallenge will be posting a new Challenge video each day for 100 days. Ordinary Americans of all ages, races and walks of life answering the question, "Why do you wear a mask?" Takes 3 minutes to shoot a video on your phone, post it to social media and tag a friend. (Think Ice Bucket Challenge. Only no ice! No buckets! No donations! Just you, your mask and your voice.) Visit our website— WhoAmIMaskChallenge.com—to find out how. Your voice could be the one that saves a life [https://www.facebook.com/WhoAmIMaskChallenge/].

On May 22, 2021, as mask resistance and Covid cases continued (but as vaccines became more available), Lucas indicated plans to bring the campaign to a close while also explaining its origination:

This thing started last summer because I wanted to feel less useless in the face of the pandemic. I didn't understand why the Hollywood community never got its act together to roll out a targeted, star-studded PSA campaign to unite Americans around the importance of masks early in the pandemic. I still don't. I'm staggered thinking of the number of lives that could have been saved. By mid–July [2020], America was hitting its second spike of infections. There were still vast swaths of Americans scoffing at the science, laughing off masks and choosing the politics of "personal freedom" over public safety. Many of them are directly responsible for the infections and deaths of the 600,000 lost to Covid. Like my mother. She was weeks away from getting her vaccine when she was infected by a person who should have been wearing a mask [https://www.facebook.com/WhoAmIMask Challenge/].

According to J. Brown (2021), "The challenge has reached 34 countries and 47 states" (para. 8) and inspired fans of the celebrities who initially posted to do the same, thus spreading the word even further.

Vaccine Promotion

Meanwhile, Dolly Parton not only contributed $1 million that directly led to the development of the Moderna vaccine, but she also sang an adaptation of one of her famous songs as she publicly got the vaccine herself (Singer, 2021; Treisman, 2021). Treisman reported:

> Parton, 75, documented the moment in a video posted to social media in which she encouraged eligible viewers to get the shot and broke into a modified rendition of "Jolene" to that effect. "Vaccine, vaccine, vaccine, vaccine, I'm begging of you please don't hesitate," she sang. "Vaccine, vaccine, vaccine, vaccine, 'cause once you're dead then that's a bit too late" [para. 3].

In the video, viewed over 4.8 million times, Parton emphasized that "I just wanted to say to all you cowards out there, don't be such a chicken squat.... Get out there and get your shot" (https://twitter.com/dolly parton/status/1366866210852323328?lang=en).

Notably, Parton has not been the only individual in the public eye to understand the value of her visibility for promoting Covid-19 vaccinations (see, e.g., Awasthi, n.d.; Macke, 2021; Sloss, 2021). Although medical procedures typically occur privately, public figures such as Parton sent powerful messages by not just telling fans that *they* should get vaccinated or making a general post to advocate for vaccinations, but instead actually *getting* their own vaccinations in front of the press. In so doing, Parton (and others) implicitly communicated that (a) the Covid-19 vaccination was safe and (b) important for personal and public health. Precisely because this type of medical procedure typically

4. Celebrity Contributions to Public Narratives 123

happens behind closed doors makes the public act more noteworthy and attention-grabbing.

Indeed, by transforming the private into the public in the medical realm, celebrities have previously employed their prominence to persuasively demonstrate that certain medical procedures might not be as bad as anticipated and that they matter. For example, actress Jennifer Garner received considerable news coverage by sharing video of herself at an annual mammogram appointment (see, e.g., C. Henderson, 2019; Shiffer, 2019) that has been viewed well over three million times (https://www.instagram.com/p/B3srFzhjUL-/?hl=en). Inspired by co-host Robin Roberts (a two-time cancer survivor), *Good Morning America*'s Amy Robach agreed to allow her mammogram to be broadcast as part of the show (Yahr, 2015). As Yahr reported, "a month later, Robach stunned viewers when she confirmed that the televised mammogram had actually revealed she had breast cancer" (para. 2). According to Yahr, Robach noted, "'The doctors told me bluntly: 'That mammogram just saved your life'" (para. 2).

However, it might not just have been Robach's life that was saved as viewers watched her mammogram and then witnessed the disclosure of her cancer diagnosis. Although I couldn't locate an empirical study that documented the clinical impact of Robach's narrative on decisions to obtain a mammogram, Cram et al. (2003) described the dramatic "Katie Couric Effect" on colonoscopies (a screening procedure for colon cancer; see also Evans, n.d., as well as related work by Kresovich & Noar, 2020). Cram et al. found "a significant increase in colonoscopy utilization coincident with a weeklong March 2000 Today Show cancer awareness campaign that featured a live, on-air colonoscopy performed on its anchor Katie Couric" (p. 1603).

Perhaps even more relevant for the issue of vaccine hesitancy, in particular, none other than the "King" himself—Elvis Presley—helped the fight against vaccine hesitancy with regard to the polio vaccine when he received his shot on national television (Hershfield & Brody, 2021; Skinner, 2020; Solly, 2020). According to Hershfield and Brody, "despite the literally crippling effects of the virus and the promising results of the vaccination, many Americans simply weren't getting vaccinated. In fact, when Presley appeared on the [Ed] Sullivan show, immunization levels among American teens were at an abysmal 0.6 percent" (para. 2). Hershfield and Brody explained that "[w]hat did prove successful was Elvis getting the vaccine in front of millions. In fact, after he publicly did so, vaccination rates among American youth skyrocketed to 80 percent after just six months" (para. 4). Acknowledging that teen peer groups also played a significant role in addressing polio vaccine hesitancy, Solly (2020, para. 12) detailed:

Elvis may not have singlehandedly vanquished polio, but he did play a part in eliminating the widely feared disease. In addition to receiving his vaccine publicly, the rock idol recorded a PSA that proclaimed "[t]he fight against polio is as tough as it ever was." Months after the "Ed Sullivan" appearance, NFIP even offered photographs signed by Elvis himself to any fan club that could prove all of its members were vaccinated.

Sixty-five years later, the Biden administration indicated that it also grasped the deep need for identifying those whom people could trust as they considered the possibility of getting the Covid-19 vaccine, including celebrity advocates, as well as an array of community-based partners, with its "We Can Do This" campaign (Diamond, 2021; M. Fernandez, 2021; Lovelace Jr., 2021). As Vice President Kamala Harris stated at the virtual kickoff event, "You are the people that folks on the ground know and rely on and have a history with…. And when people are then making a decision to get vaccinated, they're going to look to you" (Diamond, para. 4).

Among others, including Mark Cuban (owner of the Dallas Mavericks and "shark" on *Shark Tank*) and actress/producer Eva Longoria (*Desperate Housewives*), Olivia Rodrigo, an 18-year-old Disney star, joined the campaign to stress the need for younger individuals to get vaccinated as well (see, e.g., M. Fernandez, 2021; Lovelace Jr., 2021; Shevenock, 2021; Trepany, 2021). On July 14, 2021, Rodrigo visited with President Biden at the White House. In an Instagram post that has received over 5.5 million "likes" thus far, she posted a photo with President Biden as well as the following encouragement to fans:

> [I] had the absolute honor of visiting the White House today and chatting with @potus about the importance of getting vaccinated! even if you are young and not immunocompromised, getting your covid vaccination is the best thing you can do for your health and your loved ones' health. YOU have the power to save lives. check out vaccines.gov to learn more about vaccinations and to find a vaccination center near you (it's free and super easy.) thank you to everyone who has done their part in helping end this pandemic and thank you to President Biden, Vice President Harris, Dr. Fauci, and everyone at the White House for having me. EVERYONE GET VAXED IT'S SO IMPORTANT 💖 [https://www.instagram.com/p/CRU9pq4rEKj/?utm_source=ig_embed&ig_rid=ca99deda-ffb7-4e96-9f67-b0f961ab0b92].

Mask and Vaccine Opposition

However, not all celebrities presented similar commitment to this public health precaution, consistent with the pro-public health master narrative. As Yahr (2020) documented, others engaged in behavior that affirmed the counternarrative in which Covid-19 did not constitute a threat that warranted such mitigation efforts. For example, some posted photos online in which they posed without masks, and others attended events where mask-wearing got treated as optional. Yahr highlighted the example of famed country music singer Charley Pride, who died of Covid-19 on December 19. She noted that "[a]bout a month earlier, the 86-year-old singer attended the Country Music Association Awards, where he received a lifetime achievement award. But many viewers were shocked to see the ceremony taking place indoors, in front of nearly 100 people, the majority of whom were not wearing masks on camera" (para. 2). As Yahr continued, "Why did the CMA Awards have to be in person, especially with virus cases spiking in Tennessee? Why do country stars keep showing up on social media attending maskless indoor gatherings or traveling? What message is it sending to their fans?" (para. 6).

Indeed, as those individuals chose to forgo masks, they implicitly communicated that they felt safe and comfortable with doing so. According to L. Burke (2021), "In a culture that worships celebrities and amplifies their words and actions, the coronavirus pandemic has presented an opportunity for some to apply and others to confuse" (para. 1).

The disparate messages about masks and vaccines could certainly lead to confusion. For example, in stark contrast to celebrity counterparts promoting mask-wearing and vaccines, singer Eric Clapton released a song—"This Has Got to Stop." According to Uitti (2021), "In just a few hours, the track ... garnered more than half a million views on YouTube" (para. 1) and "[n]ot long after unveiling the new track, the 76-year-old musician was a trending topic on Twitter with tens of thousands of mentions due to the presumed content of the track" (para. 2). According to Frishberg (2021), the singer also purportedly refused to perform in venues where vaccine mandates might prevent anti-vaccine fans from attending, even though he did eventually do so.

On October 18, 2020, conservative radio talk show host Dennis Prager shockingly shared that he actively tried to catch Covid by "hugging thousands of people" to build natural immunity as opposed to getting the vaccine (Rohrlich, 2021; Singh, 2021). Rohrlich reported that Prager revealed to his listeners that he had, indeed, accomplished that goal of contracting Covid, which he was treating with a combination of expensive, experimental drugs (such as the Regeneron monoclonal antibody cocktail), as well as unauthorized ones (including ivermectin—the horse dewormer). According to Rohrlich, Prager told listeners that "I certainly don't gamble with my health, but I so believe science and the science of ivermectin, not the lies of *The New York Times*" (para. 10). As Rohrlich noted, "Prager's reach is extensive—his YouTube channel boasts more than 2.4 million subscribers. And there's no telling how many of them believe everything Prager says. For starters, he told his audience on Monday that there is 'no argument for young people to get vaccinated. None whatsoever'" (para. 13–14).

Personal Choices, Public Positioning, and Clashing Perspectives

As 2021 ensued, a somewhat ironic phrase became popular in some conservative circles—"My Body, My Choice," a slogan that has been associated with pro-choice in terms of abortion rights (see, e.g., Goyal et al., 2021; Warren, 2021). As Goyal et al. explained, "'My body, my choice' is the slogan of the 'medical freedom' movement spreading across the country.... Vaccine-skeptical groups, including the Tennessee Coalition for Vaccine Choice and Texans for Medical Freedom, have lifted the language and syntax of reproductive choice to promote their own agendas" (para. 3).

Arnold Schwarzenegger, former Republican governor of California, mocked such a self-focused orientation in a viral Twitter video, asserting that "and not just when we think about 'well, my freedom is being kind of disturbed here'.... No, screw your freedom. With freedom comes obligations and responsibilities" (https://twitter.com/therecount/status/1425542635423424515?lang=en). In spite of Schwarzenegger's powerful voice (along with an array of others) urging to the contrary, unfortunately, way back in March 2020, as cases began to spread across the United States, we lost our moment to agree (and collectively embark) on a singular "best" course of action. That moment slipped by as public figures poisoned messaging with the toxic combination of (a) honest confusion about how the virus could spread (cue a rush on hand sanitizer), (b) fear that medical professionals might not have enough gear (cue early dismissals from public health officials that masks could be useful), and (c) catering to a base that didn't take well to being told what to do (i.e., discourses that disputed distancing, testing, and shutdowns as the way to handle the pandemic). The adopting of "My Body, My Choice" fits with the prioritizing of personal perspectives over the public good that defined the U.S. response to Covid-19.

With the myriad voices clamoring in cybersphere as the pandemic has continued to ensue—the virus kills ... Covid isn't real ... wear a mask ... bleach could help ... take horse dewormer ... vaccines save lives ... vaccines hurt fertility—people have faced tough choices about what to believe and whom to trust as they figure out what choices to make for their own respective bodies. Unlike 65 years ago when Elvis received his vaccine on national television and many adoring fans then opted to follow suit, the complicated, layered, politically charged moment in which Covid-19 ensued could not be similarly simple or simplistic. As I've documented throughout this book (and illustrated through examples of fan comments in this chapter), fans can be influenced by celebrity statements and actions, but they also consider and react to that advocacy within the context of other concurrent interpretive communities (such as family, organizational, religious, and political influences—which may or may not converge or diverge from the rest).

In the early 2020s in the United States, perhaps no one could be like an Elvis, with such widespread appeal and credibility that could immediately impact public perception and actions. Yet, Dolly Parton might come close. According to Stevens (2020), "Through wars and social movements and a wild ride of presidential administrations, Dolly Parton has remained one of the closest things we have to a universally beloved national figure" (para. 1). Stevens noted that "[i]n a bitterly divided, hyperpartisan era, it's a marvel that Parton captures and keeps so many disparate hearts. Some of her diverse appeal stems from her unwillingness to wear her politics on her rhinestone-covered sleeve" (para. 8–9).

Even with her usual apolitical stance, Parton faced criticism for receiving a Covid-19 vaccine. While the vast majority responded favorably to her March 2, 2021, Twitter post that featured the video of her vaccination—with several even referring to her as a "national treasure"—the praise wasn't universal. One person expressed skepticism about the vaccine: "Hey Dolly, please be a doll and fill us in on how you feel after taking the covid vaccine & possible side effects As you may have heard, people have died within a few days to a couple of weeks of getting it. Hopefully that won't be your case but do keep us posted just in case!" Another individual snarled at Parton: "Dolly as you are a powerful person you must know the agenda behind this 'vaccine.' I'm so shocked and disappointed that you are promoting it and taking your fans with you and Israel. You say you are a Christian? May the Lord forgive you" (https://twitter.com/dollyparton/status/1366861968498454529?lang=en).

Four months after Parton received her vaccine, Renkl (2021) observed that "[s]he gave it a good try, a heroic try, but somehow the bonehead politicians running this state [Tennessee] managed to overcome the good will generated by its favorite daughter" (para. 3). However, that "good will" was not just dampened by some "bonehead politicians" (whose role in the pandemic I addressed in the previous chapter) but also by some who told people what they had come to want to hear and others who refused to entertain an alternate perspective that clashed with the one that they had already formed.

Colin Powell died of Covid-related complications on October 18, 2021—ironically, the same day that Dennis Prager revealed that he intentionally sought to catch Covid (see, e.g., Dunham & Mohammed, 2021; Linskey, 2021). Linskey reported that Powell "was the youngest chairman of the Joint Chiefs of Staff. He was the first Black American to become secretary of state. And in his prime, he was one of the most respected leaders in the country" (para. 1). However, sadly, according to Linskey, even the tributes became clouded as "within hours of the public announcement Monday that Colin L. Powell died of complications from covid-19 despite a full course of vaccination, some conservative officials and media personalities tried to make him something else: A prominent reason to doubt the coronavirus vaccines' utility and question the political and health officials urging Americans to get them" (para. 2).

Part of the problem in the Powell news coverage stemmed from initially missing information (Blake, 2021). According to Blake, "A bunch of mainstream news outlets left out some crucial context Monday ... that [Powell] had undergone treatment for cancer, which suppresses the immune system and makes surviving the virus significantly more difficult. As the day wore on, this [oversight] was corrected" (para. 3). However, Blake continued to note that Fox News' Tucker "Carlson did not get that memo.... Carlson pressed forward Monday night by using Powell's death to question the official case for the vaccines. And he did so while not once mentioning the crucial fact of Powell's comorbidity" (para. 5). As Moran (2021b, October 19) documented, "Personalities on Fox News were slammed for using the death of former U.S. Secretary of State Colin Powell from complications of COVID-19 to question the effectiveness of coronavirus vaccines. Hosts Tucker Carlson, Will Cain, and John Roberts each faced backlash for their commentary" (para. 1–2).

Notably, the social media posts that Moran (2021b) referenced in terms of "backlash" came from primarily nonconservative outlets or individuals, but, certainly, not all conservatives downplay the importance of the vaccination. Just two days after Powell's death and the on-air questioning about the vaccine on his own network, Fox News's Neil Cavuto tested positive for Covid-19 and expressed gratitude for being vaccinated. Fieldstadt (2021) reported:

> "While I'm somewhat stunned by this news, doctors tell me I'm lucky as well. Had I not been vaccinated, and with all my medical issues, this would be a far more dire situation," Cavuto, 63, said in a statement. Cavuto, who had open-heart surgery in 2016, was treated for cancer in the 1980s and was

4. Celebrity Contributions to Public Narratives   129

diagnosed with multiple sclerosis in 1997, has been open about his health challenges.... He said he is "surviving" Covid because he is vaccinated. "I hope anyone and everyone gets that message loud and clear. Get vaccinated, for yourself and everyone around you" Cavuto said in his statement [para. 2, 3, 5].

However, rather than "loud and clear," the messaging surrounding Covid-19 has been murky, inconsistent, and confounded by so many opposing stakeholders advancing opinions about the "correct" path forward. Even amid Biden administration vaccine mandates (Miller, 2021), organizations have struggled to navigate tensions among coworkers who disagree about Covid.

For example, those controversies bubbled prominently to the surface in the entertainment industry among stars (and coworkers) on set (see G. Evans, 2021a, 2021b; E. Lewis, 2021; Siegel et al., 2021) that also then overflowed into public discussions on social media among fans. According to Siegel et al., "Though Hollywood might appear unified when it comes to embracing such COVID-19 preventive measures as vaccines, the reality is more divided, mirroring the broader American population, where 44 percent are not fully vaccinated, according to the CDC" (para. 2).

On the ABC daytime drama *General Hospital*, tempers flared as one co-star (Steve Burton) tested positive for Covid-19 while another publicly opposed Covid vaccinations (Ingo Rademacher) (see G. Evans, 2021a). According to Evans, "Last weekend, Twitter users began retweeting social media posts by Rademacher that seemed to endorse and publicize an Aug. 21 Santa Monica 'No Vaccine Passport Rally.' Soon enough, #FireIngo began to trend" (para. 2). Evans noted that:

> The hashtag apparently was a last straw for Rademacher, who yesterday posted a vitriolic Instagram video (with no small amount of misinformation), excoriating the hashtaggers as "bigots" and "morons," and misleadingly claiming that since the CDC says vaccines have only a 95% effectiveness rate, the vaccine "was never supposed to stop the spread and is never going to stop the spread of this virus." ... He begins his video by saying, "So I'm going to address all of the morons [with] that hashtag FireIngo. I really dislike you at this point. I think that you're bigots and I think you know it. To do something like that to another person really characterizes who you are. You're a horrible, horrible person, first of all.... If you were in charge of this country you'd be a dictator" [para. 6, 10].

A few weeks later, Nancy Lee Grahn, an actor on the show and an outspoken vaccine advocate, posted on Twitter: "Thank you @valentini frank, Dominick Nuzzi @Disney & @ABCTV for following the science and taking ALL possible measures to ensure the safety of the entire @GeneralHospital cast and crew. Very grateful to be working with all of you. Today is a good day for #GH" (https://twitter.com/NancyLeeGrahn/status/1433854790262398976?ref_src=twsrc%5Etfw%7Ctwcamp%5Etweetembed%7Ctwterm%5E1433854790262398976%7Ctwgr%5E%7Ctwcon%5Es1_&ref_url=https%3A%2F%2Fwww.soapoperanetwork.com%2F2021%2F09%2Fgeneral-hospital-nancy-lee-grahn-frank-valentini-disney-abc-following-the-science).

G. Evans (2021b) reported on November 5, 2021, that Rademacher was no longer part of the *General Hospital* cast. On November 23, 2021, another longtime General Hospital cast member, Steve Burton, also announced on Instagram that he had been let go by the show, due to the vaccine mandate (https://www.instagram.com/p/CWoRbqWj5Uj/)—a video that has been viewed over 332,500 times in just six days. According to Ives (2021b, para. 3), "Mr. Burton and Mr. Rademacher were outspoken opponents of a coronavirus vaccine mandate that applied to a part of the set where actors work unmasked, known in the industry as Zone A. The mandate took effect on Nov. 1."

Fans responded passionately to Burton's post. One fan commented, "His body is his choice. We all need to stand up to these bullies whose goal is to take our freedom away. I respect Steve even more than I did before. Long time fan of his work on GH." Another echoed that "everyone must stand together to defeat tyranny. Problem is too many wouldn't know tyranny if it locked them in their homes, masked them and forced them to take experimental gene therapy poison. Just because you have been fooled into agreeing with them this time, don't think they won't come for you eventually." Some indicated plans to stop watching the show at all—"[a]fter 42 years I'm officially done with GH. I wish you and your family all the best!!!"—a comment that garnered nearly 700 "likes."

Notably, most fans uploaded supportive comments in response to Burton's Instagram post, but others affirmed the vaccine mandate. One fan asserted:

> It is a freaking health crisis that a rule was made, he had a choice and k[n]ew what the consequences would be if he did [not] follow the rules. I am sure everyone on here yelling about freedoms and rights would be in the ER if they can't breathe and want all the medical people to use all the time, effort and risk themselves to save them.... Never have people gone wacky over a vaccine, sweet lord this country wiped out small pox because they stepped up and got the shot, if this generation were around then we would have been wiped out instead of the disease.... We have a ton of laws we follow, we can't do whatever we want just because we are in America.

The same sort of saga has ensued from soundstages to stadiums as the sports world has struggled to decide the extent to which "I" can't be

4. Celebrity Contributions to Public Narratives

part of "team," at least as far as Covid-19. For example, according to Sullivan (2021), "fifty to sixty NBA players have yet to receive a single vaccine dose, league sources tell *RS*. Most are considered merely reluctant skeptics. Some of the holdouts, however, amount to their own shadow roster of **anti-vaxxers** mounting a behind-the-scenes resistance to Covid protocols—and the truth" (para. 12, emphasis original).

Yet, that stance isn't sitting well with others in the sports community. Moran (2021a, September 4) reported that "Charles Barkley has no time for professional sports stars who are refusing to receive the COVID-19 vaccine" (para. 1). According to Moran, "The 'Inside the NBA' analyst slammed them as 'selfish,' saying they were among the luckiest people during the pandemic because they've 'gotten every check' and remained well-paid even as they played to empty stadiums while others lost their jobs or died from the disease" (para. 3).

Barkley expressed frustration when reacting to Brooklyn Nets' basketball player Kyrie Irving's decision not to get vaccinated. He argued that "you don't just get vaccinated for just yourself.... You get vaccinated for your family first. You get vaccinated for your teammates second." He continued to note that "I really am proud of the Nets for putting their foot down.... The only thing that bugs me is that he's still going to make $17 million sitting at home" (https://www.cnn.com/videos/sports/2021/10/20/charles-barkley-kyrie-irving-brooklyn-nets-vaccine-comments-nd-vpx.cnn). In stark contrast, singer Chris Brown dubbed Irving as a "real hero" for taking this position and called it "his choice" (see Bowenbank, 2021; Daniels, 2021).

Allison Williams, a sports broadcaster, made her own choice to leave her decade-long job at ESPN after refusing to comply with ESPN's vaccine mandate. She posted on Twitter on September 9, 2021:

> While my work is incredibly important to me, the most important role I have is as a mother. Throughout our family planning with our doctor, as well as a fertility specialist, I have decided not to receive the COVID-19 vaccine at this time while my husband and I try for a second child.... After a lot of prayer and deliberation, I have decided I must put my family and personal health first. I will miss being on the sidelines and am grateful for the support of my ESPN family [https://twitter.com/AllisonW_Sports/status/1436042099409899533/photo/1].

In response, one person commented that "I do not feel bad for you! It's choices like this that continue to divide us. [You're] not doing anything good but only for yourself. The majority of the country is not aligned with you and the few who have this opinion. We ARE DONE WITH COVID AND 'DEATH'!" Another responded with "See ya! ZERO evidence the vaccine presents danger to pregnancies, causes people to be infertile, any of it. Just all made up. Our daughter-in-law got vaccinated, 2 shots, during her pregnancy, baby is 4 months now, adorable. Plenty of people would like your job. Sad commentary."

However, others supported her decision. One fan asserted, "Way to go! I agree whole-heartedly! It's a scary time with that jab. Mandates aren't American!" Another affirmed that "@AllisonW_Sports u r such a courageous person, ur family and community raised a great girl. Twitter users r all super liberal but the majority of Americans support and appreciate u!! It's hard to stand on principle these days—only the strongest r able to do so."

In an October 22 video posted by the *Daily Wire*, Williams emotionally claimed that "I cannot place paycheck over principle" (https://www.youtube.com/watch?v=6C4nmZjRyE0). The conservative media outlet announced that Williams was joining its staff in that same video. Fung (2021) reported:

> "Leaving ESPN was one of the most difficult decisions of my career, but it was the right thing to do," Williams said Friday. "I respect people who choose to get the COVID-19 vaccine, but it was not the appropriate medical decision for me at this time. No one should be forced to choose between their livelihood and the freedom to make their own health care choices—it is simply un-American" [para. 6].

Meanwhile, Nick Rolovich, head football coach for Washington State University, lost his job—and four assistants did as well—when he refused to comply with the WSU's vaccine mandate (Bonagura, 2021; Cobb, 2021; see also related article by Witz, 2021).

Unlike situations in which companies or institutions insisted upon vaccination, the National Football League did not require players to quit or be fired if they did not agree to the vaccine. Indeed, the NFL administered minimal punishment when Aaron Rodgers made misleading comments by implying that he had received the Covid-19 vaccination and behaving as though he were fully vaccinated (see Belson, 2021; Belson & Anthes, 2021; Hill, 2021b; Waldrop, 2021). According to Hill, "When a reporter asked him in August whether he was vaccinated, Rodgers responded, 'Yeah, I've been immunized'" (para. 5). As Hill detailed, in November, Rodgers tested positive for Covid-19, forcing him to admit that he had not, indeed, received a vaccination for the virus, even though he had been photographed violating league policy by not wearing a mask in public when unvaccinated.

Even public figures do not have to disclose personal health information, and, obviously, Rodgers is not an exception. However, Rodgers's decision to behave in a manner consistent with someone who had been vaccinated, per league rules and public health guidelines, led others—such as teammates, coaches, and members of the press—to believe that he had, indeed, received the vaccination. He further complicated the situation by perpetuating misrepresentations about the virus and the vaccine in subsequent interviews. Waldrop (2021) reported that "CNN Chief Medical Correspondent Dr. Sanjay Gupta ... [referred to Rodgers's actions as] 'very irresponsible' because 'he gives a lot of voice either intentionally or not to the anti-vaccine movement'" (para. 7). According to Waldrop, another CNN medical expert, Dr. Leana Wen, emphasized that "'[t]hese are things that are common myths.' ... 'But when it's repeated by someone with this level of celebrity and influence, it is very dangerous'" (para. 10).

Belson and Anthes (2021) referred to Rodgers as "a celebrity who transcends the nation's most popular sport, a household name on par with Tom Brady and Patrick Mahomes" (para. 2). Waldrop (2021) concurred, emphasizing that "Rodgers is not just any football player. Last year he was named the National Football League's most valuable player for the third time. He has hosted 'Jeopardy,' and he has 4.5 million followers on Twitter" (para. 4).

Rodgers pushed back on criticism and downplayed his role in public conversations about Covid-19 and the vaccination. In an interview, Rodgers claimed that "I'm an athlete, I'm not an activist" (Shapiro, 2021b, para. 6). Yet, the massive media coverage of both Rodgers's actions and utterances occurred, and, like it or not, Rodgers (and his choices regarding the Covid-19 vaccination and discourse about it) contributed to emergent public health narratives, fueling opposition to the vaccination as well as disdain of "anti-vaxxers." One medical expert provided this important insight:

> "When you're a celebrity, you are given a platform," said Dr. Paul A. Offit, the director of the Vaccine Education Center at the Children's Hospital of Philadelphia. "When you choose to do what Aaron Rodgers is doing, which is to use the platform to put out misinformation that could cause people to make bad decisions for themselves or their children, then you have done harm" [Belson & Anthes, 2021, para. 4].

Closing

Over the course of the Covid-19 pandemic, celebrities have actively engaged in public commentary about this virus and, in so doing, co-constructing the very nature of it (real or not real) as well as discussing ways to treat and prevent it and how to support those who have been impacted by it. Notably, that engagement in the public sphere hasn't been unidirectional. In this first postmodern pandemic, noncelebrities routinely comment on and "like" and "share" celebrity posts, and it's not uncommon for celebrities to do the same.

Although researchers such as Cram et al. [2003] have documented prior influence of celebrity health narratives, we lack empirical, longitudinal data on the extent to which celebrity discourse about Covid-19 impacted perceptions of the virus or decisions made about it (for a few preliminary initial studies, see Ives, 2021; Shevenock, 2021).

Based on the data that I collected for this book, I would argue that engagement by both celebrities and fans has mattered greatly. Their very public exchanges (on social and mainstream media) worked to raise awareness, encourage donations and community outreach, and consider solutions (everything from bleach to horse dewormer to masks and vaccines). That discourse didn't necessarily reveal attitude change, but it certainly reflected attitude enforcement as both celebrities and fans dug their heels into deeply entrenched divides, in some cases, quite literally, resulting in loss of life for fans who bought into belief systems of those who denied the pandemic and/or value of approved treatments or preventive measures. Perhaps even worse, though, the myriad mixed messages fueled just enough uncertainty about exactly what to do that it cost some valuable time as they paused to figure out what might be the right next move ... and, in doing so, put their lives at risk (see, e.g., Ellefson, 2021; Slisko, 2021).

CHAPTER 5

Heroes on the Frontlines of a Global Pandemic

In the December 2020 issue of *Sports Illustrated*, contributors described their respective picks for the title of "Sportsperson of the Year." Dr. Jenny Thompson did not prioritize lists of football stats as she recommended Laurent Duvernay-Tardif for the recognition. Thompson acknowledged that "[a]s one of few Canadians to win an NFL title, a key protector of MVP QB Patrick Mahomes and the starting right guard on a burgeoning dynasty in Kansas City, Laurent was already a sports hero" (2020, p. 84). However, she argued that "it's like he could see that, now, more than ever, our society needs medical heroes, and it doesn't matter whether you're the one making decisions in the intensive-care unit, or you're giving orderlies and nurses a much-needed break. He's more of a hero now than he ever would be on the field" (p. 84).

Duvernay-Tardif "opted out of last season with the Chiefs to work on the front lines in the battle against COVID-19 in his hometown of Montreal" (Costello, 2021, para. 2). He explained:

> I felt like the best thing for me was to go on the front line and help in any capacity possible. I was part of a movement of thousands of people that went back and helped, whether it was retired nurses or doctors. I think it gave me a different perspective on the medical system. Everything is so hierarchical normally, but at a time of crisis feeling everybody come together and work as a team was pretty amazing [Costello, 2021, para. 3].

That spirit of joining together in the quest of helping others became a rare beacon during a dismal time of death and despair. Throughout the past nearly two years of the pandemic as I finish this book, the medical community rallied to treat patients amid overflowing hospitals and daunting care loads. They endured the heavy load of long hours, emotional and physical exhaustion, fear, frustration, and sadness, and they reaped reactions that ran the gamut from exultation to indignance, depending on the moment in time and the perspective of those considering their efforts. Writing about Duvernay-Tardif, Thompson (2020, p. 84) commented:

> I hope that fans can appreciate his choices, even applaud them, and support whatever he and every other medical professional in society is doing right now, as we fight the relentless spread of COVID-19. This should not be about criticizing the efforts to social distance, or denying the need to wear masks and take the virus seriously. This is about stopping a deadly disease that has now claimed the lives of more than 250,000 Americans [as of December 2020] and shows no signs of slowing down.

As I bring this book to a close, I marvel at how this health crisis evolved. I could never have predicted the twists, the turns, the trauma, or the unprecedented global tragedy. As a scholar intrigued by celebrity health narratives and fandom, I did not begin to imagine how integral both would become to a saga that claimed millions of lives and affected untold numbers in physical, emotional, economic, societal, and political ways. Over the course of the past nearly two years, we have witnessed individuals step up in truly heroic ways—people who contributed to saving lives, raising awareness, doing what they could to help. I've shared in this book thus far about the stories of some who happened to be famous for something else before Covid, such as Duvernay-Tardif. However, I couldn't finish this book about fandom and Covid-19 without acknowledging how grateful citizens heralded health care professionals during the early heights of the pandemic but how, sadly, those health care professionals could not capitalize on that fandom in order to inspire compliance with recommended preventive measures by those who came to believe and trust the Covid skepticism narrative.

Fandom of "Heroes" in the Medical Community

In the stack of articles that I collected for this project, the headlines provide stark reminders of what the United States endured during the pandemic: On April 2, 2020, "New York 'like a battlefield'" (Associated Press, 2020a); on July 25, 2020, "Houston, Miami, other cities face mounting health care worker shortages as infections climb" (Sellers & Hauslohner, 2020); on October 7, 2020, "COVID-19 cases rising in 39 states—9 months into the pandemic: 'We are overwhelmed'" (Bacon & Stucka, 2020); on December 23, 2021, "COVID patients overwhelm U.S. hospitals "(Portnoy, 2021); on August 17, 2021, "American hospitals buckle under Delta, with ICUs filling up" (Sun & Heyward, 2021); and

5. Heroes on the Frontlines of a Global Pandemic

on September 30, 2021, "Ohio health care workers warn of 'astronomical COVID-19 pediatric surge" (Mitropoulos, 2021).

Regardless of the two dominant competing master narratives that filled airwaves and cyberspace beyond hospital and nursing home walls, those who worked in health care facilities encountered the terrible realities of what Covid-19 did to bodies. As I'll detail throughout this chapter, health care professionals witnessed unimaginable suffering by their patients, and they saw how the disease affected body parts, causing lasting damage and often death. They fought to secure adequate protective gear and clothing and then wore what they could get for 14-plus-hour days, only to hear non–health care workers complain about the inconvenience of wearing a mask to run into a store for a gallon of milk. They cared for too many patients whom they couldn't save and wrestled with the emotional toll of holding iPads and cell phones as loved ones said goodbye from a distance. They experienced the tragic impacts of Covid-19 as they went to work, day after day, month after month, for going on two years (for related work, please see Associated Press, 2020b; Bartick, 2020; Covert, 2021; Drash, 2020; Herzog, 2020; Stradling, 2020). The Associated Press described the scene on April 2, 2020:

> New York authorities rushed to bring in an army of medical volunteers Wednesday (para. 1) ... and the wail of ambulances in the otherwise eerily quiet streets of the city became the heartbreaking soundtrack of the crisis. As hot spots flared around the U.S. in places like New Orleans and Southern California, the nation's biggest city was the hardest hit of them all, with bodies loaded onto refrigerated morgue trucks by gurney and forklift outside overwhelmed hospitals, in full view of passing motorists (para. 2).... And the worst is yet to come [2020b, para. 4].

Seven months later, a column in *The Week* provided a daunting update:

> Hospitals across the U.S. warned they were facing critical shortages of staff and beds this week, as record numbers of Covid-19 patients began to overwhelm intensive care units and exhausted health-care workers braced for a post–Thanksgiving surge of cases (para. 1).... But unlike the first wave of the pandemic, when the disease rocketed in select places such as New York City, coronavirus cases are now soaring almost everywhere. That means there's no slack in the health-care system, and nurses and doctors can't be shifted from low-case areas to new "trouble spots" ["Hospitals buckle under a wave of Covid cases," 2020, para. 3].

The work wasn't just tiring; it was dangerous (see Andrew, 2020; Covert, 2021; Crist, 2020; Eligon, 2020; Fossi & Prazan, 2020; Moenich, 2020; Rosales, 2020; Setty, 2020; Sternlicht, 2020; for related article, see McGarry et al., 2020). "'Our members showed up and many of them made the ultimate sacrifice,' Pat Kane, executive director of the New York State Nurses Association, told NPR" (Sternlicht, para. 8). Friends and family members of Janine Paiste-Ponder, a nurse in Oakland, California, honored her memory by begging hospital officials to "make changes to protect staff, including separating negative and positive COVID-19 patients, providing more personal protective equipment, and testing asymptomatic employees" (Moench, para. 5). "'She took care of our patients and she died doing it,' said Adetola Akindele, the supervising nurse on Paiste-Ponder's unit who worked with her for 15 years, crying as she remembered her colleague" (Moench, para. 3).

Individuals filling all roles in health care facilities became vulnerable because of the pervasiveness of the virus as well as the lack of adequate protective gear. One editorial noted:

> We got a sad reminder of the precarious place health care workers put themselves in as they carry out the duties of their profession during a pandemic by the July 25 death of Joseph Costa, chief of the critical care division at Mercy Medical Center in Baltimore. He was one of the tens of thousands of health care workers on the front lines of the country's COVID-19 fight who risk their own lives to save the lives of others [*Baltimore Sun* Editorial Board, 2020, para. 1].

Especially during the early days of the pandemic, the sacrifice and commitment of health care professionals (and other essential workers) became elevated to an almost celebrity-like status by others who engaged in fan-like activities as they communicated gratitude. As a collective, communities, groups, and individuals combined to display orientations toward health care workers as objects of fandom, and, for the first three months of Covid-19 in the United States, health care workers attained widespread adoration and support that certainly mirrored fandom in other contexts.

For example, at least one Facebook group, COVID-19 Physicians Memorial, provides an ongoing space for posts about the hundreds of health care workers who have lost their lives to the virus, and members of the group also created a tribute website: https://covid19-physicians-memorial.com/?fbclid=IwAR0hvJ0ImXquXTn4U-n0r-QfiEfjVeZM-XImKgzu8G4ygE-bi85KNi-zfls. In New York City, an artist painted a "20,000-square-foot mural ... at the Queens Museum–Flushing Meadows Corona Park" (L. Cohen, 2020, para. 2). According to L. Cohen, the "massive mural [was] painted in honor of the immigrant health care workers who lost their lives while helping to fight the coronavirus," including "Dr. Ydelfonso Decoo ... remembered by friends as a grandfather whose dedication to pediatrics was only outweighed by his love and compassion for his community" (para. 1).

5. Heroes on the Frontlines of a Global Pandemic

In July 2020, "Over 160 pairs of white nursing clogs lined the US Capitol ... in memory of the nurses who've died during the coronavirus crisis" (Andrew, 2020, para. 1). According to Andrew, "The shoes were set there by members of National Nurses United.... At the vigil, the nurses implored the Senate to pass the HEROES Act, a sweeping $3 trillion bill proposed by Democrats that would, among other measures, increase production for personal protective equipment that hospitals need to treat coronavirus patients" (para. 2). Congress eventually passed the Heroes Act in October 2020 by a narrow margin of 214 to 207 (https://appropriations.house.gov/news/press-releases/house-passes-updated-heroes-act).

Indeed, especially in the early days of the pandemic, health care workers became lauded in myriad ways as individuals sought to show their gratitude for the sacrifices that the medical community made and work that they did during the pandemic (see, e.g., Barney, 2020; Cohen, 2020; Gata, 2020; Gibson, 2020; McLeod, 2020; Padgett, 2020; Weiss, 2020; Wood, 2020). Invoking the word *hero* and launching initiatives to commemorate their important service, companies and individuals acted as fans, transforming what had previously been treated as "everyday," "ordinary," and "expected" service into something extraordinary and remarkable through their tributes.

Shutterfly established its "#CreateThanks" campaign (see Weiss, 2020; https://shutterfly.wyng.com/5e8f9c1905058101c9d6fd02; https://www.instagram.com/explore/tags/createthanks/?hl=en). Shutterfly posted the following message on a designated webpage:

> Today's essential workers have emerged as everyday heroes, keeping us safe, healthy and connected. In an **overwhelming demonstration of gratitude**, we've seen kids across the country put their creativity and compassion to work making signs, cards and artworks to say thank you. We'd like to transport these messages from your front windows to the front lines by transforming select creative works of art into thank you cards and personalized gifts, and delivering them to essential organizations [https://shutterfly.wyng.com/5e8f9c1905058101c9d6fd02, para. 1–2, emphasis original].

That website now features several very cute illustrations from young artists who visually expressed their appreciation to these workers.

Honda created its "Thank a Healthcare Hero Campaign" and urged participation by "posting messages on your social media channels offering gratitude and thanks to doctors, nurses, paramedics, fire, police, and other frontline professionals placing themselves at risk in support of the public's health" (https://csr.honda.com/2020/04/03/hondas-thank-a-healthcare-hero-campaign/, para. 2). On April 2, 2020, Imperial tweeted "[t]o salute healthcare heroes across [Canada], Imperial (along with our retail brands Esso and Mobil) is providing up to $2 million in free fuel vouchers to frontline nurses, paramedics and doctors. Learn more/apply here: healthcarehero.ca" (https://twitter.com/imperialoil/status/1254871937211404289?lang=en). Nearly a month later, on April 29, 2020, the company tweeted a comment on the initial post: "**UPDATE: The response to our program has been overwhelming and all 80,000 digital vouchers, equivalent to $2 million, have been claimed. We appreciate the efforts of Canada's healthcare heroes during this time and thank them for all that they continue to do."

In Dallas, DHD Films began a campaign called "Healthcare Heroes," designed "to create a living tribute to the health care community by compiling the world's largest collection of appreciation messages for frontline workers" (Wood, 2020, para. 3; https://dhdfilms.com/healthcareheroes/). According to Wood, "Energy Transfer, an energy company headquartered in Dallas, has partnered with DHD to donate $50 for each thank you video submitted, up to $100,000, which will be gifted to Parkland's Public Health Preparedness Fund" (para. 4). The public responded, and DHD produced videos (https://www.facebook.com/DallasHDFilms/videos/2587709698006184/; https://www.facebook.com/watch/?v=2573387122900271; https://www.youtube.com/watch?v=4jdeV-Q8RCw; https://m.facebook.com/watch/?v=2573387122900271&_rdr). Even though DHD didn't attract quite as many videos as hoped, Energy Transfer donated $100,000 on July 14, 2020 (Prajean, 2020).

Adobe invited individuals to "#HonorHeroes with Creativity During COVID-19" (Adobe Communications Team, 2020) and developed a beautiful virtual gallery of art (https://www.adobe.com/heroes.html). The company also teamed with Jimmy Kimmel to brighten the day of one nursing home nurse. According to Gata, Kimmel called to thank her and also arranged for Adam Levine to join the call. "To make the big surprise even better, Adam and Jimmy presented Samantha with $10,000 for herself, plus food delivery gift cards for all the nurses in her department" (Gata, 2020, para. 4).

Community-based health facilities also encouraged community members to "#ThankAHealthCareHero" (see Padgett, 2020). For example, as Padgett noted, "At Scott Memorial [based in Scottsburg, Indiana], we honor all our providers and employees.... I hope you will join me and add your voice to the chorus of appreciation for our community's healthcare heroes by posting your own message of thanks on your favorite social media, with the hashtag #ThankAHealthCareHero" (para. 5). In Michigan, Beaumont began "Home Beams for Health Care Teams" (para. 1). Beaumont's website provided these instructions.

5. Heroes on the Frontlines of a Global Pandemic 141

Every evening at 8 p.m., beginning March 31, families are encouraged to step outside their front door and shine a flashlight toward their nearest hospital to show support for health care heroes across Southeast Michigan. Families are also encouraged to swap out their porch light with a blue lightbulb as a sign of support for health care heroes and first responders [https://www.beaumont.org/health-wellness/press-releases/beaumont-encourages-community-to-honor-health-care-heroes-with-home-beams-for-health-care-teams; para. 2; see also MacLeod, 2020].

In my hometown of Athens, Ohio, "employees from Hopewell Health Centers decorated the walkway at O'Bleness Hospital with encouraging messages ... [that] ranged from 'Heroes wear scrubs' and 'O'Bleness is the bomb diggity' to 'You're a hero'" (Hulvachick, 2020, para. 1–2). According to Hulvachick, "Trimble Elementary has been sending cards to the hospital by grateful students. The Laurels of Athens [an assisted living facility] reached out as well, sending flowers to healthcare workers" (para. 12).

One of the many film projects to chronicle the pandemic is *Bravery and Hope: 7 Days on the Front Line*, a documentary that "follows emergency physicians and critical care specialists struggling to save patients suffering from COVID-19" (Barney, 2020, para. 3). According to Barney, "[t]he documentary captures the toll the disease has taken on one of the poorest and worst-stricken neighborhoods in New York City and the nation" (para. 5). *Bravery and Hope* won two Emmy Awards (Grobar & Johnson, 2021) and nearly 2.5 million tuned in for its original airdate on May 15, 2020 (http://www.thefutoncritic.com/ratings.aspx?id=broadcast_20200515).

Much of the initial fandom of health care workers faded by May 2020. In part, national attention shifted to escalating racial tensions and protests in the United States after George Floyd's murder (see, e.g., Madrigal & Meyer, 2020; Taylor, 2021), and I would argue that increasingly divided perspectives about the pandemic dampened enthusiasm about honoring members of the medical community. However, on July 5, 2021, New York City hosted its Hometown Heroes Parade, a special event paying tribute to essential workers who helped the city survive Covid-19 (see Sonkin et al., 2021). According to Sonkin et al., "The iconic stretch [Canyon of Heroes] has been used to honor world leaders, victorious sport teams, soldiers and celebrities for at least a century but Wednesday's parade is the first in Big Apple history that exclusively commemorated the everyday working person" (para. 5).

Yet, that parade constituted a rarity in 2021, one year into the pandemic, in terms of acts of fandom for health care professionals. As I detail in the next section, the fading of fandom for health care workers contrasted sharply with the escalating need for medical professionals as the pandemic ensued. After getting so much appreciation and adoration in the early stages of Covid-19 to feeling snubbed and disregarded just a few short months later, public reaction has been at least part of the emotional roller coaster that has been Covid-19 for those in the medical community. A health care worker posted the following on the public Emergency Nurse Facebook page, dated July 30, 2020:

> Remember 3 months ago when everyone cared about healthcare employees? We received lots of check-in phone calls and texts and countless prayers for safety and well-being, all to remind us that we were essential ... and appreciated. There were signs stuck into the ground in front of every hospital saying "Heroes work here" and employees were proud to be there. But all of that support has seemed to disappear. But you know what hasn't disappeared? The stress on the healthcare workers during this pandemic. And if you think for one second that three months ago was the worst of it, here is some news for you ... it's not done. It's worse.... Regardless of personal stances on COVID... be nice to healthcare workers and hospital employees, because the stress is real [https://www.facebook.com/emergencynursing/photos/pb.1617866958511359.-2207520000../2425887521042628/?type=3&eid=AR Af7U0psvzHGdW9ekX3O3uEWSWnszoeCjbMaCkq9W1lDj1NHTHp7d2 XHH8wQuUwl6fMcMu44zNzlrct].

Fandom Goes Only So Far....

Madrigal and Meyer wrote in June 2020 that "[f]or several weeks at the beginning of the outbreak in the U.S., the need to control the virus took precedence over other concerns. Now, for many people, the pandemic is no longer the most pressing national issue" (para. 20). Although many moved on to other concerns and started to resume their pre-pandemic lives, health care professionals continued (and, as I finish this book, continue) to toil. Just a few days ago, I scrolled on Facebook after a relaxing Thanksgiving at home with my family. I saw a post from a family friend who went to school with one of my daughters. She's a nurse, and, in her post, she described the emotional toll that became part of her Thanksgiving as she worked another shift with now mostly preventable severe cases of Covid. She's been treating Covid patients for nearly two years now, and she's tired.... Tired of Covid.... Tired of excuses.... Just tired. As I read her post, I thought about how sad that I was for her to be that tired in her late 20s and the impact that caring for Covid patients has had on her young life.

Several health care workers have tried to communicate more broadly in the public sphere in a quest to educate and enlighten others about

5. Heroes on the Frontlines of a Global Pandemic

Covid-19 from their perspectives as health care providers and to motivate them to take precautions. According to Kindelan (2020, para. 1), "Lizzy Pesch, an occupational therapist, has been treating patients with COVID-19 for the past nine months, working long hours and dealing with the unpredictable and devastating toll of the disease." Pesch wrote a poem that eventually got circulated on social media (including the Dr. Amy Acton Facebook page) as well as featured on *Good Morning America* (see Kindelan, 2020). A few especially powerful lines from the poem include: "We healthcare workers are falling apart; When I get dressed for work, it's not just a job; When I lose another patient, it's in my car that I sob; You see I am human, I bleed just like you; And with each death that I witness, a part of me dies too" (Kindelan, para. 21–23). DeGregory (2021) chronicled one nurse's 12-hour shift. As DeGregory asserted, "If everyone could see what she sees, she says, the horror and hopelessness her nurses live with every day, the anguish the patients' families endure, maybe they'd believe" (para. 37).

Another nurse, Megan Dunaway, posted on the public Tallahassee Memorial HealthCare Facebook page on August 29, 2021, imploring people to take the virus seriously:

> I'm posting this in honor of my staff in the ER who are working relentlessly, and seeing horrific outcomes.... I hope you read it, I hope you share it, I hope you restrain from commenting negatively. Controversy is the last thing I want from this share. I simply hope you start supporting, stop fighting, and start thinking before coming to the ER, "is this an emergency?" ... To the Tallahassee Community: Instead of googling and arguing about what may or may not be real, here are actual events, witnessed by this 1 tiny nurse, in this 1 tiny ER in this 1 tiny town. In the past 10 shifts, I have personally taken care of at MINIMUM 1 critical patient with COVID per shift, all to have died. Daily. From COVID. Unvaccinated. Young. No underlying illness. There are no beds in our hospital COVID units or ICUs (though daily we work tirelessly to make space). I am caring for these patients for hours/days in our ER, in addition to emergencies walking in. I get to know them in their darkest hour, their families, then finally, I get a bed for them at the hospital, I hug them goodbye. I have had to stop checking up on them the next day, because my heart cannot handle hearing one more time, that none of them made it. This is my reality. Which means this is YOUR reality. You live right here in Tallahassee with me. This is YOUR community. This is not google researched. These are not skewed facts. This is my actual account. Right here in Tallahassee. We, as a community, are in crisis. Stop fighting over what is real or not. Stop fighting over whether you should get the vaccine or not. Stop fighting over whether to wear a mask or not. I can only share with you my experience.... PLEASE extend grace to our staff. We are working so hard, and we are tired. When you yell at us, when you treat us like we are not a human being, it is infuriating, as one of my major roles is to protect

my staff. If you are not being seen quick enough to your expectation, please take comfort in the fact it means you will not be dying today.... I have been a nurse for 18 years, most of it ICU and Emergency Nursing, so by the nature of the beast, I have seen some things I would wish on no one. But this, by far, is the most horrific thing I have ever experienced. Let's come together as a community and support each other. May we get through this TOGETHER, Megan [https://www.facebook.com/TallahasseeMemorial/photos/a.162195 950486361/4479901345382445/?type=3; see also Walton, 2021].

Yet, accomplishing that vision of everyone "coming together" has remained elusive. Bartick (2020, para. 1) explained her experience:

As a hospitalist treating COVID-19 patients in the Boston area, a hot-spot, I seem to live in two conflicting worlds. At the peak of the epidemic, I would go to work and witness the sickness and death that COVID can bring. Then I would look on Facebook, and be met with angry voices writing from locales that have seen little of COVID. People were angry about wearing masks, about staying at home, about job losses. And as the pandemic has worn on, they have become angry about haircuts and all things reopening.

In addition to individual appeals, major medical groups have implored citizens to wear masks and get vaccinated (American Association of Critical-Care Nurses, 2021; Khan et al., 2020; "Major medical groups urge Americans," 2020). In the summer of 2020, "[m]ore than 150 prominent US medical experts, scientists, teachers, nurses, and others ... signed a letter urging political leaders to shut down the country and start over to contain the surging coronavirus pandemic" (Erdman et al., 2020, para. 1). Nicol (2021, para. 2) reported that "[m]ore than 800 Florida physicians [demanded] Gov. Ron DeSantis permit local school boards to install mask mandates as the COVID-19 delta variant continues to spread."

In my own community, the local newspaper, the *Athens Messenger*, put a joint message from multiple health care agencies on the front page, noting that "[w]ith COVID cases on the rise, The Messenger believes this information is front-page worthy. In order for health professionals to continue helping us, we need to help them" ("Area medical professionals speak candidly," 2021, p. A1). Those agencies wrote: "For the first time, the local health systems across Athens, Fairfield, Gallia, Hocking, Jackson, Madison, Mason (WV), Meigs, Noble, Pickaway, Ross, Scioto, Vinton, and Washington counties are coming together to ask for your help" (p. A1). They noted that "[a]t times, we are all asked to put others before ourselves. During the pandemic, our call is no different. Using our knowledge of science and compassion to help others, we ask that you act soon. Help us change the trajectory of COVID-19 for our communities by protecting yourself and your loved ones" (p. A1). Notably, over a year earlier, health facilities in northeast Ohio had issued the same sort of plea (see Loreno, 2020).

Given their personal testimony and professional expertise, the appeals of health care professionals fit neatly with the master narrative about Covid-19 from a pro-science perspective but not so well at all for those who embrace the more skeptical narrative in which Covid-19 can be easily remedied; in which mask-wearing, vaccinations, and other mitigation efforts might cause more harm than good; and wherein public health officials remain suspect. For example, on November 30, 2021, Lara Logan made the following statement as a guest on a Fox News show:

> What you see on Dr. Fauci, this is what people say to me, that he doesn't represent science to them. He represents Josef Mengele ... the Nazi doctor who did experiments on Jews during the Second World War and in the concentration camps.... And I am talking about people all across the world are saying this. Because the response from COVID, what it has done to countries everywhere, what it has done to civil liberties, the suicide rates, the poverty, it has obliterated economies [Mastrangelo, 2021, para. 2].

According to Barr (2021), Logan's statement garnered considerable criticism, and "Jonathan Greenblatt, the chief executive of the Anti-Defamation League, an organization that works to combat antisemitism, issued a statement to *The Washington Post* on Tuesday saying that 'there's absolutely no comparison between mask mandates, vaccine requirements, and other covid-19 mitigation efforts to what happened to Jews during the Holocaust'" (para. 10).

However, an array of sentiments and conspiracy theories persist on myriad platforms, advancing the skeptical counternarrative and encouraging fans of shows such as Lara Logan's *Lara Logan Has No Agenda* on the Fox Nation streaming service to distrust voices from the established medical community, fostering resistance to public health guidance. That resistance impacts not only those who have been working to stop the spread of the virus but also those who become ill and those who must care for them if they do.

That narrative has constrained the mitigation efforts of local public health officials (Alexander, 2021; Becker, 2020; Brown, 2020; Colby, 2020; Morris, 2020). Although they don't face vehemence on the same level as Dr. Fauci, Morris reported that, in Kansas alone, "[m]ore than a quarter of all the public health administrators ... quit, retired, or got fired this year [2020], according to Vicki Collie-Akers, an associate professor of population health at the University of Kansas. Some got death threats. Some had to hire armed guards" (para. 10). According to Alexander, "Across the United States, public health workers are in bad shape.

Over 61 percent say they have received job-related threats, and more than half report at least one mental health symptom" (para. 2).

Moreover, perpetuation of the Covid-skepticism narrative has contributed to what some refer to as "compassion fatigue" among some very tired health care workers (see, e.g., Erb, 2021; Gross, 2020; Hollingsworth, 2021; Salcedo, 2021; Yong, 2021). In an article for *The Atlantic* that chronicled the choice by many health care providers to leave the profession as the pandemic has ensued, Yong quoted one health care worker who lamented that "[o]nce, Americans clapped for health-care heroes; now 'we're at war with a virus and its hosts are at war with us'" (para. 12).

According to Hollingsworth (2021, para. 23), "Dr. Ryan Stanton recently had a patient who began their conversation by saying, 'I'm not afraid of any China virus.' From that point on, he knew what he was up against in dealing with the patient's politics and misguided beliefs about the virus." Dr. Andrea Jones, a family medicine doctor in Nebraska, shared that "she has been screamed at by hospitalized COVID-19 patients who refuse to believe they have the virus. On other occasions, she has told family members that a patient's heart is damaged, or their liver is failing, and the patient's family members have laughed in her face" (Hansen, 2021, para. 15). As Hansen reported, "That's ridiculous, they say. That can't be from COVID-19. It can't make anyone this sick" (para. 16). Hollingsworth provided yet another example:

> The COVID-19 patient's health was deteriorating quickly at a Michigan hospital, but he was having none of the doctor's diagnosis. Despite dangerously low oxygen levels, the unvaccinated man didn't think he was that sick and got so irate over a hospital policy forbidding his wife from being at his bedside that he threatened to walk out of the building. Dr. Matthew Trunsky didn't hold back in his response: "You are welcome to leave, but you will be dead before you get to your car,'" he said [para. 1–2].

According to the director of the Centers for Disease Control and Prevention, Dr. Rochelle Walensky, "Studies show that those who are unvaccinated continue to be more likely to be infected, more likely to be in the hospital and more likely to have severe complications from Covid-19" (Syal, 2021, para. 8). Frustrated by continuing to handle cases that could largely have been prevented through vaccinations and troubled over battling what they consider to be unfounded perceptions of the virus at the near-two-year mark of the pandemic, health care workers have experienced the pendulum shifting from their feeling appreciated, valued, and elevated to being disputed, disregarded, and dismissed (see Erb, 2021; Hansen, 2021; Karkowsky, 2021; Salcedo, 2021; Sircar, 2021).

As one doctor wrote in an op-ed for the *Los Angeles Times*, "I had cared for hundreds of COVID patients. We all had, without being able to take breaks long enough to help us recover from this unending ordeal. Compassion fatigue was setting in. For those of us who hadn't left after the hardest year of our professional lives, even hope was now in short supply" (Sircar, 2021, para. 6). Another shared, "'[w]hat makes me the maddest,' one of my doctor friends told me, 'is that these people will reject science right until the second they need everything I have to keep them alive, and then they feel that they can come to our door and be entitled to that help and that hard work'" (Karkowsky, 2021, para. 11).

In Closing

So many voices entered the public sphere to share their perspectives on Covid-19—athletes and sports organizations as they wrestled with uncertainties about how to proceed during a global pandemic ... politicians (and their advocates in the media) as they positioned themselves and the virus in preferred ways ... celebrities who raised awareness and provided resources ... health care professionals who shared their personal experiences and pleas for compliance with public health recommendations. As all did so, they co-constructed the meaning of Covid 19, foregrounding the sources, stories, and statistics that made most sense to them and framing emergent narratives for others who read their posts, watched their interviews or shows, and believed them to be credible and convincing.

As I've argued in this book, these emergent interpretive communities extended, at least in part, from fandom of those in the public eye—athletes, politicians, performers—and even groups of people, such as health care professionals, frontline workers, first responders as they became celebrated by organizations, and celebrities who urged the rest of us to applaud their work and sacrifices.

In our first postmodern pandemic, a plethora of perspectives filled social media, eventually morphing into two master health narratives—a pro-science narrative and a narrative skeptical of Covid and primary efforts to stop its spread. As individuals participated in their respective interpretive communities, they came to understand Covid through the lens of the master narrative that made most sense to them ... the one that rang "most true" (see W. Fisher, 1984) and, by extension, what then ran counter to that set of beliefs. W. Fisher explained:

> The idea of human beings as storytellers indicates the generic form of all symbol construction; it holds that symbols are created and communicated

ultimately as stories meant to give order to human experience and to induce others to dwell in them to establish ways of living in common, in communities in which there is sanction for the story that constitutes one's life. And one's life is, as suggested by Burke, a story that participates in the stories of those who have lived, who live now, and who will live in the future [p. 6].

The Covid-19 pandemic illustrates the consequentiality of public health narratives—both the contrasting master narratives about the virus in the United States and the many, many individual stories around the world that became part of those narratives. As this book has described, those stories mattered. Both master narratives and individual stories shaped and impacted so many others, contributing to intricate, interwoven, interconnected webs of influence in the public sphere as well as in families, friendships, local communities, organizations, and interpretive communities of fans that span geographical borders.

Indeed, the stories of Covid-19 affected all who lived during it, albeit in myriad ways—emotionally, physically, economically, socially, politically, etc. As the world strives to move forward from this deadly virus, its stories continue to evolve, with each diagnosis, death, disclosure, and discrepancy. Its legacy remains to be written. I'm hoping that such a legacy will, at least in part, leave lasting lessons for those who must endure the next once-in-a-century pandemic.

References

Abbott, A. (2021, February 3). Covid's mental-health toll: How scientists are tracking a surge in depression. *Nature*. https://www.nature.com/articles/d41586-021-00175-z.
ABC6/Fox28 poll (2020, August 26). ABC6/FOX28 poll regarding DeWine impeachment threat receives more than 18,000 votes. https://abc6onyourside.com/news/local/abc6fox28-poll-regarding-dewine-impeachment-threat-receives-more-than-18000-votes.
Ables, K. (2020, October 1). Covid "long haulers" have nowhere else to turn—so they're finding each other online. *Washington Post*. https://www.washingtonpost.com/technology/2020/10/01/long-haulers-covid-facebook-support-group/.
Abutaleb, Y. (2020, October 29). Trump's $250 million coronavirus ad campaign had 'partisan' edge, down to the celebrities chosen to participate. *Washington Post*. https://www.washingtonpost.com/health/2020/10/29/trump-covid-advertising-celebrities/.
Achenbach, J., & Brulliard, K. (2020, October 28). State and local leaders order new restrictions amid autumn's coronavirus surge. *Washington Post*. https://www.washingtonpost.com/health/coronavirus-surge-new-restrictions/2020/10/28/b88c0dd2-1939-11eb-aeec-b93bcc29a01b_story.html.
Achenbach, J., Wan, W., Brulliard, K., & Janes, C. (2020, July 19). The crisis that shocked the world: America's response to the coronavirus. *Washington Post*. https://www.washingtonpost.com/health/2020/07/19/coronavirus-us-failure/.
Aden, R.C. (2007). *Huskerville: A story of Nebraska football, fans, and the power of place*. McFarland.
Aiello, M. (2020, April 8). Andrew Cuomo threatens to hang up on brother Chris during their greatest on-air fight yet. E! https://www.eonline.com/news/1138933/andrew-cuomo-threatens-to-hang-up-on-brother-chris-during-their-greatest-on-air-fight-yet.
Alba, M. (2020, September 28). Redfield voices alarm over influence of Trump's new coronavirus task force advisor. NBC News. https://www.nbcnews.com/politics/politics-news/redfield-voices-alarm-over-influence-trump-s-new-coronavirus-task-n1241221.
Alexander, B. (2021, September 7). The GOP's war on public health officials. *Washington Monthly*. https://washingtonmonthly.com/2021/09/07/the-gops-war-on-public-health-officials/.
Alfonso, F., III, & Vogt, A. (2021, November 27). US announces travel restrictions over new Covid-19 variant. CNN. https://www.cnn.com/world/live-news/new-covid-variant-south-africa-11-27-21/index.html.
Ali, R. (2020, March 17). Vanessa Hudgens apologizes for 'insensitive' coronavirus remarks that sparked outrage. *USA Today*. https://www.usatoday.com/story/entertainment/celebrities/2020/03/17/vanessa-hudgens-walking-back-her-controversial-coronavirus-comments/5071421002/.
Allaire, C. (2020, July 1). One thing celebrities can do is take a stand on masks. *Vogue*.

https://www.vogue.com/article/celebrities-take-a-stance-on-masks-jennifer-aniston.

Allard, S. (2020, May 5). *The New York Times* deconstructs celebrity of Ohio's Dr. Amy Acton in video. https://www.citybeat/com/news/blog/21121959/the-new-york-times-deconstructs-celebrity-of-ohios-dr-amy-acton-in-video.

Allen, C.M. (2020, August 14). Can college football settle debate on managing risk in coronavirus pandemic? Play ball. *Fort Worth Star-Telegram*. https://www.star-telegram.com/opinion/cynthia-m-allen/article244945702.html.

Altungul, O., & Karahüseyinoğlu, M.F. (2017). Determining the level of fanaticism and football fanship to university athletes. *Journal of Education and Training Studies*, 5, 171–176. DOI: 10.11114/jets.v5i11.2742.

American Association of Critical-Care Nurses (2021, September 20). Hear us out campaign reports nurses' COVID-19 reality. https://www.aacn.org/newsroom/hear-us-out-campaign-reports-nurses-covid-19-reality.

Aminosharei, N. (2020, May 27). Susan Lucci on how her 103-year-old mother inspired her to fight the COVID-19 nursing home crisis. *Harper's Bazaar*. https://www.harpers bazaar.com/culture/a32677872/susan-lucci-aarp-nursing-home-covid-19/.

Anderson, C. (2020, July 2). Over 1,000 Ohioans send 'thank you' card to former ODH Director Dr. Acton for leadership during COVID-19 pandemic. Fox19. https://www.fox19.com/2020/07/02/over-ohioans-send-thank-you-card-former-odh-director-dr-acton-leadership-during-covid-pandemic/.

Anderson, S.M. (2020). United we stand, divided we kneel: Examining perceptions of the NFL anthem protest on organizational reputation. *Communication & Sport*, 8, 591–610. DOI: 10.1177/2167479519893661.

Andrew, S. (2020, July 22). Nurses planted more than 160 pairs of shoes on the Capitol lawn to remember colleagues who've died from coronavirus. CNN. https://www.cnn.com/2020/07/22/us/nurses-shoes-us-capitol-coronavirus-deaths-trnd/index.html.

Andrews, T.M. (2020, July 29). Madonna keeps making controversial covid-19 claims, calling a misinformation-spreading doctor her 'hero.' *Washington Post*. https://www.washingtonpost.com/technology/2020/07/29/madonna-instagram-covid-coronavirus-stella-immanuel-bathtub/.

Andrews, T.M., & Paquette, D. (2020, July 29). Trump retweeted a video with false covid-19 claims. One doctor in it has said demons cause illnesses. *Washington Post*. https://www.washingtonpost.com/technology/2020/07/28/stella-immanuel-hydroxychloroquine-video-trump-americas-frontline-doctors/.

Ang, I. (1996). *Living room wars: Rethinking media audiences for a postmodern world*. Routledge.

AP (2020, August 26). New virus cases decline in the U.S. and experts credit masks. *Times-Union*, 8B.

AP News (2020, November 2). Disney plans 4,000 more layoffs. https://apnews.com/article/business-orlando-florida-california-coronavirus-pandemic-133743026aad007f4c9803b9351c49ba.

Applebaum, A. (2020, October 3). Trump is a super-spreader of disinformation. *The Atlantic*. https://www.theatlantic.com/ideas/archive/2020/10/trump-super-spreader-disinformation/616604/.

Aquilina, T. (2020, October 28). Khloé Kardashian reveals she had COVID-19 amid backlash over Kim's private island party. Yahoo! Finance. https://finance.yahoo.com/news/khlo-kardashian-reveals-she-had-173549194.html.

"Area medical professionals speak candidly to community" (2021, September 14). *The Athens Messenger*, A1.

Arnold, C. (2018). *Pandemic 1918*. St. Martin's Griffin.

Aronson, E., & Tavris, C. (2020, July 12). The role of cognitive dissonance in the pandemic. *The Atlantic*. https://www.theatlantic.com/ideas/archive/2020/07/role-cognitive-dissonance-pandemic/614074/.

Aschburner, S. (2020, March 12). Coronavirus pandemic causes NBA to suspend season

References

after player tests positive. *National Basketball Association.* https://www.nba.com/news/coronavirus-pandemic-causes-nba-suspend-season.

Associated Press (2020a, April 2). New York 'like a battlefield.' *The Journal Gazette*, 3A.

Associated Press (2020b, June 16). Health workers feel the toll of virus fight. https://nypost.com/2020/06/16/health-workers-feel-the-toll-of-coronavirus-fight/.

Associated Press (2020c, June 28). Arizona nurses facing impact. *The Journal Gazette*, 3A.

Associated Press (2020d, July 4). NASCAR's Jimmie Johnson copes with coronavirus at home, with wife, kids. https://www.tampabay.com/news/health/2020/07/04/nascars-jimmie-johnson-copes-with-coronavirus-at-home-with-wife-kids/.

Associated Press (2020e, July 17). Tina Charles medically excused for WNBA season. *Boston Globe.* https://www.bostonglobe.com/2020/07/17/sports/tina-charles-medically-excused-wnba-season/.

Associated Press (2020f, September 2). The Rock, his family tested positive for the coronavirus. https://www.washingtonpost.com/health/the-rock-his-family-tested-positive-for-the-coronavirus/2020/09/02/8a5be3a2-ed87-11ea-bd08-1b10132b458f_story.html.

Astor, M., & Weiland, N. (2020, July 8). Coronavirus surge in Tulsa 'more than likely' linked to Trump rally. *New York Times.* https://www.nytimes.com/2020/07/08/us/politics/coronavirus-tulsa-trump-rally.html.

Aw, E. C-X., & Labrecque, L.I. (2020). Celebrity endorsement in social media contexts: Understanding the role of parasocial interactions and the need to belong. *Journal of Consumer Marketing, 37*(7), 895–908. DOI:10.1108/JCM-10-2019-3474.

Awasthi P. (n.d.). Nicki Minaj to Jennifer Aniston: Celebrities who got COVID-19 vaccine, and those who said no to it. *WION.* https://www.wionews.com/photos/nicki-minaj-to-jennifer-aniston-celebrities-who-got-covid-19-vaccine-and-those-who-said-no-to-it-413731#blake-lively-and-ryan-reynolds-413707.

Babayan, S. (2020, August 7). When comedian Laurie Kilmartin's mom was dying of COVID-19, she tweeted her way through the pain. *LA Magazine.* https://www.lamag.com/culturefiles/laurie-kilmartin-covid-19/.

Babcock, M. (1988). *Go big red: The ultimate fan's guide to Nebraska Cornhusker football.* St. Martin's Press.

Bacon, J., & Stucka, M. (2020, October 7). COVID-19 cases rising in 39 states—9 months into the pandemic: 'We are overwhelmed.' *USA Today.* https://www.usatoday.com/story/news/health/2020/10/07/united-states-coronavirus-cases-nine-states-records/5906943002.

Baek, Y.M., Bae, Y., & Jang, H. (2013). Social and parasocial relationships on social network sites and their differential relationships with users' psychological well-being. *Cyberpsychology, Behavior, and Social Networking, 16*(7), 512–517.

Baer, S.K. (2020, September 28). More than 1 million people around the world have now died from the coronavirus. *Buzzfeed News.* https://www.buzzfeenews.com/article/skbaer/coronavirus-global-death-toll-1-million.

Baig, J. (2020, August 10). Trump calls Birx's Covid-19 warnings pathetic—but the real test is what she does next. *NBC News.* https://www.nbcnews.com/think/opinion/trump-calls-birx-s-covid-19-warnings-pathetic-real-test-ncna1236232.

Bailey, A. (2020, July 20). Dr. Anthony Fauci to throw out first pitch for Nationals-Yankees opener. *USA Today.* https://www.usatoday.com/story/sports/mlb/2020/07/20/dr-anthony-fauci-opening-day-mlb-yankees-nationals-5475633002.

Baker, P., & Haberman, M. (2020, July 20). After dismissing coronavirus surge, Trump wants to talk about the virus again. *New York Times.* https://www.nytimes.com/2020/07/20/us/politics/trump-coronavirus-briefings.html.

Baker, P., & Haberman, M. (2020, October 2). Trump tests positive for the coronavirus. *New York Times.* https://www.nytimes.com/2020/10/02/us/politics/trump-covid.html.

Balmert, J. (2020, August 24). Ohio House Speaker Bob Cupp opposes GOP-led effort to impeach Gov. Mike DeWine. *Cincinnati Enquirer.* https://www.cincinnati.com/

story/news/2020/08/24/conservative-lawmakers-want-impeach-gov-mike-dewine-over-covid-19-response/3428359001/.

Baltimore Sun Editorial Board (2020, July 31). The death of Joseph Costa and the risk of being a health care worker during the COVID-19 pandemic: Commentary. *Baltimore Sun.* https://www.baltimoresun.com/opinion/editorial/bs-ed-0803-covid-healthcare-workers-20200731-gdwgpqkwczdixnnfwe5rippa4y-story.html.

Balz, D. (2020, December 27). After a year of pandemic and protest, and a big election, America is as divided as ever. *Washington Post.* https://www.washingtonpost.com/graphics/2020/politics/elections-reckoning/.

Banco, E. (2021, November 12). Emails reveal new details of Trump White House interference in CDC Covid planning. *Politico.* https://www.politico.com/news/2021/11/12/trump-cdc-covid-521128.

Barney, C. (2020, May 14). 'Bravery and hope: 7 days on the front line,' a compelling look inside the battle against COVID-19. *Mercury News.* https://www.mercurynews.com/2020/05/14/bravery-and-hope-7-days-on-the-front-line-a-compelling-look-inside-the-battle-against-covid-19/.

Barr, J. (2021, November 30). Lara Logan draws outrage for comparing Fauci to Nazi doctor Josef Mengele on Fox News. *Washington Post.* https://www.washingtonpost.com/media/2021/11/30/media-lara-logan-fox-fauci-mengele-comparison/.

Barry, J.M. (2018). *The great influenza: The story of the deadliest pandemic in history.* Penguin Books.

Barry, J.M. (2020, August 18). A warning for the United States from the author of 'The Great Influenza.' *New York Times.* https://www.nytimes.com/2020/08/18/opinion/coronavirus-economy.html.

Bartick, M. (2020, June 9). Confronting COVID-19 and social media: A hospitalist speaks out on re-opening. Harvard Medical School. https://postgraduateeducation.hms.harvard.edu/trends-medicine/confronting-covid-19-social-media-hospitalist-speaks-out-re-opening.

Barton, K.M., & Lampley, J.M. (Eds.). (2014). *Fan culture: Essays on participatory fandom in the 21st century.* McFarland.

Bash, D., & Stracqualursi, V. (2020, October 3). Chris Christie tests positive for Covid-19. CNN. https://www.cnn.com/2020/10/03/politics/chris-christie-coronavirus/index.html.

Batchlor, E. (2021, September 1). I'm a Black doctor. My mom still won't get vaccinated. *The Atlantic.* https://www.theatlantic.com/ideas/archive/2021/09/im-a-black-doctor-i-cant-persuade-my-mom-to-get-vaccinated/619933/.

Baym, N. (2000). *Tune in, log on: Soaps, fandom, and online community.* SAGE.

Baym, N. (2010). *Personal connections in the digital age* (pp. 72–149). Polity.

BBC (2020, March 31). Coronavirus: Three out of four Americans under some form of lockdown. https://www.bbc.com/news/world-us-canada-52103066.

Beck, C.S. (1995). Personal stories and public activism: The implications of Michael J. Fox's public health narrative for policy and perspectives. In E.B. Ray (Ed.), *Health communication in practice: A case study approach* (pp. 335–345). Erlbaum.

Beck, C.S. (2001). *Communicating for better health: A guide through the medical mazes.* Allyn & Bacon.

Beck, C.S., Chapman, S., Simmons, N., Tenzek, K.E., & Ruhl, S.M. (2015). *Celebrity health narratives and the public health.* McFarland.

Becker, J. (2020, August 9). This contact tracer is fighting two contagious: The virus and fear. *New York Times.* https://www.nytimes.com/2020/08/09/us/california-contact-tracing.html.

Beech, H. (2020, September 25). 'I feel sorry for Americans': A baffled world watches the U.S. *New York Times.* https://www.nytimes.com/2020/09/25/world/asia/trump-united-states.html.

Bella, T. (2021, September 14). Conservative radio show host who spurned vaccines, mocked AIDS patients dies of covid-19. *Washington Post.* https://www.washingtonpost.com/nation/2021/09/14/bob-enyart-conservative-radio-covid/.

References

Bellafante, G. (2020, August 7). Lifestyles of the rich and reckless: Posh pandemic parties. *New York Times*. https://www.nytimes.com/2020/08/07/nyregion/coronavirus-rich-parties.html.

Bellware, K., Wagner, J., O'Grady, S., Shaban, H., Shammas, B., Knowles, H., Thebault, R., & Sonmez, F. (2020, August 3). Fauci amplifies Birx's warning about 'new phase' of coronavirus spread in U.S. *Washington Post*. https://www.washingtonpost.com/nation/2020/08/03/coronavirus-covid-live-updates-us/.

Belson, K. (2021, November 9). N.F.L. fines Aaron Rodgers, Packers for Covid-19 protocol violations. *New York Times*. https://www.nytimes.com/2021/11/09/sports/football/packers-rodgers-lazard-fined-covid.html.

Belson, K., & Anthes, E. (2021, November 8). Scientists fight a new source of vaccine misinformation: Aaron Rodgers. *New York Times*. https://www.nytimes.com/2021/11/08/sports/football/aaron-rodgers-vaccine.html.

Bennett, A., & Robards, B. (Eds.). (2014). *Mediated youth cultures: The internet, belonging and new cultural configurations*. Palgrave MacMillan.

Berman, R. (2020, August 17). No, COVID-19 is not a metaphor. *The Atlantic*. https://www.theatlantic.com/politics/archive/2020/08/cuomo-new-york-coronavirus/615352/.

Bernstein, L. (2020, June 9). A long road home: Hugo Sosa survived the ICU. But for coronavirus patients like him that's just the start of the recovery. *Washington Post*. https://www.washingtonpost.com/health/2020/06/09/coronavirus-ventilator-rehabilitation/?arc404=true.

Bernstein, L. (2021, February 18). Pandemic cut U.S. life expectancy by a year during the first half of 2020. *Washington Post*. https://www.washingtonpost.com/health/life-expectancy-covid-us/2021/02/17/ae9b71fe-713c-11eb-93be-c10813e358a2_story.html.

Besser, R.E. (2020, October 2). COVID in the White House should be American's wake-up call. *Scientific American*. https://www.scientificamerican.com/article/covid-in-the-white-house-should-be-americas-wake-up-call/.

Biressi, A. (2020). President Trump: Celebrity-in-chief and the desecration of political authority. *Celebrity Studies*, *11*(1), 125–139. https://doi.org/10.1080/19392397.2020.1704391.

Birnbaum, J. (2021, March 6). Major sports leagues lost jaw-dropping amounts of money in 2020. *Forbes*. https://www.forbes.com/sites/justinbirnbaum/2021/03/06/major-sports-leagues-lost-jaw-dropping-amount-of-money-in-2020/?sh=2c80035169c2.

Blake, A. (2021, August 24). How those ivermectin conspiracy theories convinced people to buy horse dewormer. *Washington Post*. https://www.washingtonpost.com/politics/2021/08/24/how-rights-ivermectin-conspiracy-theories-led-people-buying-horse-dewormer/.

Blake, A. (2021, October 19). Colin Powell's death epitomizes the willful carelessness of vaccine skeptics like Tucker Carlson. *Washington Post*. https://www.washingtonpost.com/politics/2021/10/19/willful-carelessness-tucker-carlson-his-vaccine-skeptic-ilk/.

Blake, A., & Rieger, J.M. (2020, November 3). Timeline: The 201 times Trump has downplayed the coronavirus threat. *Washington Post*. https://www.washingtonpost.com/politics/2020/03/12/trump-coronavirus-timeline/.

Blinder, A., Higgins, L, & Guggenheim, B. (2020, December 11). College sports has reported at least 6629 virus cases: There are many more. *New York Times*. https://www.nytimes.com/2020/12/11/sports/coronavirus-college-sports-football.html.

Blistein, J. (2020, May 12). 'Rise Up New York': How NYC star power highlighted life at the COVID-19 epicenter. *Rolling Stone*. https://www.rollingstone.com/tv/tv-news/rise-up-new-york-how-nyc-star-power-highlighted-life-at-the-covid-19-epicenter-997739/.

Blodgett, B.M. (2020). Media in the post #gamergate era: Coverage of reactionary fan anger and the terrorism of the privileged. *Television & New Media*, *21*(2), 184–200.

Blomeley, A. (2021, March 3). How the COVID-19 pandemic is forcing a reckoning within celebrity culture. *Crimson White*. https://cw.ua.edu/79901/culture/how-the-covid-19-pandemic-is-forcing-a-reckoning-within-celebrity-culture/.

References

Bonagura, K. (2021, October 20). Washington State football coach Nick Rolovich fired: How it happened, what comes next and more. ESPN. https://www.espn.com/college-football/story/_/id/32427102/washington-state-football-coach-nick-rolovich-fired-how-happened-comes-next-more.

Booth, P. (2015). *Playing fans: Negotiating fandom and media in the digital age.* University of Iowa Press.

Borchardt, J. (2021, September 14). Gov. Mike DeWine says he would mandate masks in schools if it weren't for legislature. *Cincinnati Enquirer.* https://www.cincinnati.com/story/news/politics/2021/09/14/covid-19-ohio-gov-mike-dewine-childrens-hospitals-give-update/8330666002/.

Bowe, J. (2020, December 28). Watch: Camila Banus tests positive for COVID-19. *Daytime Confidential.* https://daytimeconfidential.com/2020/12/29/watch-camila-banus-tests-positive-for-covid-19.

Bowenback, S. (2021, October 20). Chris Brown calls Kyrie Irving a "real hero" for refusing COVID-19 vaccine: "I stand with my brother." *Billboard.* https://www.billboard.com/articles/news/9648210/chris-brown-supports-kyrie-irving-vaccine-stance.

Boyd, D. (2014). *It's complicated: The social lives of networked teens.* Yale University Press.

Branswell, H. (2021, September 20). Covid-19 overtakes 1918 Spanish flu as deadliest disease in American history. *Statnews.* https://www.statnews.com/2021/09/20/covid-19-set-to-overtake-1918-spanish-flu-as-deadliest-disease-in-american-history/.

Brar, F. (2020, May 6). Bebe Rexha teamed up with a mental health expert to offer advice about coronavirus anxiety. *Shape.* https://www.shape.com/celebrities/news/bebe-rexha-coronavirus-anxiety-mental-health.

Bremmer, I. (2020, August 6). The next global depression is coming and optimism won't slow it down. *Time.* https://time.com/5876606/economic-depression-coronavirus/.

Bricker, T. (2020, April 6). How Andrew Cuomo and Chris Cuomo's sibling rivalry captured the heart of America. E! https://www.eonline.com/news/1137769/how-andrew-cuomo-and-chris-cuomo-s-sibling-rivalry-captured-the-heart-of-america.

Brockmeier, J., & Carbaugh, D. (2001a). Introduction. In J. Brockmeier & D. Carbaugh (Eds.), *Narrative and identity: Studies in autobiography, self, and culture* (pp. 1–22). John Benjamins Publishing Company.

Brockmeier, J., & Carbaugh, D. (Eds.). (2001b). *Narrative and identity: Studies in autobiography, self, and culture.* John Benjamins Publishing Company.

Brown, J. (2021, January 27). Who am I?—'Regular people' saving lives through mask challenge. *Laurens County Advertiser.* https://www.laurenscountyadvertiser.net/2021/01/27/who-am-i-regular-people-saving-lives-through-mask-challenge/.

Brown, S. (2020, June 1). Oprah Winfrey donates $12 million for COVID-19 relief in five cities. *Atlanta Voice.* https://www.theatlantavoice.com/articles/oprah-winfrey-donates-12-million-for-covid-19-relief-in-five-cities/.

Brown, W.J., & Basil, M.D. (1995). Media celebrities and public health: Responses to 'Magic' Johnson's HIV disclosure and its impact on AIDS risk and high-risk behaviors. *Health Communication,* 7(4), 345–370. DOI: 10.1207/s15327027hc0704_4.

Brown, W.J., & Basil, M.D. (2010). Parasocial interaction and identification: Social change processes for effective health interventions. *Health Communication,* 25(7), 601–602. https://doi.org/10.1080/10410236.2010.496830.

Brown, W.J., Basil, M.D., & Bocarnea, M.C. (2003). The influence of famous athletes on health beliefs and practices: Mark McGwire, child abuse prevention, and androstenedione. *Journal of Health Communication,* 8, 41–57. DOI: 10.1080/10810730390152352.

Brown, W.J., & De Matviuk, M.A.C. (2010). Sports celebrities and public health: Diego Maradona's influence on drug use prevention. *Journal of Health Communication,* 15, 358–373. DOI: 10.1080/10810730903460575.

Brulliard, K. (2020, November 12). At dinner parties and game nights, casual American life is fueling the coronavirus surge. *Washington Post.* https://www.washingtonpost.com/health/2020/11/12/covid-social-gatherings/.

Budak, C., Muddiman, A., & Stroud, N. (2021, February 3). How did U.S. television news networks cover the pandemic? Here's a scorecard. *Washington Post*. https://www.washingtonpost.com/politics/2021/02/03/how-did-different-us-television-news-networks-cover-pandemic-heres-scorecard/.

Bump, P. (2020, August 4). Trump actually doesn't appear to understand how bad the pandemic is. *Washington Post* https://www.washingtonpost.com/politics/2020/08/04/trump-actually-doesnt-appear-understand-how-bad-pandemic is/.

Bump, P. (2021, February 17). Rush Limbaugh created the politics that Trump used to win the White House. *Washington Post*. https://www.washingtonpost.com/politics/2021/02/17/rush-limbaugh-created-politics-that-trump-used-win-white-house/.

Burke, K. (1950/1969). *A rhetoric of motives*. University of California Press.

Burke, L. (2021, August 29). After rapper launches anti-mask, anti-vaccine rant, Black doctors speak out. *Michigan Chronicle*. https://michiganchronicle.com/2021/08/29/after-rapper-launches-anti-mask-anti-vaccine-rant-black-doctors-speak-out/.

Burnasheva, R., & Suh, Y.G. (2020). The moderating role of parasocial relationships in the associations between celebrity endorser's credibility and emotion-based responses. *Journal of Marketing Communications*. https://doi.org/10.1080/13527266.2020.1862894.

Burnett, S., McCarthy, T., & Murphy, S. (2020, June 18). Heat, virus no deterrent for Trump fans camped outside arena. *AP News*. https://apnews.com/article/ok-state-wire-virus-outbreak-donald-trump-us-news-racial-injustice-7d81b3efbb3170ca6e471cb7e08b1b9e.

Burns, G. (2020, July 18). Freddie Freeman details his battle with COVID-19. *Atlanta Journal-Constitution*. https://www.ajc.com/sports/atlanta-braves/freddie-freeman-details-his-battle-with-covid-19/BJ2Z4RIMLRGGTNT7ETQWTKZS5A/.

Burstein, D. (2020a, April 13). Broadway star Danny Burstein on harrowing coronavirus experience: 'Strength through stillness' (guest column). *Hollywood Reporter*. https://www.hollywoodreporter.com/lifestyle/arts/broadway-star-danny-burstein-his-harrowing-coronavirus-experience-strength-stillness-guest-column-1289839/.

Burstein, D. (2020b, August 10). Broadway star Danny Burstein on his struggles after COVID-19: 'I'm not really sure how I'm doing' (guest column). *Hollywood Reporter*. https://www.hollywoodreporter.com/lifestyle/arts/broadway-star-danny-burstein-his-struggles-covid-19-guest-column-1305904/.

Butterworth, M.L. (2020). Sport and the quest for unity: How the logic of consensus undermines Democratic culture. *Communication & Sport*, 8, 452–472. DOI: 10.1177/2167479519900160.

Calvin, B.C. (2021, April 7). More governors publicly vaccinated, but Florida's kept mum. AP News. https://apnews.com/article/florida-coronavirus-pandemic-ron-desantis-2e4204216f20068636c01dd5478c16d1.

Campbell, F. (2020, August 25). Ohio lawmaker draws up Articles of Impeachment against Gov. DeWine over COVID response. *ABC6*. https://abc6onyourside.com/news/local/ohio-lawmaker-draws-up-articles-of-impeachment-against-gov-dewine-over-covid-response.

Carino, J. (2020, August 11). She beat the Spanish flu, and now 107-year-old New Jersey woman beat COVID-19. *USA Today*. https://www.usatoday.com/story/news/nation/2020/08/11/covid-19-107-year-old-nj-woman-coronavirus/3342231001/.

Cassilo, D., & Sanderson, J. (2019). From social isolation to becoming an advocate: Exploring athletes' grief discourse about lived concussion experiences in online forums. *Communication & Sport*, 7, 678–696.

Cathey, L. (2020, August 9). Timeline: Tracking Trump alongside scientific developments on hydroxychloroquine. ABC News. https://abcnews.go.com/Health/timeline-tracking-trump-alongside-scientific-developments-hydroxychloroquine/story?id=72170553.

Ceccarelli, L. (2020). The polysemic facepalm: Fauci as rhetorically savvy scientist citizen. *Philosophy & Rhetoric*, 53(3), 239–245. DOI: 10.5325/philrhet.53.3.0239.

References

Chan, A. (2020, May 11). "Rise Up New York": The 10 best moments. *Billboard*. https://www.billboard.com/articles/news/9375995/rise-up-new-york-telethon-best-moments.

Chapman, M. (2020, July 28). "Profoundly disturbing": Trump slammed on CNN for obsessing over whether people "like him" during crises. https://www.rawstory.com/2020/07/profoundly-disturbing-trump-slammed-on-cnn-for-obsessing-over-whether-people-like-him-during-crises/.

Chappell, B. (2020, March 31). CNN anchor Chris Cuomo says he tested positive for the coronavirus. NPR. https://www.npr.org/sections/coronavirus-live-updates/2020/03/31/824555135/chris-cuomo-says-he-tested-positive-for-coronavirus.

Chen, J., & McGeorge, R. (2020, October 23). Spillover effects of the COVID-19 pandemic could drive long-term health consequences for non-COVID-19 patients. *Health Affairs Blog*. DOI: 10.1377/hblog20201020.566558 https://www.healthaffairs.org/do/10.1377/hblog20201020.566558/full/.

Chiu, A. (2020, February 25). Rush Limbaugh on coronavirus: "The common cold" that's being "weaponized" against Trump. *Washington Post*. https://www.washingtonpost.com/nation/2020/02/25/limbaugh-coronavirus-trump/.

Chiu, A., & Bever, L. (2021, May 14). Are they experimental? Can they alter DNA? Experts tackle lingering coronavirus vaccine fears. *Washington Post*. https://www.washingtonpost.com/lifestyle/2021/05/14/safe-fast-vaccine-fear-infertility-dna/.

Chiu, A., Shepherd, K., Shammas, B., & Itkowitz, C. (2020, April 24). Trump claims controversial comment about injecting disinfectants was "sarcastic." *Washington Post*. https://www.washingtonpost.com/nation/2020/04/24/disinfectant-injection-coronavirus-trump/.

Christie, C. (2020, October 21). I should have worn a mask. *Wall Street Journal*. https://www.wsj.com/articles/i-should-have-worn-a-mask-11603315968.

Chung, S., & Cho, H. (2017). Fostering parasocial relationships with celebrities on social media: Implications for celebrity endorsement. *Psychology & Marketing*, 34(4), 481–495. DOI: 10.1002/mar.21001.

Cillizza, C. (2020, August 26). Some Ohio Republicans are trying to impeach the state GOP governor over coronavirus. CNN. https://www.cnn.com/2020/08/26/politics/ohio-mike-dewine-covid-19-coronavirus/index.html.

Click, M.A. (Eds.). (2019). *Anti-fandom: Dislike and hate in the digital age*. New York University Press.

Clifford, K. (2020, May 9). General Hospital alum Rick Springfield calls on The Young and the Restless' Doug Davidson for his new song, The Wall Will Fall. *Soap Central*. https://www.soapcentral.com/general-hospital/news/2020/0509-rick_springfield_wall_will_fall_doug_davidson.php.

Cloud, D. (2018). *Reality bites: Rhetoric and the circulation of truth claims in U.S. political culture*. Ohio State University Press.

Cobb, D. (2021, October 20). Washington State coach Nick Rolovich, four assistants fired for cause over COVID-19 vaccine mandate. CBS Sports. https://www.cbssports.com/college-football/news/washington-state-coach-nick-rolovich-four-assistants-fired-for-cause-over-covid-19-vaccine-mandate/.

Cohen, E.L. (2020, October 19). Stars—They're sick like us! The effects of a celebrity exemplar on COVID-19 related risk cognitions, emotions, and preventative behavioral intentions. *Science Communication*. https://doi.10.1177/1075547020960465.

Cohen, L. (2020, May 29). Massive mural of doctor who died of Covid-19 honors immigrant frontline workers in New York City. CBS News. https://www.cbsnews.com/news/massive-mural-of-doctor-who-died-of-covid-19-honors-frontline-workers-in-new-york-city/.

Cohen, P. (2020, December 26). A 'great cultural depression' looms for legions of unemployed performers. *New York Times*. https://www.nytimes.com/2020/12/26/arts/unemployed-performer-theatre-arts.html.

Colby, C. (2020, July 21). As COVID-19 misinformation abounds, Missouri's public health departments struggle to be heard. *Columbia Daily Tribune*. https://

www.columbiatribune.com/story/news/coronavirus/2020/07/21/as-covid-19-misinformation-abounds-missourirsquos-public-health-departments-struggle-to-be-heard/42505561/.

Collins, F. (2021, February 23). NIH launches new initiative to study "long COVID." National Institutes of Health. https://www.nih.gov/about-nih/who-we-are/nih-director/statements/nih-launches-new-initiative-study-long-covid.

Concha, J. (2020, July 28). Fauci baseball card shatters Topps 24-hour record with 51,512 sold. *The Hill.* https://www.thehill.com/homenews/media/509383-fauci-baseball-card-shatters-topps-24-hour-record-with-51512-sold.

Conger, K., Gebeloff, R., & Oppel Jr., R. (2020, July 20). Native Americans feel devastated by the virus yet overlooked in the data. *New York Times.* https://www.nytimes.com/2020/07/30/us/native-americans-coronavirus-data.html.

Contreras, C. (2020, April 13). Andrew Cuomo reflects on 'somewhere between a father and a brother' for Chris Cuomo. https://www.eonline.com/news1140246/andrew-cuomo-reflects-on-being-somewhere-between-a-father-and-a-brother-for-chris-as-kids.

Cooky, C., & Antunovic, D. (2020). "This isn't just about us": Articulations of feminism in media narratives of athlete activism. *Communication & Sport, 8,* 692–711. DOI: 10.1177/2167479519896360.

Coombs, D.S., & Cassilo, D. (2017). Athletes and/or activists: LeBron James and Black Lives Matter. *Journal of Sport and Social Issues, 41,* 425–444. DOI: 10.1177/0193723517719665.

Cooper, B., Descutner, D., & Alspach, S. (1994). From celebrity entrepreneur to civic hero: Donald Trump's campaign of self-transformation. In S.J. Drucker & R.S. Cathcart (Eds.), *American heroes in a media age* (pp. 188–202). Hampton Press.

Coppins, M. (2020, March 11). Trump's dangerously effective coronavirus propaganda. *The Atlantic.* https://www.theatlantic.com/politics/archive/2020/03/trump-coronavirus-threat/607825/.

Costello, B. (2021, November 25). Laurent Duvernay-Tardif loving Jets chance after year on front lines fighting COVID. *New York Post.* https://nypost.com/2021/11/25/laurent-duvernay-tardif-loving-jets-chance-after-year-on-front-lines-fighting-covid/.

Covert, B. (2021, April 16). 'They just feel that they've been violated.' *The Atlantic.* https://www.theatlantic.com/health/archive/2021/04/the-pandemic-broke-americas-health-care-workers/618600/.

COVID-19 Response Fund Stewardship Report (2020, July). Feeding America. https://www.feedingamerica.org/sites/default/files/2020-08/Feeding%20America%-20COVID-19%20Response%20Stewardship%20Report_July2020_updated.pdf.

"Covid surge overwhelms hospitals across America" (2020, November 27). *The Week, 7.*

Cram, P., Fendrick, A.M., Inadomi, J., Cowen, M.E., Carpenter, D., & Vijan, S. (2003). The impact of a celebrity promotional campaign on the use of the colon cancer screening: The Katie Couric effect. *Archives of Internal Medicine,* 163(13), 1601–1605. DOI: 10.1001/archinte.163.13.1601.

Crist, C. (2020, June 9). Almost 600 health care workers dead from COVID-19. https://www.webmd.com/lung/news/20200610/almost-600-health-care-workers-have-died-from-covid-19.

Crosby, A.W. (2003). *America's forgotten pandemic: The influenza of 1918* (2nd ed.). Cambridge University Press.

Crowley, M. (2020, July 28). 'Nobody likes me,' Trump complains, renewing defense of dubious science. *New York Times.* https://www.nytimes.com/2020/07/28/us/politics/trump-nobody-likes-me-walks-out-briefing.html.

Crump, J. (2020, July 27). Anti-mask US senator who called coronavirus a hoax tests positive for Covid-19. *Independent.* https://www.independent.co.uk/news/world/americas/us-politics/jason-rapert-coronavirus-hoax-face-mask-arkansas-asa-hutchinson-a9640156.html.

Cuomo, A. (2020). *American crisis. Leadership lessons from the COVID-19 pandemic.* Crown.

References

Dahlberg, T. (2020, April 6). Coronavirus will make timeline for sports, too. *Journal Gazette*, 2B.

Daniels, K. (2021, October 22). Chris Brown says Kyrie Irving refusing COVID-19 vaccine is a "damn good choice." *New York Daily News*. https://www.nydailynews.com/snyde/ny-chris-brown-praises-kyrie-irving-covid-19-vaccine-20211022-o3vxadajpjasdpqmmhwnfj3e74-story.html.

Darcy, O. (2020, March 12). How Fox News misled viewers about the coronavirus. CNN Business. https://www.cnn.com/2020/03/12/media/fox-news-coronavirus/index.html.

Dastagir, A.E. (2021, August 25). What Trump getting booed can teach us about this COVID moment. *USA Today*. https://www.usatoday.com/story/life/health-wellness/2021/08/25/trump-booed-at-rally-for-encouraging-covid-vaccination-we-can-learn/5579328001/.

Davis, M. (2020, April 12). Lexington's Laura Bell Bundy recovering from coronavirus. Kentucky Sports Radio. https://kentuckysportsradio.com/main/lexingtons-laura-bell-bundy-recovering-from-coronavirus/.

Dawsey, J., & Itkowitz, C. (2020, October 2). Trump says he and first lady have tested positive for coronavirus. *Washington Post*. https://www.washingtonpost.com/politics/hope-hicks-close-trump-aide-tests-positive-for-coronavirus/2020/10/01/af238f7c-0444-11eb-897d-3a6201d6643f_story.html.

Dean, J. (2017). Politicising fandom. *The British Journal of Politics and International Relations*, 19(2), 408–424. DOI: 10.1177/1369148117701754.

Deb, S. (2020, July 13). Russell Westbrook says he tested positive for the coronavirus. *New York Times*. https://www.nytimes.com/2020/07/13/sports/basketball/russell-westbrook-coronavirus.html.

Decker, T. (2021, September 9). Theodore Decker: As pandemic drags on, only a shadow remains of the Mike DeWine we knew. *Columbus Dispatch*. https://www.dispatch.com/story/news/columns/2021/09/09/ohio-governor-mike-dewine-no-longer-stands-firm-covid/5711180001/.

DeGregory, L. (2021, September 2). Twelve hours in a Florida covid ICU. *Tampa Bay Times*. https://www.tampabay.com/news/health/2021/09/02/twelve-hours-in-a-florida-covid-19-icu/.

Del Rosario, A. (2020, July 9). Conan' writer Laurie Kilmartin opens up about mom's COVID-19 death. *Hollywood Reporter*. https://www.hollywoodreporter.com/news/conan-writer-laurie-kilmartin-tweets-mom-covid-19-death-1302622.

Delle Donne, E. (2020, July 15). An open letter about my health. *The Players Tribune*. https://www.theplayerstribune.com/en-us/articles/elena-delle-donne-wnba-season-lyme-disease?fbclid=IwAR1zlVHpG3YenKGp4-wKLdb2p2oXadqKujXIIW5RghtY3CVDJGW0lZwy0YQ.

Dellenger, R. (2020, August 5). "14 days of Hell": Athletes revealing serious COVID-19 symptoms provide another hurdle to a 2020 season. *Sports Illustrated*. https://www.si.com/college/2020/08/05/college-football-coronavirus-covid-cases-opt-outs.

Diamond, D. (2020, April 1). Fauci gets security detail after receiving threats. *Politico*. https://www.politico.com/news/2020/04/01/fauci-coronavirus-security-160901.

Diamond, D. (2021, April 1). "We can do this": Biden unveils pro-vaccine TV ads, network of grass-roots leaders to push shots. *Washington Post*. https://www.washingtonpost.com/health/2021/04/01/biden-pro-vaccine-tv-ads/.

Dibble, J.L., Hartmann, T., & Rosaen, S.F. (2016). Parasocial interaction and parasocial relationship: Conceptual clarification and a critical assessment of measures. *Human Communication Research*, 42, 21–44. DOI: 10.1111/hcre.12063 https://www.politico.com/news/2021/03/29/trump-fauci-birx-cnn-documentary-478422.

Dicker, G. (2020, October 2). My Pillow guy Mike Lindell shouts out unproven COVID-19 "cure" to Trump. *Huffington Post*. https://www.huffpost.com/entry/my-pillow-guy-mike-lindell-donald-trump-oleandrin_n_5f76ff71c5b6dd94f1e91938.

Digiovanna, M. (2020, July 19). Angels' Julio Teheran discusses his battle with coronavirus. *Los Angeles Times*. https://www.latimes.com/sports/angels/story/2020-07-19/julio-teheran-late-arrival-angels-training-camp-coronavirus.

Din, B. (2021, March 29). Trump lashes out at Fauci and Birx after CNN documentary. *Politico*. https://www.politico.com/news/2021/03/29/trump-fauci-birx-cnn-documentary-478422.

Dodd, D. (2020, August 16). Battle over playing 2020 college football season intensifies as no one can get on the same page. CBS Sports. https://www.cbssports.com/college-football/news/battle-over-playing-2020-college-football-season-intensifies-as-no-one-can-get-on-the-same-page/.

Dohrmann, G. (2018). *Superfans*. Ballantine Books.

"Donald Trump interview" (2020, August 3). https://www.rev.com/blog/transcripts/donald-trump-interview-transcript-with-axios-on-hbo.

Donnelly, P. (2020). We are the games: The COVID-19 pandemic and athletes' voices. *Sociologia Del Deporte* (SD), *1* (1), 35–40. DOI: http://doi.org/10.466661/sociol deporte.5009.

Dove, J., Gage, A., Kriz, P., Tabaddor, R.R., & Owens, B.D. (2020). COVID-19 and review of current recommendations for return to athletic play. *Rhode Island Medical Journal*, September, 15–20.

Dowd, M. (2020a, March 27). Let's kick coronavirus's ass. *New York Times*. https://www.nytimes.com/2020/03/27/opinion/sunday/cuomo-new-york-coronavirus.html.

Dowd, M. (2020a, October 3). Reality bursts the Trumpworld bubble. *New York Times*. https://www.nytimes.com/2020/10/03/opinion/sunday/trump-coronavirus-covid.html.

Drash, W. (2020, July 16). Georgia hospital worker sounds alarm: "I have never seen anything like this." NPR. https://www.npr.org/sections/coronavirus-live-updates/2020/07/16/891997539/georgia-hospital-worker-sounds-alarm-i-have-never-ever-seen-anything-like-this.

Duboff, J. (2016, September). Who's really pulling the strings (and pressing "send") on the social-media accounts of the famous. *Vanity Fair*. https://www.vanityfair.com/style/2016/09/celebrity-social-media-accounts.

Duffett, M. (2013). *Understanding fandom*. Bloomsbury.

Dugan, C. (2021, June 25). All My Children star Susan Lucci mourns death of her mother at 104: She "was a survivor and thriver." *People*. https://people.com/tv/susan-lucci-mourns-her-mothers-death-at-104/.

Dunham, W., & Mohammed, A. (2021, October 19). Colin Powell, top U.S. soldier and diplomat, dies of COVID-19 complications. Reuters. https://www.reuters.com/world/us/ex-joint-chiefs-staff-powell-dies-covid-complications-facebook-post-2021-10-18/.

Durkee, A. (2020, July 21). Nearly a third of Americans believe Covid-19 death toll conspiracy theory. *Forbes*. https://www.forbes.com/sites/alisondurkee/2020/07/21/nearly-a-third-of-americans-believe-covid-19-death-toll-conspiracy-theory/?sh=2c22048240ab.

Dutton, N., Consalvo, M., & Harper, T. (2011). Digital pitchforks and virtual torches: Fan responses to the *Mass Effect* news debacle. *Convergence: The International Journal of Research into New Media Technologies*, *17*(3), 287–305.

"Dynasty cast reuniting." (2021, March 5). Dynasty cast reuniting to support long covid research. BBC. https://www.bbc.com/news/uk-england-gloucestershire-56295505.

Eades, C. (2020, May 26). Don't miss the All My Children online reunion series. *Soaps In Depth*. https://www.soapsindepth.com/posts/all-my-children/online-reunion-series.

Ecarma, C. (2021, September 3). Anti-vax radio hosts keep dying from COVID. *Vanity Fair*. https://www.vanityfair.com/news/2021/09/anti-vax-radio-hosts-dying-covid.

Elfer, H. (2021, September 18). Judge refuses woman's demand that hospital treat her husband with horse dewormer ivermectin. *Independent*. https://www.independent.co.uk/news/world/americas/covid-ivermectin-hospital-treatment-denied-b1922668.html.

Elfrink, T. (2020, July 30). Rep. Louie Gohmert, GOP mask skeptic who tested positive for virus, says he'll take hydroxychloroquine. *Washington Post*. https://www.

washingtonpost.com/nation/2020/07/30/louie-gohmert-covid-hydroxychloroquine/.

Eligon, J. (2020, December 23). Black doctor dies of Covid-19 after complaining of racist treatment. *New York Times*. https://www.nytimes.com/2020/12/23/us/susan-moore-black-doctor-indiana.html.

Ellefson, L. (2021, September 20). Washington State kids blame dad's COVID death on Tucker Carlson "misinformation about vaccines." *The Wrap*. https://www.thewrap.com/kids-blame-tucker-carlson-father-death/.

Emba, C. (2021, June 2). Opinion: Naomi Osaka's silence speaks volumes. *Washington Post*. https://www.washingtonpost.com/opinions/2021/06/02/naomi-osaka-withdraw-french-open-media-depression/.

"Emma Samms on GH status and Dynasty reunion." (2021, March 22). *Soap Opera Digest*, 46(12), 13.

Erb, R. (2021, September 15). A Michigan doctor goes to Facebook over dying, unvaccinated COVID patients. Bridge Michigan. https://www.bridgemi.com/michigan-health-watch/michigan-doctor-goes-facebook-over-dying-unvaccinated-covid-patients.

Erdman, S.L., Howard, J., Christensen, J., & Hetter, K. (2020, July 23). Shut down the country and start over to contain COVID-19, US medical experts urge political leaders. CNN. https://www.cnn.com/2020/07/23/health/shutdown-us-contain-coronavirus-wellness/index.html.

Escalas, J.E., & Bettman, J.R. (2017). Connecting with celebrities: How consumers appropriate celebrity meanings for a sense of belonging. *Journal of Advertising*, 46(2), 297–308.

ESPN News Services (2020, March 12). NCAA tournaments canceled over coronavirus. https://www.espn.com/mens-college-basketball/story/_/id/28893285/ncaa-tournaments-canceled-coronavirus.

Evans, G. (2021a, August 27). Covid controversy checks in to ABC's "General Hospital' when cast clash over vax mandate." *Deadline*. https://deadline.com/2021/08/general-hospital-ingo-rademacher-covid-vaccine-steve-burton-nancy-lee-grahn-1234823321/.

Evans, G. (2021b, November 8). Ingo Rademacher out at ABC's "General Hospital," last airdate set. *Deadline*. https://deadline.com/2021/11/ingo-rademacher-general-hospital-last-airdate-set-1234870108/.

Evans, J.R. (n.d.). The "Katie Couric effect" explained: How the journalist spurred the nation to get colonoscopies. SurvivorNet. https://www.survivornet.com/articles/the-katie-couric-effect-explained-how-the-journalist-spurred-the-nation-to-get-colonoscopies/.

Faghy, M.A., Ashton, R.E., Maden-Wilkinson, T.M., Copeland, R.J., Bewick, T., et al. (2020). Integrated sports and respiratory medicine in the aftermath of COVID-19. *The Lancet*, 8. DOI: https:// doi.org/10.1016/S2213–2600(20)30307–6.

Fairman, M. (2020, December 28). Days Camila Banus tests positive for COVID-19. Michael Fairman TV. https://michaelfairmantv.com/days-camila-banus-tests-positive-for-covid-19/2020/12/28/.

Falk, W. (2020, November 20). Denial's catastrophic cost. *The Week*. https://theweek.com/articles/950898/denials-catastrophic-cost.

Fandos, N. (2020, July 21). Republicans heap criticism on Liz Cheney, calling her disloyal to Trump. *New York Times*. https://www.nytimes.com/2020/07/21/us/politics/liz-cheney-house-republicans.html.

Farhi, P. (2021, September 1). Four conservative talk show hosts bashed coronavirus vaccine. Then they got sick. *Washington Post*. https://www.washingtonpost.com/lifestyle/media/conservative-talk-radio-covid-deaths/2021/08/31/a912a89c-0a66-11ec-aea1-42a8138f132a_story.html.

Farr, C. (2020, September 24). Stanford researchers say they won't be silenced after criticizing Trump's coronavirus advisor Dr. Scott Atlas. CNBC. https://www.cnbc.com/2020/09/24/stanford-researchers-say-they-wont-be-silenced-after-criticizing-trumps-coronavirus-advisor-dr-scott-atlas.html.

Feeding America (2020, July). COVID-19 Response Fund Stewardship Report. Feeding America. https://www.feedingamerica.org/sites/default/files/2020-08/Feeding%20America%20COVID-19%20Response%20Stewardship%20Report_July2020_updated.pdf.

Feinsand, M. (2020, July 6). Play ball: MLB announces 2020 regular season. https://www.mlb.com/news/mlb-announces-2020-regular-season.

Fernández, A. (2020a, April 9). Sandra Bullock donates 6,000 KN95 masks to health care workers in Los Angeles. *People.* https://people.com/movies/sandra-bullock-donates-n95-masks-health-care-workers/.

Fernández, A. (2020b, May 21). See Julia Roberts' cute reaction to speaking with Dr. Anthony Fauci: "This is such a thrill." *People.* http://people.com/movies/julia-roberts-cute-reaction-speaking-dr-anthony-fauci/.

Fernandez, M. (2021a, July 16). The hunt for celebrity COVID vaccine endorsements. *Axios.* https://www.axios.com/why-celebrity-vaccine-endorsements-are-hard-4aa2227a-c529-4750-8be6-ac6fee6aee61.html.

Fernandez, M. (2021b, September 15). NIH launches massive project to study long COVID. *Axios.* https://www.axios.com/nih-launches-massive-project-study-long-covid-5ad4d89c-3c5e-40ce-a901-a4ca865bc755.html.

Ferré-Sadurní, L., & Goodman, J.D. (2021, August 10). Cuomo resigns amid scandals, ending decade-long run in disgrace. *New York Times.* https://www.nytimes.com/2021/08/10/nyregion/andrew-cuomo-resigns.html.

Fieldstadt, E. (2021, October 20). Fox News' anchor Neil Cavuto has Covid, urges vaccines. NBC News. https://www.nbcnews.com/news/us-news/fox-news-anchor-neil-cavuto-has-covid-19-urges-vaccines-n1281951.

Finan, E. (2021a, March 11). *Dynasty*'s Emma Samms on living with long haul COVID: "It's so hard to catch my breath." *People.* https://people.com/health/dynastys-emma-samms-on-living-with-long-haul-covid-its-so-hard-to-catch-my-breath/.

Finan, E. (2021b, March 16). Emma Samms reunites with former *Dynasty* castmates to raise money for long-haul COVID survivors. *People.* https://people.com/health/dynasty-cast-reunites-raise-money-long-haul-covid/.

Fish, S. (1980). *Is there a text in this class?* Harvard University Press.

Fisher, A. (2020, October 2). Trumpworld delighted in cruelty. Now that Trump has COVID, it demands empathy. *Business Insider.* https://www.businessinsider.com/trumpworld-delighted-cruelty-trump-positive-covid-test-demands-empathy-coronavirus-2020-10.

Fisher, W. (1984). Narrative as human communication paradigm: The case of public moral argument. *Communication Monographs*, 51, 1–22.

Flood, B. (2021, March 3). Liberal journalists, pundits delete fawning Cuomo tweets, backtrack on unified pandemic praise. Fox News. https://www.foxnews.com/media/cuomo-tweets-deleted-liberal-reporters-pundits-backtrack.

Florka, N. (2020, September 10). Public trust in CDC, Fauci, and other top health officials is evaporating, poll finds. https://www.statnews.com/09/10/trust-cdc-fauci-evaporating/.

Fossi, C., & Prazan, P. (2020, July 17). Health care workers becoming infected with COVID-19. NBC Miami. https://www.nbcmiami.com/news/local/health-care-workers-becoming-infected-with-covid-19/2264165/.

France-Presse, A. (2020, April 28). Canadian stars join in coronavirus broadcast fundraiser. *Jakarta Post.* https://www.thejakartapost.com/life/2020/04/28/canadian-stars-join-in-coronavirus-broadcast-fundraiser.html.

France-Presse, A. (2021, June 16). Republicans introduce bill to fire Fauci, face of US COVID response. https://newsinfo.inquirer.net/1446764/republicans-introduce-bill-to-fire-fauci-face-of-us-covid-response.

Francis, D.B. (2018). Young Black men's information seeking following celebrity depression disclosure: Implications for mental health communication. *Journal of Health Communication*, 23(7), 687–694. https://doi.org/10.1080/10810730.2018.1506837.

Frank, A. (1995). *The wounded storyteller: Body, illness, and ethics.* University of Chicago Press.

Frederick, E.L., Lim, C.H., Clavio, G., & Walsh, P. (2012). Why we follow: An examination of parasocial interaction and fan motivations for following athlete archetypes on Twitter. *International Journal of Sport Communication*, 5, 481–502.

Frederick, E., Sanderson, J., & Schlereth, N. (2017). Kick these kids off the team and take away their scholarships: Facebook and perceptions of athlete activism at the University of Missouri. *Journal of Issues in Intercollegiate Athletics*, 10, 17–34.

Freeman, H. (2020a, April 17). Rita Wilson on coronavirus and chloroquine: 'I was so ill I could hardly stand.' *Guardian*. https://www.theguardian.com/film/2020/apr/17/rita-wilson-tom-hanks-coronavirus-choloroquine-covid.

Freeman, H. (2020b, July 6). Tom Hanks on surviving coronavirus. *Guardian*. https://www.theguardian.com/film/2020/jul/06/tom-hanks-on-surviving-coronavirus-i-had-crippling-body-aches-fatigue-and-couldnt-concentrate.

Frenkel, S., & Alba, D. (2020, July 28). Misleading virus video, pushed by the Trumps, spreads online. *New York Times*. https://www.nytimes.com/2020/07/28/technology/virus-video-trump.html.

Frenkel, S., Decker, B., & Alba, D. (2020, May 20). How the "Plandemic" movie and its falsehoods spread widely online. *New York Times*. https://www.nytimes.com/2020/05/20/technology/plandemic-movie-youtube-facebook-coronavirus.html.

Frishberg, H. (2021, September 20). Eric Clapton plays venue with vax mandate—despite saying he wouldn't. *New York Post*. https://nypost.com/2021/09/20/eric-clapton-plays-venue-with-vax-mandate-despite-saying-he-wouldnt/.

Froelich, P. (2020, July 11). Texas millennial dies after attending "COVID party" thinking virus was a "hoax." *New York Post*. https://nypost.com/2020/07/11/texas-millennial-dies-after-attending-covid-19-party/.

Fung, K. (2021, October 22). Allison Williams joins conservative news outlet after leaving ESPN over vaccine mandate. *Newsweek*. https://www.newsweek.com/allison-williams-joins-conservative-news-outlet-after-leaving-espn-over-vaccine-mandate-1641759.

Gabler, E., & Rabin, R.C. (2020, July 27). The doctor behind the disputed Covid data. *New York Times*. https://www.nytimes.com/2020/07/27/science/coronavirus-retracted-studies-data.html.

Galily, Y. (2019). "Shut up and dribble?" Athletes activism in the age of twittersphere: The case of LeBron James. *Technology in Society*, 58. DOI: https://doi.org/10.1016/j.techsoc.2019.01.002.

Gallagher, B. (2020, April 7). Rachael Ray announced $4 million donation to COVID-19 relief plans through her two charities. *Daily Mail*. https://www.dailymail.co.uk/tvshowbiz/article-8198199/Rachael-Ray-announces-4-million-donation-COVID-19-relief-plans-two-charities.html.

Galocha, A., & Berkowitz, B. (2021, February 21). 500,000 dead, a number almost too large to grasp. *Washington Post*. https://www.washingtonpost.com/nation/interactive/2021/500000-covid-deaths-visualized/.

Gamillo, E. (2021, September 24). Covid-19 surpasses 1918 flu to become deadliest pandemic in American history. *Smithsonian Magazine*. https://www.smithsonianmag.com/smart-news/the-covid-19-pandemic-is-considered-the-deadliest-in-american-history-as-death-toll-surpasses-1918-estimates-180978748/.

Garcia-Hodges, A., Talmazan, Y., & Yamamoto, A. (2020, March 24). Tokyo Olympics postponed over coronavirus concerns. NBC News. https://www.nbcnews.com/news/world/tokyo-2020-olympics-postponed-over-coronavirus-concerns-n1165046.

Gardner, S. (2020, July 16). WNBA MVP Elena Delle Donne will still be paid by Mystics despite denied medical waiver. *USA Today*. https://www.usatoday.com/story/sports/wnba/mystics/2020/07/16/elena-delle-donne-washington-mystics-paying-wnba-mvp-full-salary/5453980002/.

Gata, J. (2020, June 1). A #HealthCareHero got the surprise of her life. 98.1/CHFI. https://www.chfi.com/2020/06/01/a-healthcarehero-got-the-surprise-of-her-life/

Geraghty, L. (2018, May). Hallowed place, toxic space: "Celebrating" Steve Bartman and

Chicago Cubs' fan pilgrimage. *Participations: Journal of Audience & Reception Studies, 15*(1), 348–365.
Gergen, K. (1991). *The saturated self: Dilemmas of identity in contemporary life*. BasicBooks.
Gergen, K. (1994). *Realities and relationships: Soundings in social construction*. Harvard University Press.
Gergen, K. (1999). *An invitation to social construction*. SAGE.
Gergen, M. (2001). *Feminist reconstructions in psychology: Narrative, gender, and performance*. SAGE.
"Germany fears spiraling" (2020, October 8). *Guardian*. https://www.theguardian.com/world/2020/oct/08/germany-fears-spiralling-covid-spread-as-cases-rise-suddenly.
Giambalvo, E. (2020, August 11). Big Ten becomes first major college football conference to cancel fall season. *Washington Post*. https://www.washingtonpost.com/sports/2020/08/11/big-ten-cancels-fall-college-football-season/.
Gillmor, D., Corman, S., & Simeone, M. (2021, July 11). The power of local celebrities in the fight against vaccine hesitancy. *Scientific American*. https://www.scientificamerican.com/article/the-power-of-local-celebrities-in-the-fight-against-vaccine-hesitancy/.
Gillom, M. (2020, November 19). Why Trump's Operation Warp Speed is credited with helping race for COVID-19 vaccine. CBC. https://www.cbc.ca/news/health/operation-warp-speed-trump-pfizer-moderna-vaccine-1.5806820.
Giorgis, H. (2020, April 14). The problem with celebrities urging fans to donate during a pandemic. *The Atlantic*. https://www.theatlantic.com/culture/archive/2020/04/celebrities-shouldnt-ask-average-people-to-donate-now/610468/.
Gleeson, S. (2020, August 11). President Donald Trump says not playing college football this fall is a "tragic mistake." *USA Today*. https://www.usatoday.com/story/sports/ncaaf/2020/08/11/president-trump-not-playing-college-football-fall-tragic-mistake/3342712001/.
Goffman, E. (1959). *The presentation of self in everyday life*. Doubleday.
Gold, L., & Robinson, N. (2020, May 20). Andrew Cuomo is no hero. He's to blame for New York's coronavirus catastrophe. *Guardian*. https://www.theguardian.com/commentisfree/2020/may/20/andrew-cuomo-new-york-coronavirus-catastrophe.
Goldberg, L. (2020, April 30). "Parks and Recreation" reunion delivers a heartfelt message of hope. *Hollywood Reporter*. https://www.hollywoodreporter.com/tv/tv-news/parks-recreation-reunion-delivers-a-heartfelt-message-hope-1292756/.
Goldmacher, S. (2021, August 31). G.O.P. governors fight mandates as the party's covid politics harden. *New York Times*. https://www.nytimes.com/2021/08/31/us/politics/republican-governors-covid-19.html.
Golliver, B. (2020, July 29). Ridiculed and alone, Rudy Gobert was the face of coronavirus in sports: Now he's ready to return. *Washington Post*. https://www.washingtonpost.com/sports/2020/07/29/rudy-gobert-coronavirus-nba-return/.
Goodykoontz, B. (2020, October 5). Trump's "don't be afraid of COVID" tweet may be the most irresponsible one in history. *Arizona Republic*. https://www.azcentral.com/story/entertainment/media/2020/10/05/trump-fear-covid-tweet/3629483001/.
Gowen, A., & Bailey, H. (2020, November 12). "Catastrophic" lack of hospital beds in Upper Midwest as coronavirus cases surge. *Washington Post*. https://www.washingtonpost.com/national/coronavirus-midwest/2020/11/12/90508b72-250f-11eb-952e-0c475972cfc0_story.html.
Goyal, R., Hegele, A., & Tenen, D. (2021, May 22). Op-ed: How "my body, my choice" came to define the vaccine skepticism movement. *Los Angeles Times*. https://www.latimes.com/opinion/story/2021-05-22/vaccine-hesitancy-language-covid.
Graber, M. (2020, September 16). Do you speak Fox? *The Atlantic*. https://www.theatlantic.com/culture/archive/2020/09/fox-news-trump-language-stelter-hoax.
Gray, J. (2005). Antifandom and the moral text: Television without pity and textual dislike. *American Behavioral Scientist, 48*(7), 840–858. DOI: 10.1177/0002764273171.
Gray, J., Sandvoss, C., & Harrington, C.L. (Eds.). (2017). *Fandom: Identities and communities in a mediated world* (2nd ed.). New York University Press.

Grobar, M., & Johnson, T. (2021, September 28). News & documentary Emmys. *Deadline*. https://deadline.com/2021/09/news-and-documentary-emmys-2021-winners-list-1234846419/.

Grodin, D., & Lindlof, T.R. (Eds.) (1996). *Constructing the self in a mediated world*. Sage.

Gross, J. (2020, July 7). Nurses who battled virus in New York confront friends back home who say it's a hoax. *New York Times*. https://www.nytimes.com/2020/07/07/us/coronavirus-nurses.html.

Grynbaum, M.B. (2020, March 25). Trump's briefings are a ratings hit. Should networks cover them live? *New York Times*. https://www.nytimes.com/2020/03/25/business/media/trump-coronavirus-briefings-ratings.html.

Grzeszczak, J. (2020, July 23). Republican support for wearing masks leaps to 58% after Trump wears one in public for first time. *Newsweek*. https://www.newsweek.com/republican-support-wearing-masks-leaps-58-after-trump-wears-one-public-first-time-1520043.

Gubrium, J.F., & Holstein, J.A. (2009). *Analyzing narrative reality*. SAGE.

Gunter, B. (2014). *Celebrity capital*. Bloomsbury Academic.

Guynn, J. (2020a, October 2a). Trump and COVID-19: Facebook, Twitter and YouTube race to contain disinformation about president's diagnosis. *USA Today*. https://www.usatoday.com/story/tech/2020/10/02/trump-coronavirus-facebook-twitter-youtube-misinformation-disinformation/3592616001/.

Guynn, J. (2020b, October 2b). Trump's COVID-19 diagnosis is not slowing virulent anti-mask movement on Facebook. *USA Today*. https://www.usatoday.com/story/tech/2020/10/02/facebook-anti-face-mask-groups-trump-covid-19/3597593001/.

Haberman, M. (2021, March 1). Trump and his wife received coronavirus vaccine before leaving the White House. *New York Times*. https://www.nytimes.com/2021/03/01/us/politics/donald-trump-melania-coronavirus-vaccine.html.

Haberman, M., & Sanger, D.E. (2020, March 23). Trump says coronavirus cure cannot "be worse than the problem itself." *New York Times*. https://www.nytimes.com/2020/03/23/us/politics/trump-coronavirus-restrictions.html.

Haberman, M., & Thomas, K. (2020, October 7). Trump calls his illness "a blessing from God." *New York Times*. https://www.nytimes.com/2020/10/07/us/politics/trump-coronavirus-blessing.html.

Hale, D.M. (2020, October 29). Trevor Lawrence positive for COVID-19, will miss Boston College-Clemson. ESPN. https://www.espn.com/college-football/story/_/id/30219908/trevor-lawrence-positive-covid-19-miss-boston-college-clemson.

Hall, A. (2020, April 11). Atlanta Braves' Freddie Freeman opens up to ESPN *E60* on life, COVID, baseball. ESPN Press Room. https://espnpressroom.com/us/press-releases/2021/04/atlanta-braves-freddie-freeman-opens-up-to-espn-e60-on-life-covid-baseball/.

Halon, Y. (2021, March 16). Trump urges all Americans to get COVID vaccine: "It's a safe vaccine" and it "works." Fox News. https://www.foxnews.com/media/trump-urges-all-americans-to-get-covid-vaccine-its-a-safe-vaccine.

Hamilton, B., Anderson, L., Anglem, N., Armstrong, S., Baker, S., Beable, S. et al. (2020). Medical considerations for supporting elite athletes during the post-peak phase of the New Zealand COVID-19 pandemic: A New Zealand sporting code consensus. *New Zealand Medical Journal*, 133, 107–116.

Hansen, M. (2021, September 5). Nebraska doctors despondent as preventable COVID wave slams state. Nebraska Public Media. https://nebraskapublicmedia.org/en/news/news-articles/nebraska-doctors-despondent-as-preventable-covid-wave-slams-state/.

Haque, U. (2020, June 10). America is giving up on coronavirus—and the consequences will be devastating. *Eudaimonia*. https://eand.co/whats-the-price-of-living-in-america-your-life-7f2e6b7b6c05.

Hardy, L.J., Mana, A., Mundell, L., Neuman, M., Benheim, S., & Otenyo, E. (2021, September 1). Who is to blame for COVID 19? Examining politicized fear and health behavior through a mixed methods study in the United States. *PLOS One*. https://doi.org/10.1371/journal.pone.0256136.

Harig, B. (2020, May 24). Tiger Woods and Peyton Manning edge Phil Mickelson and Tom Brady to win The Match. *ESPN*. https://www.espn.com/golf/story/_/id/29217016/tiger-woods-peyton-manning-edge-phil-mickelson-tom-brady-win-match.

Harmon, K.G., Pottinger, P.S., Baggish, A.L., Drezner, J.A. Luks, A.M., Thompson, A.A., et al. (2020). Comorbid medical conditions in young athletes: Considerations for preparticipation guidance during the COVID-19 pandemic. *Sports Health*, 12, 456–458. DOI: 10.1177/1941738120939079.

Harrington, N.G. (2020). On changing beliefs in the closed human mind. *Health Communication*, 35(14), 1715–1717. DOI: 10.1080/10410236.2020.1837444.

Harrison, P. (2020, July 20). Jack Nicklaus confirms he and wife had COVID-19. *Buckeye Wire*. https://buckeyeswire.usatoday.com/2020/07/20/jack-nicklaus-confirms-he-wife-battled-covid19-ohio-state-coronavirus/.

Harter, L.M., Japp, P., & Beck, C.S. (Eds.) (2005a). *Narratives, health, and healing: Communication theory, research, and practice*. Erlbaum.

Harter, L.M., Japp, P., & Beck, C.S. (2005b). Vital problematics of narrative theorizing about health and healing. In L.M. Harter, P. Japp, & C.S. Beck (Eds.), *Narratives, health, and healing: Communication theory, research, and practice* (pp. 7–30). Erlbaum.

Harven, M. (2021, May 27). Could COVID-19 change celebrity culture? 1A. https://the1a.org/segments/celebrity-lockdown-who-weekly/.

Harvey, M. (2017). *Celebrity influence: Politics, persuasion, and issue-based advocacy*. University Press of Kansas.

Havey, N.F. (2020). Partisan public health: How does political ideology influence support for COVID-19 related misinformation? *Journal of Computational Social Science*, 3, 319–342. https://doi.org/10.1007/s42001-020-00089-2.

Hawkins, D., & Iati, M. (2020, July 11). Coronavirus update: Democratic Louisiana governor issues mask mandate as state's death toll rises. *Washington Post*. https://www.washingtonpost.com/nation/2020/07/11/coronavirus-update-us/.

Hawkins, D., & Pietsch, B. (2021, July 28). New CDC guidance confuses and frustrates some Americans as delta variant surges. *Washington Post*. https://www.washingtonpost.com/health/2021/07/28/mask-mandate-nevada-vegas/.

Head, A.J., Braun, S., MacMillan, M., Yurkofsky, J., & Bull, A.C. (2020, September 15a). The shape of the coronavirus news story. https://projectinfolit.org/pubs/covid19-first-100-days/shape-of-coronavirus-story/index.html.

Head, A.J., Braun, S., MacMillan, M., Yurkofsky, J., & Bull, A.C. (2020, September 15b). Visual messaging of the coronavirus news story. https://projectinfolit.org/pubs/covid19-first-100-days/visual-messaging/index.html.

Hellekson, K., & Busse, K. (Eds.). (2006). *Fan fiction and fan communities in the age of the internet*. McFarland.

Henderson, A. (2020, June 30). "Throwing a hissyfit": Sen. Rand Paul slammed by critics after attacking Dr. Fauci at Senate hearing. *AlterNet*. https://www.alternet.org/2020/06/throwing-a-hissyfit-sen-rand-paul-slammed-by-critics-after-attacking-dr-fauci-at-senate-hearing/.

Henderson, C. (2019, October 17). Jennifer Garner shares playful mammogram video to mark breast cancer awareness month. *USA Today*. https://www.usatoday.com/story/entertainment/celebrities/2019/10/17/jennifer-garner-shares-mammogram-video-breast-cancer-awareness/4014620002/.

Hendrix, S. (2020, July 9). Six months, six countries, six families—and one unrelenting, unforgiving epidemic. *Washington Post*. https://www.washingtonpost.com/graphics/2020/world/coronavirus-pandemic-lives-upended/.

Hershfield, H., & Brody, I. (2021, January 18). How Elvis got Americans to accept the polio vaccine: Campaigns to change behavior thrive on three factors: social influence, social norms vivid examples. *Scientific American*. https://www.scientificamerican.com/article/how-elvis-got-americans-to-accept-the-polio-vaccine/.

Highfield, T., Harrington, S., & Bruns, A. (2013). Twitter as a technology for audiencing and fandom. *Information, Communication & Society, 16*(3), 315–339. DOI: 10.1080/1369118X.2012.756053.

Hill, J. (2021a, June 2). Naomi Osaka is part of a larger war within sports. *The Atlantic.* https://www.theatlantic.com/ideas/archive/2021/06/naomi-osaka-french-open-press-conferences-mental-health/619066/.

Hill, J. (2021b, November 5). Why Aaron Rodgers felt free to mislead people. *The Atlantic.* https://www.theatlantic.com/ideas/archive/2021/11/aaron-rodgers-vaccine-nfl/620623/.

Hills, M. (2002). *Fan cultures.* Routledge.

Hills, M. (2018, May). An extended foreword: From fan doxa to toxic fan practices. *Participations: Journal of Audience & Reception Studies, 15*(1), 105–126.

Hinck, A. (2019). *Politics for the love of fandom.* Louisiana State University Press.

Hochman, D. (2020, December). 18 weeks. *AARP Bulletin, 81*, 8–21.

Hodges, L. (2020, December 29). A quiet and "unsettling" pandemic toll: Students who've fallen off the grid. NPR. https://www.npr.org/2020/12/29/948866982/a-quiet-and-unsettling-pandemic-toll-students-whove-fallen-off-the-grid.

Holcombe, M., & Waldrop, T. (2021, March 10). This covid long-hauler is afraid to take a shower a year after her infection because of the amount of hair she has lost. CNN. https://www.cnn.com/2021/03/10/us/long-covid-mother-family-year-later-trnd/index.html.

Hollingsworth, H. (2021, October 4). Doctors grow frustrated over COVID-19 denial, misinformation. *US News.* https://www.usnews.com/news/us/articles/2021-10-04/doctors-grow-frustrated-over-covid-19-denial-misinformation.

Holstein, J.A., & Gubrium, J.F. (2000). *The self we live by: Narrative identity in a postmodern world.* Oxford University Press.

Hoppin, S. (2016). Applying the narrative paradigm to the vaccine debates. *American Communication Journal, 18*(2), 45–55.

Horton, D., & Wahl, R.R. (1956). Mass communication and para-social interaction observations on intimacy at a distance. *Psychiatry, 19*(3), 215–229. DOI: 10.1080/00332747.1956.11023049.

"Hospitals buckle under a wave of Covid cases" (2020, December 4). *The Week,* 5.

Huang, P. (2021, July 22). Public health experts call on CDC to change its mask guidance. NPR. https://www.npr.org/sections/health-shots/2021/07/22/1019311989/public-health-experts-call-on-cdc-to-endorse-masking-indoors.

Hulvalchick, A. (2021, October 16). Frontline workers at O'Bleness have spirits lifted by kind gestures. *Athens Messenger,* A1, A3.

Hunt, K. (2020, July 21). Liz Cheney attacked over Fauci support during GOP meeting. https://www.aol.com/article/news/2020/07/21/liz-cheney-attacked-over-fauci-support-during-gop-meeting.

Hwang, K., & Zhang, Q. (2018). Influence of parasocial relationship between digital celebrities and their followers on followers' purchase and electronic word-of-mouth intentions, and persuasion knowledge. *Computers in Human Behavior, 87,* 155–173.

"Impeachment is foolishness" (2020, August 30). *Toledo Blade.* https://www.toledoblade.com/opinion/editorials/2020/08/30/impeachment-is-foolishness-ohio-governor-mike-dewine/stories/20200827152.

Ingles, J., & Kasler, K. (2020, August 25). There's little will to impeach Gov. Mike DeWine, from either party. WVXU. https://www.wvxu.org/post/theres-little-will-impeach-gov-mike-dewine-either-party.

Irwin, E. (2020, October 3). The pandemic depression is over: The pandemic recession has just begun. *New York Times.* https://www.nytimes.com/2020/10/03/upshot/pandemic-economy-recession.html.

Isaac, M. (2020, April 7). Jack Dorsey vows to donate $1 billion to fight the coronavirus. *New York Times.* https://www.nytimes.com/2020/04/07/technology/jack-dorsey-donate-1-billion-coronavirus.html.

Italie, L. (2021, March 9). From a prolonged pandemic, a rethink of life's milestones.

References

ABCNews. https://abcnews.go.com/Lifestyle/wireStory/prolonged-pandemic-rethink-lifes-milestones-76335343.

Ives, M. (2021a, May 1). Celebrities are endorsing Covid vaccine: Does it help? *New York Times.* https://www.nytimes.com/2021/05/01/health/vaccinated-celebrities.html.

Ives, M. (2021b, November 24). Two actors leave the soap opera "General Hospital" over its vaccine mandate. *New York Times.* https://www.nytimes.com/2021/11/24/arts/television/general-hospital-actors-vaccine-mandate.html.

Jackson, D., Fritze, J., Collins, M., & Subramanian, C. (2020, October 5). "Don't be afraid of it." Trump returns to White House after three-day hospitalization for COVID-19. *USA Today.* https://www.usatoday.com/story/news/politics/2020/10/05/trump-return-white-house-despite-battle-covid-19/3620877001/.

Jackson, D., Trevisan, F., Pullen, E., & Silk, M. (2020). Towards a social justice disposition in communication and sport scholarship. *Communication & Sport, 8*, 435–451. DOI: 10.1177/2167479520932929.

Jacobs, A. (2020, April 28). Trump's bleach statements echo claims by pseudo-scientists. *The Hindu.* https://www.thehindu.com/news/international/trumps-bleach-statements-echo-claims-by-pseudo-scientists/article31457387.ece.

Jenkins, H. (2008). *Convergence culture: When old and new media collide.* New York University Press.

Jenkins, H. (2013). *Textual poachers: Television fans and participatory culture.* Routledge.

Jenkins, H., Ito, M., & Boyd, D. (2016). *Participatory culture in a networked era.* Polity.

Jenkins, S. (2020, August 11). College football is caught in the coronavirus culture war: The only smart choice is caution. *Washington Post.* https://washingtonpost.com/sports/2020/08/11/college-football-coronavirus-culture-war.

Jong-Fast, M. (2020, March 22). Why we are crushing on Andrew Cuomo right now. *Vogue.* https://www.vogue.com/article/andrew-cuomo-why-we-love-him-now-coronavirus.

Jong-Fast, M. (2021, March 20). My Cuomo "crush" turned out to be Stockholm Syndrome. *The Daily Beast.* https://www.thedailybeast.com/my-cuomo-crush-turned-out-to-be-stockholm-syndrome.

Joyce, E. (2020, September 30). App State student, Ledford grad who died of COVID-19 complications remembered as selfless and kind. *Winston-Salem Journal.* https://journalnow.com/news/local/app-state-student-ledford-grad-who-died-of-covid-19-complications-remembered-as-selfless-and/article_179c6614-0283-11eb-8807-53d1edb82130.html.

JWB3 Media Insights (2020, May 11). How essential is sports? Consumer attitudes on sports during the coronavirus pandemic. https://secureservercdn.net/166.62.107.20/bkp.b31.myftpupload.com/wp-content/uploads/2020/05/JWB3-Media-Sports-Pandemic-Insights-May-2020.pdf.

Kaminski, M., Szymanska, C., & Nowak, J.K. (2021). Whose tweets on COVID-19 gain the most attention: Celebrities, political, or scientific authorities? *Cyberpsychology, Behavior, and Social Networking, 24*(2), 123–128. DOI: 10.1089/cyber.2020.0336.

Karkowsky, C.E. (2021, August 11). Vaccine refusers risk compassion fatigue. *The Atlantic.* https://www.theatlantic.com/ideas/archive/2021/08/health-care-workers-compassion-fatigue-vaccine-refusers/619716/.

Karl, J. (2021, November 11). Lawsuit threats, empty seats, and a "COVID mobile": Trump's disastrous Tulsa rally was even more of a train wreck than originally thought. *Vanity Fair.* https://www.vanityfair.com/news/2021/11/trumps-disastrous-tulsa-rally-was-even-more-of-a-train-wreck-than-originally-thought.

Karni, A., & Haberman, M. (2020, October 3). A White House long in denial confronts reality. *New York Times.* https://www.nytimes.com/2020/10/03/us/politics/white-house-coronavirus.html.

Kasabian, P. (2020, March 17). Russell Wilson, Ciara donate 1M meals to Seattle community amid coronavirus. *Bleacher Report.* https://bleacherreport.com/articles/2881659-russell-wilson-ciara-donate-1m-meals-to-seattle-community-amid-coronavirus.

Keown, T. (2021, July 21). Olympics in 2021 spur frustration in Tokyo: "People just want their lives back." ESPN. https://www.espn.com/olympics/story/_/id/31849476/2021-olympics-spur-frustration-tokyo-people-just-want-their-lives-back.

Kercheval, B., & Sallee, B. (2020, August 10). Trevor Lawrence sparks united #WeWantToPlay movement, players association goal as 2020 season hangs in balance. CBS Sports. https://www.cbssports.com/college-football/news/d-j-uiagaleleis-preparation-for-the-pressure-of-leading-clemson-football-began-long-ago/.

Kessler, G. (2020, July 23). DeVos' claim that children are "stoppers" of covid-19. *Washington Post*. https://www.washingtonpost.com/politics/2020/07/23/devoss-claim-that-children-are-stoppers-covid-19/.

Khan, A., Bisgrove, J.T., Krishnamoorthi, V.R. Salisbury-Afshar, E., Chen, A., & Arora, V. (2020, September 24). We are doctors. Trump's rallies show he doesn't care about you—or any of us. *Newsweek*. https://www.newsweek.com/we-are-doctors-trumps-rallies-show-he-doesnt-care-about-you-any-us-opinion-1533969.

Khazan, O. (2020, September 22). A failure of empathy led to 200,000 deaths. It has deep roots. *The Atlantic*. https://www.theatlantic.com/politics/archive/2020/09/covid-death-toll-us-empathy-elderly/616379/.

Kilmartin, L. (2018). *Dead people suck: A guide for survivors of the newly departed*. Macmillan.

Kim, A. (2020, July 29). Kaepernick and Fauci will be honored as Robert F. Kennedy Human Rights award laureates. CNN. https://www.cnn.com/2020/07/29/us/kennedy-award-fauci-kaepernick-trnd-index.html.

Kim, D.K.D., & Kreps, G.L. (2020, August 27). An analysis of government communication in the United States during the COVID-19 pandemic: Recommendation for effective government health risk communication. *World Medical and Health Policy*, 10. https://doi.org/10.1002/wmh3.3636.

Kim, J., & Song, H. (2016). Celebrity's self-disclosure on Twitter and parasocial relationships: A mediating role of social presence. *Computers in Human Behavior*, 62, 570–577. DOI: 10.1016/j.chb.2017.03.083.

Kim, S. (2020, October 6). Donald Trump "gasping for air" video raises questions about president's health. *Newsweek*. https://www.newsweek.com/coronavirus-donald-trump-breathing-difficulty-gasping-air-white-house-hospital-discharge-1536598.

Kindelan, K. (2020, December 21). "We health care workers are falling apart," the therapist writes in a moving poem about Covid-19. *Good Morning America*. https://www.goodmorningamerica.com/wellness/story/health-care-workers-falling-therapist-writes-moving-poem-74750620.

Klein, K. (2020, October 10). The CDC finally admits that the coronavirus can linger in the air. *Los Angeles Times*. https://www.latimes.com/opinion/story/2020-10-08/cdc-aerosol-coronavirus.

Kleinman, A. (1988). *The illness narratives: Suffering, healing, and the human condition*. Basic Books.

Klepper, D. (2020, July 29). Misinformation on coronavirus is proving highly contagious. Associated Press. https://abcnews.go.com/Health/wireStory/misinformation-virus-proving-highly-contagious-72056314.

Kloots, A., & Kloots, A. (2021). *Live your life*. HarperCollins.

Kluch, Y. (2020). "My story is my activism!": (Re-)definitions of social justice activism among college athlete activists. *Communication & Sport*, 8, 566–590.

Kosenko, K.A., Binder, A.R., & Hurley, R. (2015). Celebrity influence and identification: A test of the Angelina effect. *Journal of Health Communication*, 21(3), 318–326. https://www.tandfonline.com/doi/abs/10.1080/10810730.2015.1064498.

Kresovich, A., & Noar, S. (2020). The power of celebrity health events: Meta-analysis of the relationship between audience involvement and behavioral intentions. *Journal of Health Communication*, 25(6), 501–513. https://doi.org/10.1080/10810730.2020.1818148.

Kristof, N. (2020, October 3). Trump's diagnosis is a wake-up call for America: Forget the snark. Just wear a mask. *New York Times.* https://www.nytimes.com/2020/10/03/opinion/sunday/trump-coronavirus-infection.html.

LaGatta, E. (2020, March 27). TV ratings, cocktails up for DeWine's daily briefings. *Columbus Dispatch.* https://www.dispatch.com/entertainment/20200327/tv-ratings-cocktails-up-for-dewinersquos-daily-coronavirus-briefings.

Lal, Y. (2021). Chinese celebrity fans during the COVID-19 pandemic. *Transformative Works and Cultures, 35,* 87–96. DOI: 10.3983/twc.2021.2011.

Lamerichs, N., Nguyen, D., Melguizo, M., Radojevic, R., Lange-Bohmer, A. (2018). Elite male bodies: The circulation of alt-Right memes and the framing of politicians on social media. *Participations: Journal of Audience & Reception Studies, 15*(1). https://doi.org/10.1177/2056305119898777.

Lange, J. (2020, December 8). Coronavirus has an optics issue. *The Week.* https://theweek.com/articles/953798/coronavirus-optics-issue.

Lange, J. (2021, January 15). Trump's vaccine delay is getting suspicious. *The Week.* https://theweek.com/articles/960969/trumps-vaccine-delay-getting-suspicious.

Langellier, K.M., & Peterson, E.E. (2004). *Storytelling in daily life.* Temple University Press.

Lee, C.E., Welker, K., & Alba, M. (2020, July 3). "We need to live with it": White House readies new message for the nation on coronavirus. NBC News. https://www.nbcnews.com/politics/politics-news/we-need-live-it-white-house-readies-new-message-nation-n1232884.

Lee, D. (2020, December 1). Tale of two families: How COVID is making America's income and race gap bigger. *Los Angeles Times.* https://www.latimes.com/politics/story/2020-12-01/how-covid-19-is-making-americas-income-and-race-gap-bigger.

Lee, J. (2020). Mental health effects of school closures during COVID-19. *The Lancet, 4*(6). DOI: https://doi.org/10.1016/S2352-4642(20)30109-7.

Leibovich, M. (2020, July 17). Treacherous times for Dr. Fauci in the sacred cow business. *New York Times.* https://www.nytimes.com/2020/07/17/us/fauci-trump.html.

Leitch, W. (2020, August 13). College football cancelled amid COVID-19? Not if Trump (or greedy colleges) can help it. NBC News. https://www.nbcnews.com/think/opinion/college-football-cancelled-amid-covid-19-not-if-trump-or-ncna1236562.

Lenthang, M., & Johnson, C. (2020, July 6). "How do you get through the hardest time in your life? Family": Nick Cordero's heartbroken wife Amanda Kloots shares video showing how her family supported her over the past 95 days during his battle with COVID. *Daily Mail.* https://www.dailymail.co.uk/news/article-8495449/Amanda-Kloots-shares-video-showing-family-supported-amid-Nick-Corderos-COVID-battle.html.

Leonard, E., & Boucher, A. (2020, April 13). Ryan Seacrest donates $1 million to help coronavirus relief efforts in N.Y.C. and L.A. *People.* https://people.com/tv/ryan-seacrest-donates-1-million-first-responders-coronavirus-pandemic/.

Leonhardt, D. (2021, November 8). U.S. Covid deaths get even redder. *New York Times.* https://www.nytimes.com/2021/11/08/briefing/covid-death-toll-red-america.html?referringSource=articleShare&fbclid=IwAR0jVY7gWN-NhLu-SW4N6VKWEZSx00nUm0_mQNST47v0ic237B-h9D0zqhM.

Lerman, R., Shepherd, K., & Telford, T. (2020, July 28). Twitter penalizes Donald Trump, Jr., for posting hydroxychloroquine misinformation amid coronavirus pandemic. *Washington Post.* https://www.washingtonpost.com/nation/2020/07/28/trump-coronavirus-misinformation-twitter/.

Levenson, E. (2021, September 11). College football fans and traditions are back, even with Covid-19 still here. CNN. https://www.cnn.com/2021/09/11/us/college-football-fans-covid/index.html.

Levin, D. (2020, August 22). Covid in the classroom? Some schools are keeping it quiet. *New York Times.* https://www.nytimes.com/2020/08/22/us/school-reopenings-coronavirus-reporting.html.

Levin, D., & Taylor, K. (2020, September 10). "Science versus politics": School district defies governor's reopening order. *New York Times.* https://www.nytimes.com/2020/09/10/us/des-moines-school-opening-coronavirus.html.

Lewis, E. (2021, September 4). "General Hospital" actress Nancy Lee Grahn thanks Frank Valentini, Disney, and ABC for following "the science." *Soap Opera Network.* https://www.soapoperanetwork.com/2021/09/general-hospital-nancy-lee-grahn-frank-valentini-disney-abc-following-the-science.

Lewis, J.R. (2020, November 18). What is driving the decline in people's willingness to take the COVID-19 vaccine in the United States. *JAMA Health Forum, 1*(11):e201393. doi:10.1001/jamahealthforum.2020.1393.

Li, D.K. (2020, July 20). Surgeon General makes impassioned pleas to Fox News viewers to wear face coverings in public. NBC News. https://www.nbcnews.com/news/us-news/surgeon-general-makes-impassioned-plea-fox-news-viewers-wear-face-n1234344.

Li, D.K., & Arkin, D. (2020, March 31). CNN anchor Chris Cuomo tests positive for coronavirus. NBC News. https://www.nbcnews.com/news/us-news/cnn-anchor-chris-cuomo-tests-positive-coronavirus-n1173176.

Lindlof, T.R. (1988). Media audiences as interpretive communities. *Annals of the International Communication Association, 11*(1), 81–107. DOI: 10.1080/23808985.1988.11678680.

Linker, D. (2020, December 24). Our pandemic half-lives. *The Week.* https://theweek.com/articles/956645/pandemic-halflives.

Linskey, A. (2021, October 19). High-profile and fully vaccinated but immunocompromised: Colin Powell's death wrongly seized upon to undermine utility of coronavirus vaccines. *Washington Post.* https://www.washingtonpost.com/politics/powell-vaccine-skeptics/2021/10/19/a1679ddc-303b-11ec-a1e5-07223c50280a_story.html.

Lipton, E., Goodnough, A., Shear, M.D., Twohey, M., Mandavilli, A., Fink, S., et al. (2020, June 15). The CDC waited "its entire existence for this moment." What went wrong? *New York Times.* https://www.nytimes.com/2020/06/03/us/cdc-coronavirus.html.

Livingstone, S. (1990). *Making sense of television: The psychology of audience interpretations.* Routledge.

"The Locher Room celebrates its 1st anniversary." (2021, April 2). *Soap Opera Digest.* https://www.soapoperadigest.com/content/the-locher-room-marks-1st-anniversary/.

Long, H., & Siegel, R. (2020, December 24). Families on brink of eviction, hunger describe nightmare Christmas as $900 billion relief bill hangs in limbo. *Washington Post.* https://www.washingtonpost.com/business/2020/12/24/trump-congress-stimulus-unemployment-reaction/.

Lookadoo, K., Hubbard, C., & Nisbett, G. (2021). We're all in this together: Celebrity influencer disclosures about COVID-19. *Atlantic Journal of Communication.* https://www.tandfonline.com/doi/abs/10.1080/15456870.2021.1936526.

Lopez, S. (2020, October 3). Column: When his mom died of COVID, virus skeptics chimed in on social media. Will Trump's illness convince them? Yahoo News. https://news.yahoo.com/column-lost-loved-ones-covid-140014467.html.

Loreno, D. (2020, July 23). NE Ohio hospitals issue joint letter to stress seriousness of pandemic: "We are asking for your help." Fox 8. https://fox8.com/news/ne-ohio-hospitals-issue-joint-letter-to-stress-seriousness-of-pandemic-we-are-asking-for-your-help/.

Lovelace Jr., B. (2021, April 22). Biden administration to use celebrities, athletes in campaign to combat Covid vaccine hesitancy. CNBC. https://www.cnbc.com/2021/04/22/white-house-to-use-celebrities-athletes-in-ad-campaign-to-combat-covid-vaccine-hesitancy.html.

Ludlow, R. (2020, June 11). Dr. Amy Acton resigns as state health director amid coronavirus pandemic. *USA Today.* https://www.usatoday.com/story/news/nation/

References

2020/06/11/amy-acton-ohio-health-director-resigns-amid-coronavirus-pandemic/5345010002/.

Lyall, S., & Epstein, R.J. (2020, October 2). Trump's Covid news meets a landscape primed for mistrust. *New York Times*. https://www.nytimes.com/2020/10/02/us/politics/trump-virus-trust.html.

Macke, J. (2021, September 16). Steve Martin, Martha Stewart and more stars who've spoken out about getting the COVID-19 vaccine. *US Magazine*. https://www.usmagazine.com/celebrity-news/pictures/stars-whove-spoken-out-about-getting-the-covid-19-vaccine/.

MacLeod, M.K. (2020, May 30). Beaumont encourages community to honor #HealthCareHeroes. https://patch.com/michigan/royaloak/beaumont-encourages-community-honor-healthcareheroes.

Madere, C.M. (2018). Introduction. In C.M. Madere (Ed.), *Celebrity media effects: The persuasive power of the stars* (pp. 1–4). Lexington Books.

Madhani, A., Alonso-Zaldivar, R., & Lemire, J. (2020, August 4). Chasm grows between Trump and government experts. AP News. https://apnews.com/article/virus-outbreak-ap-top-news-health-united-states-politics-ee505d5a774598babc6b4b925d7bfa6f.

Madrigal, A.C., & Meyer, R. (2020, June 7). America is giving up on the pandemic. *The Atlantic*. https://www.theatlantic.com/science/archive/2020/06/america-giving-up-on-pandemic/612796/.

"Major medical groups urge Americans to wear face masks" (2020, July 6). Staywell. https://demo.staywellhealthlibrary.com/content/daily-news-feed-v1/major-medical-groups-urge-americans-to-wear-face-masks/.

Mandavilli, A. (2020, July 4). 239 experts with 1 big claim: The coronavirus is airborne. *New York Times*. https://www.nytimes.com/2020/07/04/health/239-experts-with-one-big-claim-the-coronavirus-is-airborne.html.

Mandese, J. (2020, April 1). "You wanted a reality show host as president, well now you're on *Survivor*." *Media Post*. https://www.mediapost.com/publications/article/349342/you-wanted-a-reality-show-host-as-president-well.html.

Mann, R.H., Clift, B.C., Boykoff, J., & Bekker, S. (2020). Athletes as community; athletes in community: Covid-19, sporting mega-events and athlete health protection. *British Journal of Sports Medicine*, 54, 1071–1072. DOI: 10.1136/bjsports-2020-102433.

Marcin, T. (2020, September 3). The Rock describes his fight with COVID-19 in powerful new video. *Mashable*. https://mashable.com/article/the-rock-coronavirus-video/.

Marcotte, A. (2020, June 24). Red-state reopening has been a disaster—and Republican hopes for a comeback are collapsing. *Salon*. https://www.salon.com/2020/06/24/red-state-reopening-has-been-a-disaster—and-republican-hopes-for-a-comeback-are-collapsing/.

Marot, M (2020, July 6). Knocked out of Brickyard: Johnson copes at home with virus. Associated Press. https://apnews.com/article/f4190c76f260d603e9942eab2cff96c2.

Marr, L.C. (2020, July 30). Yes, the coronavirus is in the air. *New York Times*. https://www.nytimes.com/2020/07/30/opinion/coronavirus-aerosols.html.

Marr, M. (2020, August 3). "Real wives" star Peter Thomas has coronavirus: He thinks he got it from selfies. *Miami Herald*. https://www.miamiherald.com/entertainment/celebrities/article244682487.html.

Martin, J., & Burns, A. (2020, March 17). Once political b-listers, governors lead nation's coronavirus response. *New York Times*. https://www.nytimes.com/2020/03/17/us/politics/governors-coronavirus-trump.html.

Martinez, P. (2020, May 12). "Rise Up New York!": Star-studded virtual telephone raises $115 million for New Yorkers. CBS News. https://www.cbsnews.com/news/rise-up-new-york-tina-fey-virtual-telethon-raises-115million/.

Mason, C. (2020, December 29). After sharing that she's tested positive, Days of Our Lives' Camila Banus claps back at "all the idiots talking negativity." https://soaps.sheknows.com/days-of-our-lives/news/587948/camila-banus-covid-criticism-reaction-days-of-our-lives/.

Massie, G. (2021, June 20). Dr. Fauci says he puts "very little weight in the craziness of condemning me." *Independent*. https://www.independent.co.uk/news/world/americas/fauci-covid19-scientist-critics-b1869439.html.

Mastrangelo, D. (2021, December 1). Dr. Fauci compared to Nazi doctor by Fox News host. https://www.mystateline.com/news/politics/dr-fauci-compared-to-nazi-doctor-by-fox-news-host/.

Mathis-Lilley, B. (2020, June 25). White House official: Americans will "just have to live with" massive coronavirus surge. *Slate*. https://slate.com/news-and-politics/2020/06/larry-kudlow-americans-just-have-to-live-with-covid-19.html.

May, C. (2021, April 16). "One world: Together at home": 1 year later, 100% of $127.9M raised is helping millions fight COVID-19. *Global Citizen*. https://www.globalcitizen.org/en/content/one-world-together-at-home-1-year-later/.

Mazziotta, J. (2021, May 25). Alyssa Milano says long-haul COVID has "impacted every part of my health." *People*. https://people.com/health/alyssa-milano-wants-people-to-get-vaccinated-as-she-continues-to-deal-with-long-haul-covid/.

McBain, S. (2020, April 17). Andrew Cuomo, the charismatic, controlling, combative anti–Trump. *The New Statesman*. https://www.newstatesman.com/uncategorized/2020/04/andrew-cuomo-charismatic-controlling-combative-anti-trump.

McCarriston, S. (2020, March 12). Coronavirus: MLS suspends season due to COVID-19 concerns; U.S. Soccer cancels friendlies. CBS Sports. https://www.cbssports.com/soccer/news/manchester-united-vs-villarreal-europa-league-final-predictions-united-miss-maguire-emery-wont-capitalize/.

McDonnell, A., & Wheeler, M. (2019). @realDonaldTrump: Political celebrity, authenticity, and para-social engagement on Twitter. *Celebrity Studies*, *10*(3). https://doi.org/10.1080/19392397.2019.160157.

McEvoy, J. (2021, May 27). Rush Limbaugh's replacements named: Here's who is taking over the influential radio slot. *Forbes*. https://www.forbes.com/sites/jemimamcevoy/2021/05/27/rush-limbaughs-replacements-named-heres-who-is-taking-over-the-influential-radio-slot/?sh=37f6e9364c10.

McGarry, B.E., Porter, L., & Grabowski, D.C. (2020, July 28). Nursing home workers now have the most dangerous jobs in America. They deserve better. *Washington Post*. https://www.washingtonpost.com/opinions/2020/07/28/nursing-home-workers-now-have-most-dangerous-jobs-america-they-deserve-better/.

McGraw, D. (2020, June 25). COVID-19 and the college football debate. *Quillette*. https://quillette.com/2020/06/25/covid-19-and-the-college-football-debate/.

McGraw, M., & Oprysko, C. (2020, March 29). Inside the White House during "15 days to slow the spread." *Politico*. https://www.politico.com/news/2020/03/29/inside-the-white-house-coronavirus-response-153058.

McGraw, M., & Stein, S. (2021, April 23). It's been exactly one year since Trump suggested injecting bleach. We've never been the same. *Politico*. https://www.politico.com/news/2021/04/23/trump-bleach-one-year-484399.

McNamara, M. (2020, May 19). Column: Why I'm glad to say goodbye to "Some Good News." *Los Angeles Times*. https://www.latimes.com/entertainment-arts/story/2020-05-19/coronavirus-john-krasinski-some-good-news-goodbye.

Meah, A. (n.d.). 35 inspirational Jim Valvano quotes on success. https://www.awakenthegreatnesswithin.com/35-inspirational-jim-valvano-quotes-on-success/.

Messer, L., & Kindelan, K. (2020, July 5). Broadway star Nick Cordero dies at 41 after long battle with COVID-19. *Good Morning America*. https://www.goodmorningamerica.com/culture/story/broadway-star-nick-cordero-dies-41-long-battle-71004829.

Meyer, R. (2020, July 2). The week America lost control of the pandemic. *The Atlantic*. https://www.theatlantic.com/science/archive/2020/07/week-america-lost-control-pandemic/613831/.

Meyrowitz, J. (1985). *No sense of place: The impact of electronic media on social behavior*. Oxford University Press.

Miller, Z. (2021, September 9). Sweeping new vaccine mandates for 100 million

Americans. AP News. https://apnews.com/article/joe-biden-business-health-coronavirus-pandemic-executive-branch-18fb12993f05be13bf760946a6fb89be.

Miller, Z., Colvin, J., & Madhani, A. (2020, October 7). Trump, out of sight, tweets up storm, says he "feels great." *Denver Post*. https://www.denverpost.com/2020/10/07/trump-covid-19-recovery.

Mitropoulos, A. (2021, September 30). Ohio health care workers warn of "astronomical" COVID-19 pediatric surge. ABC News. https://abcnews.go.com/Health/ohio-health-care-workers-warn-astronomical-covid-19/story?id=80309375.

Moench, M. (2020, July 21). Oakland nurse dies of COVID-19, fellow health care workers call for more protection. *San Francisco Chronicle*. https://www.sfchronicle.com/health/article/Oakland-nurse-dies-of-COVID-19-fellow-health-15423100.php.

Moran, L. (2021a, September 4). Charles Barkley hits anti-vaccine sports stars with a blunt reminder. Yahoo! Entertainment. https://www.yahoo.com/entertainment/charles-barkley-hits-anti-vaccine-065447176.html.

Moran, L. (2021b, October 19). Fox News hosts trashed for "disgraceful" spin on Colin Powell's death. AOL. https://www.aol.com/news/fox-news-hosts-trashed-disgraceful-062434665.html?guccounter=1&guce_referrer=aHR0cHM6Ly93d3cuZ29vZ2xlLmNvbS8&guce_referrer_sig=AQAAAEL4ftunsgZTwdPbCPrvdLQ2dy3yq21kbt7RbfMn5wrDIAfMh-KjkY-tDSJrCAqeWdGtMn4aVypCR16O-3Ap1lRND4aS-8fzJjSpUy0IWPrZlZMmR9jF1EDKt4RuaIKU05ubdOj2kvsPxEk2aQFJ8EHknv49HR5KfoqubS0xyzAT.

Morris, F. (2020, December 28). "Toxic individualism": Pandemic politics driving health care workers from small towns. NPR. https://www.npr.org/2020/12/28/950861977/toxic-individualism-pandemic-politics-driving-health-care-workers-from-small-town.

Moser, B. (2021, February 17). Rush Limbaugh did his best to ruin America: How the right-wing talk radio icon corrupted the Republican Party, spread hate, racism, and lies, and laid the groundwork for Trumpism. *Rolling Stone*. https://www.rollingstone.com/politics/politics-features/rush-limbaugh-dead-trump-ruined-america-1129222/.

Mosk, M. (2020, April 5). George W. Bush in 2005: "If we wait for a pandemic to appear, it will be too late to prepare." ABC News. https://abcnews.go.com/Politics/george-bush-2005-wait-pandemic-late-prepare/story?id=69979013.

"Most Ohioans approve" (2020, September 25). https://www.wkyc.com/article/news/health/coronavirus/dewine-approval-rating-poll/95-2a30e2d0-ab4b-4652-848e-24003c40f1c9.

Murakami, S., Park, J., & Slodkowski, A. (2021, July 8). Olympics host city Tokyo bans spectators amid COVID-19 emergency. Reuters. https://www.reuters.com/world/asia-pacific/japan-set-declare-state-emergency-tokyo-area-through-aug-22-minister-2021-07-08/.

Murphy, C. (2021, August 20). Melissa Joan Hart reveals she has breakthrough case of COVID-19 in emotional Instagram video: "I'm mad." *Health*. https://www.health.com/condition/infectious-diseases/coronavirus/melissa-joan-hart-instagram-covid.

Murphy, H. (2020, August 20). Drug pitched to Trump for Covid-19 comes from a deadly plant. *New York Times*. https://www.nytimes.com/2020/08/20/health/covid-oleandrin-trump-mypillow.html.

Murray, S., & Ouellette, L. (Eds.). (2009). *Reality TV* (2nd ed.). New York University Press.

Myrick, J.G., & Willoughby, J.F. (2021). The "celebrity canary in the coal mine for the coronavirus": An examination of a theoretical model of celebrity illness disclosure effects. *Social Science & Medicine*, 279, [113963]. https://doi.org/10.1016/j.socscimed.2021.113963.

Natale, N. (2021, May 15). "Dynasty" star Emma Samms opens up about her symptoms as a COVID long-hauler. *Prevention*. https://www.prevention.com/health/a35811128/emma-samms-covid-long-hauler-symptoms/.

National Institutes of Health (2021, September 15). NIH builds large nationwide study population of tens of thousands to support research on long-term effects of COVID-19. https://www.nih.gov/news-events/news-releases/nih-builds-large-nationwide-study-population-tens-thousands-support-research-long-term-effects-covid-19.

Nazaryan, A. (2020, July 28). Trump complains that Americans like Fauci more than him. Yahoo. https://www.news.yahoo.com/trump-complains-that-americans-like-fauci-more-than-him-232251216.html.

"NCAA tournaments canceled over coronavirus" (2020, March 12). ESPN News Services. https://www.espn.com/mens-college-basketball/story/_/id/28893285/ncaa-tournaments-canceled-coronavirus.

Neddenriep, K. (2020, March 19). Cancellation of IHSAA basketball tournament leaves 64 teams in Indiana asking, "What if?" *Indianapolis Star.* https://www.indystar.com/story/sports/high-school/2020/03/19/indiana-high-school-boys-basketball-tournament-canceled-fate-spring-sports-uncertain/2878545001/.

Nelson, J. (2020, October 12). Jon Bon Jovi & Dorothea: Livin' on love. *People, 94*(15), 30–36.

Nersessian, M. (2020, May 1). "Stronger Together" special raises more than $8M for Food Banks Canada. CTVNews. https://www.ctvnews.ca/entertainment/stronger-together-special-raises-more-than-8m-for-food-banks-canada-1.4920366.

Nichols, M. (2020, May 21). Laura Bell Bundy shares her experience with coronavirus, credits Eastern medicine practices. *Variety.* https://variety.com/2020/legit/news/laura-bell-bundy-coronavirus-1234610951/.

Nicol, R. (2021, August 12). More than 800 Florida physicians implore Gov. DeSantis to allow local school mask mandates. https://floridapolitics.com/archives/449821-800-physicians-desantis-school-mask-mandates/.

Niemietz, B. (2020, June 26). Dick Cheney crosses party lines to promote face masks. *New York Daily News.* https://www.nydailynews.com/news/national/ny-dick-cheney-liz-cheney-wear-a-mask-20200626-3f2l4xeyqnbidh3ftyivl2o3d4-story.html.

Nirappil, F. (2020, December 20). A Black doctor alleged racist treatment before dying of covid-19: "This is how Black people get killed." *Washington Post.* https://www.washingtonpost.com/health/2020/12/24/covid-susan-moore-medical-racism/.

Noar, S., & Austin, L. (2020). (Mis)communicating about COVID-19: Insights from health and crisis communication. *Health Communication, 35*(14), 1735–1739. https://doi.org/10.1080/10410236.2020.1838093.

Norcia, A. (2020, June 11). The hollow inspiration of "Some Good News." *New York Times Magazine.* https://www.nytimes.com/2020/06/11/magazine/the-hollow-inspiration-of-some-good-news.html.

Norris, R. (2020, April 20). iHeartRadio announces commencement speeches podcast for 2020 graduates who won't get a ceremony. *Country Living.* https://www.countryliving.com/life/a32161904/commencement-speeches-podcast-iheartradio-2020-graduates/.

North, A. (2020, April 27). How the pandemic turned Michigan Gov. Gretchen Whitmer into an unlikely firebrand. *Vox.* https://www.vox.com/2020/4/27/21232964/gretchen-whitmer-coronavirus-michigan-vp-vice-president.

Novak, M. (2020, July 28). Who are "America's frontline doctors," the pro–Trump, pro-hydroxychloroquine weirdos banned from social media? *Gizmodo.* https://gizmodo.com/who-are-americas-frontline-doctors-the-pro-trump-pro-1844528900.

Obama, B. (2020, June 7). Opinion: Class of 2020, "you don't have to accept the world as it is." *Washington Post.* https://www.washingtonpost.com/opinions/2020/06/07/barack-obama-class-2020-you-dont-have-to-accept-world-it-is/.

O'Kane, C. (2020, July 24). Fauci says "serious threats" have been made against him and his family. CBS News. https://www.cbsnews.com/news/fauci-threats-wife-daughters-family/.

"One World: Together at Home." (2020, April 6). *Global Citizen.* https://www.globalcitizen.org/en/content/gloria-estefan-fundraise-nurses-us-covid-19/.

O'Rourke, C. (2020, September 2). The Latina progressive who faced down Texas Republicans. *Politico.* https://www.politico.com/news/magazine/2020/09/02/latina-progressive-texas-lina-hidalgo.

Osterholm, M., & Kashkari, N. (2020, August 7). Here's how to crush the virus until vaccines arrive. *New York Times.* https://www.nytimes.com/2020/08/07/opinion/coronavirus-lockdown-unemployment-death.html.

Ott, B. (2017). The age of Twitter: Donald J. Trump and the politics of debasement. *Critical Studies in Media Communication, 34*(1), 59–68. https://doi-org.proxy.library.ohio.edu/10.1080/15295036.2016.1266686.

Ouellett, L., & Murray, S. (2009). Introduction. In S. Murray & L. Ouellette (Eds.), *Reality TV: Remaking television culture* (pp. 1–22). New York University Press.

Padgett, M. (2020, April 6). Thank a healthcare hero. Scott Memorial Health. https://www.scottmemorial.com/news/thank-a-healthcare-hero.

Paletta, D., & Abutaleb, Y. (2021, June 1). Anthony Fauci's pandemic emails: "All is well despite some crazy people in this world." *Seattle Times.* https://www.seattletimes.com/nation-world/dr-anthony-faucis-pandemic-emails-all-is-well-despite-some-crazy-people-in-this-world/.

Park, A. (2013, May 27). The Angelina effect. *Time.* https://time.com/3450368/the-angelina-effect/.

Park, D. (2020, June 6). My friends are way too relaxed about COVID-19 now. https://www.scarymommy.com/friends-disagree-social-distancing/.

Parker, A., & Rucker, P. (2020, July 27). One question still dogs Trump: Why not try harder to solve the coronavirus crisis? *Washington Post.* https://www.washingtonpost.com/politics/trump-not-solve-coronavirus-crisis/2020/07/26/7fca9a92-cdb0-11ea-91f1-28aca4d833a0_story.html.

Parsley, A. (2021, October 27). Donald Trump was more focused on reelection than preventing COVID deaths, Dr. Deborah Birx says. *People.* https://people.com/politics/dr-birx-says-donald-trump-more-focused-reelection-deaths-from-covid-19/.

Pat, G. (2020, March 17). The Cuomo brothers had the most "brother argument" of all time live on national television. https://barstoolsports.com/blog/2102256/the-cuomo-brothers-just-had-the-most-brother-argument-of-all-time-on-live-tv.

Paulson, M. (2021, January 21). "Moulin Rouge!" was their ticket. Then 2020 happened. *New York Times.* https://www.nytimes.com/2021/01/21/theater/moulin-rouge-broadway-coronavirus.html.

Paz, C. (2020, November 2). All the president's lies about the coronavirus. *The Atlantic.* https://www.theatlantic.com/politics/archive/2020/11/trumps-lies-about-coronavirus/608647/.

Pederson, P.M., Ruihley, B.J., & Li, B. (Eds.) (2021). *Sport and the pandemic: Perspectives on Covid-19's impact on the sport industry.* Routledge.

Pengelly, M. (2021, August 23). "You are not a horse": FDA tells Americans stop taking dewormer for Covid. *Guardian.* https://www.theguardian.com/us-news/2021/aug/23/fda-horse-message-ivermectin-covid-coronavirus.

Penney, J. (2017). Social Media and Citizen Participation in "Official" and "Unofficial" Electoral Promotion: A Structural Analysis of the 2016 Bernie Sanders Digital Campaign. *Journal of Communication, 67*(3), 402–423. doi:10.1111/jcom.12300.

PEOPLE Staff (2020, April 29). PEOPLE, LeBron James and more to honor the Class of 2020 with primetime special *Graduate Together. People.* https://people.com/human-interest/people-lebron-james-honor-class-of-2020-graduate-together-special/.

Perez, A.M. (2020, May 12). COVID-19 changes celebrity culture. https://news.miami.edu/stories/2020/05/covid-19-changes-celebrity-culture.html.

Pérez-Peña, R. (2020, September 28). Coronavirus deaths pass one million worldwide. *New York Times.* https://www.nytimes.com/2020/09/28/world/covid-1-million-deaths.html.

Perry, D., Acquavella, K., & Anderson, R. (2020, July 29). Timeline of how the COVID-19 pandemic affected the 2020 Major League Baseball season. CBS Sports. https://

www.cbssports.com/mlb/news/mlb-grades-rays-red-sox-padres-giants-ace-quarter-mark-report-cards-dodgers-yankees-not-far-behind/.

Peters, J.W. (2020, July 30). Will Herman Cain's death change Republican views on the virus and masks? *New York Times*. https://www.nytimes.com/2020/07/30/us/politics/herman-cain-gop-coronavirus.html.

Peterson, K. (2020, July 22). Liz Cheney parries criticisms from fellow Republicans. *Wall Street Journal*. https://www.wsj.com/articles/rep-cheney-parries-criticism-from-fellow-republicans-11595372153.

Petronio, S. (2010). Communication privacy management theory: What do we know about family privacy regulation? *Journal of Family Theory & Review, 2*(3), 175–196.

Pinsker, J. (2020, October 2). Don't expect Trump's diagnosis to change the minds of pandemic skeptics. *The Atlantic*. https://www.theatlantic.com/family/archive/2020/10/trump-positive-coronavirus-test-pandemic-skeptics/616593/.

Pitofsky, M. (2020, November 10). Stevie Wonder, Céline Dion and other stars to perform at Thanksgiving concert honoring nurses. *The Hill*. https://thehill.com/blogs/in-the-know/in-the-know/525276-stevie-wonder-celine-dion-and-other-stars-to-perform-at.

Pitofsky, M. (2021, April 12). Fareed Zakaria pays tribute to his mother after she died of COVID-19 complications. *The Hill*. https://thehill.com/media/547783-fareed-zakaria-pays-tribute-to-his-mother-after-she-died-of-covid-19-complications.

Place, N. (2021, June 7). "They don't let you put the window down": Dr. Fauci reveals level of security he's under during Kelly and Ryan interview. *Independent*. https://www.independent.co.uk/news/world/americas/us-politics/anthony-fauci-car-window-security-b1861333.html.

Plante, K.S., Dwivedi, V., Plante, J.A., Fernandez, D., Mirchandani, D., Bopp, N. et al. (2021). Antiviral activity of oleandrin and a defined extract of Nerium oleander against SARS-CoV-2. *Biomedicine and Pharmacotherapy, 138*, 111457. DOI: 10.1016/j.biopha.2021.111457.

Pleat, Z. (2020, July 23). Sinclair gives "Plandemic" conspiracy theorists a platform to spread their lies about Dr. Fauci and the coronavirus. Media Matters. https://www.mediamatters.org/sinclair-broadcast-group/sinclair-gives-plandemic-conspiracy-theorists-platform-spread-their-lieshttps://www.mediamatters.org/sinclair-broadcast-group/sinclair-gives-plandemic-conspiracy-theorists-platform-spread-their-lies.

Poniewozik, J. (2020, July 21). Trump's briefings, "The Apprentice" and the perils of the second season. *New York Times*. https://www.nytimes.com/2020/07/21/arts/television/trump-briefing.html.

Porter, T. (2020, July 24). Fauci says he has been assigned personal security after receiving "serious threats" to his family. *Business Insider*. https://www.businessinsider.com/fauci-given-personal-security-after-threats-family-2020-7.

Portnoy, J. (2021, December 23). Covid patients overwhelm U.S. hospitals. *The Seattle Times*. https://www.seattletimes.com/nation-world/covid-patients-overwhelm-u-s-hospitals-people-are-dying-because-we-cannot-get-to-them-fast-enough/.

Powell, C. (2020, March 12). Dawn Staley issues statement in wake of NCAA tournament cancellation. *Sports Illustrated*. https://www.si.com/college/southcarolina/basketball/staley-tourney-cancelled.

Prajean, J. (2020, July 14). Energy transfer came through with a $100K check for Parkland Foundation's Dallas healthcare heroes. https://mysweetcharity.com/2020/07/energy-transfer-came-through-with-a-100k-check-for-parkland-foundations-dallas-healthcare-heroes/.

Pramuk, J. (2020, May 1). White House blocks Fauci from testifying at House coronavirus hearing. CNBC. https://www.cnbc.com/2020/05/01/anthony-fauci-blocked-from-testifying-at-house-coronavirus-hearing.html.

Proctor, W. (2018). "I've seen a lot of talk about the #blackstormtrooper outrage, but not a single example of anyone complaining": *The Force Awakens*, canonical fidelity and non-toxic fan practices. *Participations: Journal of Audience & Reception Studies*, 15(1). http://eprints.bournemouth.ac.uk/30771/.

Proctor, W., & Kies, B. (2018). Editors' introduction: On toxic fan practices and the new culture wars. *Participations: Journal of Audience & Reception Studies*, 15(1). http://eprints.bournemouth.ac.uk/30957/1/on%20toxic%20fan%20practices.pdf.

Puente, M. (2020, October 2). First lady Melania Trump's face masks: Sometimes yes, sometimes no. *USA Today*. https://www.usatoday.com/story/entertainment/celebrities/2020/10/02/melania-trump-face-masks-sometimes-she-wears-sometimes-doesnt/5893940002/.

Purves, M., & WHIO Staff. (2020, August 10). Reports: Big Ten schools vote to cancel fall football season. https://www.whio.com/sports/ohio-state/reports-big-ten-schools-vote-cancel-fall-football-season/NACF57MM3RFBZFQQDWNKJYGGQE/.

Quinn, C. (2020, March 26). The people are speaking, and wow, do they adore Mike DeWine's handling of the coronavirus. *Plain Dealer*. https://www.cleveland.com/news/2020/03/the-people-are-speaking-and-wow-do-they-adore—mike-dewines-handling-of-the-coronavirus.html.

Rabin, R.C. (2021, April 2). Vaccinated Americans are at low risk while traveling but must still wear masks, the C.D.C. says. *New York Times*. https://www.nytimes.com/2021/04/02/science/cdc-travel-vaccinated.html.

Rafiquddin, S. (2021, September 18). Doctors treating unvaccinated Covid patients are succumbing to compassion fatigue. *Guardian*. https://www.theguardian.com/us-news/2021/sep/18/doctors-caring-unvaccinated-covid-patients.

"Read the full transcript" (2020, May 16). *New York Times*. https://www.nytimes.com/2020/05/16/us/obama-graduation-speech-transcript.html.

Reichels, A. (2020, March 25). Area hopefuls taking delay in stride. *Journal Gazette*, B1.

Reimann, N. (2020, August 24). Some Americans are tragically still drinking bleach as a coronavirus "cure." *Forbes*. https://www.forbes.com/sites/nicholasreimann/2020/08/24/some-americans-are-tragically-still-drinking-bleach-as-a-coronavirus-cure/?sh=53bfc0576748.

Reinhard, C.D. (2018). *Fractured fandoms: Contentious communication in fan communities*. Lexington Books.

Reinikainen, H., Munnukka, J., Maity, D., & Luoma-aho, V. (2020). "You really are a great big sister"—parasocial relationships, credibility, and the moderating role of audience comments in influencer marketing. *Journal of Marketing Management*, 36(1), 1–20. DOI:10.1080/0267257X.2019.1708781.

Reisman, N. (2020, July 31). How Cuomo's popularity could be sustained amid pandemic. Spectrum News 1. https://spectrumlocalnews.com/nys/central-ny/ny-state-of-politics/2020/07/31/cuomo-s-popularity-could-be-sustained-amid-pandemic.

Renau, A. (2020, April 6). John Krasinski gathered the original Hamilton cast on Zoom to surprise a young fan. Upworthy. https://www.upworthy.com/some-good-news-hamilton-cast.

Renkl, M. (2021, July 19). Dolly Parton tried. But Tennessee is squandering a miracle. *New York Times*. https://www.nytimes.com/2021/07/19/opinion/tennessee-dolly-parton-covid-vaccine.html.

Renwick, D. (2020, October 8). Loved ones of Covid victims appalled by Trump's "don't be afraid" tweet. *Guardian*. https://www.theguardian.com/world/2020/oct/08/loved-ones-covid-victims-appalled-trump-tweet.

Reuters Staff (2020, March 24). Reaction to postponement of the Tokyo 2020 Olympics. Reuters. https://www.reuters.com/article/us-health-coronavirus-olympics-reaction/reaction-to-postponement-of-the-tokyo-2020-olympics-idUSKBN21B24V.

Richardson, S. (2020, June 12). Former Ohio health director Dr. Amy Acton will join Sesame Street characters for a coronavirus town hall Saturday. *Plain Dealer*. https://www.cleveland.com/open/2020/06/former-ohio-health-director-dr-amy-acton-will-join-sesame-street-characters-for-a-coronavirus-town-hall-saturday.html.

References

Rico, K. (2020, June 10). "Days of Our Lives" star Judi Evans hospitalized with COVID-19. *Variety.* https://variety.com/2020/tv/news/judi-evans-days-of-our-lives-coronavirus-1234629803/.

Rinker, K. (2020, December 11). A nationwide mask of disunity. *Journal Gazette*, 7A.

Robins-Early, N., Miller, H., & Cook, J. (2020, July 28). How quack doctors and powerful GOP operatives spread misinformation to millions. *Huffington Post.* https://www.huffpost.com/entry/how-quack-doctors-and-powerful-gop-operatives-spread-misinformation-to-millions_n_5f208048c5b66859f1f33148.

Rogers, K. (2020, July 15). After attacks from Trump aides, Fauci says "let's stop this nonsense" and focus on virus. *New York Times.* https://www.nytimes.com/2020/07/15/us/politics/fauci-navarro-coronavirus.html.

Rogers, K., & Weiland, N. (2020, July 27). Trump announced, then canceled, a Yankees pitch. Both came as a surprise. *New York Times.* https://www.nytimes.com/2020/07/27/us/politics/trump-yankees-fauci.html.

Rohrlich, J. (2021, October 18). Dennis Prager announces he has COVID after hugging "thousands" to get it. *Daily Beast.* https://www.thedailybeast.com/dennis-prager-announces-he-has-covid-after-hugging-thousands-to-get-it.

Rooney, D. (2020, April 13). Broadway star Danny Burstein on harrowing coronavirus experience: "Strength through stillness" (guest column). *Hollywood Reporter.* https://www.hollywoodreporter.com/lifestyle/arts/broadway-star-danny-burstein-his-harrowing-coronavirus-experience-strength-stillness-guest-column-1289839/.

Rosales, I. (2020, June 12). Nurse in COVID-19 ICU quits after colleagues get sick at St. Petersburg hospital. ABC WFTS. https://www.abcactionnews.com/news/region-pinellas/nurse-in-covid-19-icu-unit-quits-after-colleagues-get-sick-at-st-petersburg-hospital.

Rosenberg, G. (2020, June 11). Amy Acton stepping down as Ohio Health Department director. WOSU. https://news.wosu.org/news/2020-06-11/amy-acton-stepping-down-as-ohio-health-department-director.

Rosenthal, E. (2011). Betty Ford's momentous contributions to cancer awareness. *Oncology Times*, 33(15), 7–8.

Rosenwald, B. (2021, September 13). Talk radio's Covid death trend a metastasization of conservative media culture. NBC News. https://www.nbcnews.com/think/opinion/talk-radio-s-covid-death-trend-metastasization-conservative-media-culture-ncna1279023.

Rosman, K. (2021, June 10). The story of a famous covid widow. *New York Times.* https://www.nytimes.com/2021/06/10/books/amanda-kloots-nick-cordero-live-your-life.html.

Rucker, P., Dawsey, J., Parker, A., & Costa, R. (2020, October 2). Invincibility punctured by infection: How the coronavirus spread in Trump's White House. *Washington Post.* https://www.washingtonpost.com/politics/trump-virus-spread-white-house/2020/10/02.

Rugg, A. (2020). Incorporating the protests: The NFL, social justice, and the constrained activism of the "Inspire Change" campaign. *Communication & Sport*, 8, 611–628. DOI: 10.1177/2167479519896325.

Rupar, A. (2020, August 4). "They are dying. That's true. It is what it is." Trump's Axios interview was a disaster. *Vox.* https//www.vox.com/2020/8/4/21354055/trump-axios-interview-jonathan-swan.

Rusoja, E.A., & Thomas, B.A. (2021). The COVID-19 pandemic, Black mistrust, and a path forward. *EClinical Medicine*, 35. DOI: htttps://doi.org/10.1016/j.eclinm.2021.100868.

Russo, R.D. (2021, August 22). College football 2021: Return to normal wrapped in change. AP News. https://apnews.com/article/sports-college-football-football-health-utah-utes-football-be9c91d43fe864619e1f8166ca1ca17b.

Ryan, L. (2020, March 27). Inside the Dr. Amy Acton internet fan club. https://www.ideastream.org/news/inside-dr-amy-acton-s-internet-fan-club.

Sacchetti, M. (2020, July 30). "I'm scared." *Washington Post.* https://www.washingtonpost.com/nation/2020/07/18/im-scared/?arc404=true.

Salcedo, A. (2021, September 24). Doctor who has lost over 100 patients to covid says some deny virus from their deathbeds: "I don't believe you." *Washington Post*. https://www.washingtonpost.com/nation/2021/09/24/michigan-doctor-plea-unvaccinated/.

Samore, T., Fessler, D.M.T., Sparks, A.M., & Holbrook, C. (2021). Of pathogens and party lines: Social conservatism positively associates with COVID-19 precautions among U.S. Democrats but not Republicans. PLOS One. https://doi.org/10.1371/journal.pone.0253326.

Sanchez, C. (2020, July 1). Celebrities take on the "Wear a Damn Mask" challenge as coronavirus cases soar. *Harper's Bazaar*. https://www.harpersbazaar.com/celebrity/latest/a33023419/celebrity-wear-a-damn-mask-challenge/.

Sanders, E. (2020, April 23). The problem with celebrity "charity." Whitman Wire. https://whitmanwire.com/opinion/2020/04/23/the-problem-with-celebrity-charity/.

Sandvoss, C. (2013). Toward an understanding of political enthusiasm as media fandom: Blogging, fan productivity and affect in American politics. *Participations*, *10*(1). http://www.participations.org/Volume%2010/Issue%201/12a%20Sandvoss%2010%201.pdf.

Sandvoss, C., Gray, J., & Harrington, C.L. (2017). Introduction: Why still study fans? In J. Gray, C. Sandvoss, & C.L. Harrington (Eds.), *Fandom: Identities and communities in a mediated world* (2nd ed., pp. 1–28). New York University Press.

Scheyder, E., & Brown, N. (2020, October 2). "Anyone can get it," Trump supporters shocked at diagnosis, unwavering in support. Yahoo News. https://www.yahoo.com/now/anyone-trump-supporters-shocked-diagnosis-185400949.html.

Schmidt, S.H., Frederick, E.L., Pegoraro, A., & Spencer, T.C. (2019). An analysis of Colin Kaepernick, Megan Rapinoe, and the national anthem protests. *Communication & Sport*, *7*, 653–677.

Schmittel, & Sanderson, J.A. (2014). Talking about Trayvon in 140 characters: Exploring NFL players' tweets about the George Zimmerman verdict. *Journal of Sport & Social Issues*, *39*, 332–345.

Schnurr, S. (2020, Marc 24). Brothers Chris Cuomo and Governor Andrew Cuomo teasing each other on live TV is a must-see. E! https://www.eonline.com/news/1133863/governor-andrew-cuomo-and-chris-cuomo-teasing-each-other-on-live-tv-is-a-must-see.

Schoenberg, N. (2020, September 10. Comparing COVID-19 with previous national crises such as Vietnam War, Spanish Flu: Historians weigh in on the similarities and differences. *Chicago Tribune*. https://www.chicagotribune.com/lifestyles/ct-life-covid-compare-national-crises-09092020-20200910-ovkxyg36fje6bkfr45k3fr4jta-story.html.

Schouten, A.P., Janssen, L., & Verspaget, M. (2019). Celebrity vs. influencer endorsements in advertising: The role of identification, credibility, and product-endorser fit. *International Journal of Advertising*, *39*(2).

Schuetz, R.A. (2020, October 2). Lina Hidalgo quietly postponing Harris County foreclosures with executive orders. *Houston Chronicles*. https://www.houstonchronicle.com/business/article/Lina-Hidalgo-using-executive-orders-to-postpone.

Schwartz, K., Exner-Cortens, D., McMorris, C.A., Makarenko, E., Arnold, P., Van Bavel, M., et al. (2021). COVID-19 and student well-being: Stress and mental health during return-to-school. *Canadian Journal of School Psychology*, *36*(2), 166–185. https://doi.org/10.1177/08295735211001653.

Sciutto, J., & LeBlanc, P. (2020, June 1). Dr. Anthony Fauci hasn't spoken with Trump in two weeks. CNN. https://www.cnn.com/2020/06/01/politics/fauci-trump-two-weeks/index.html.

Segal, J.Z. (2005). *Health and the rhetoric of medicine*. Southern Illinois University Press.

Segers, G. (2020, November 5). Whitmer on Trump's response to kidnapping plot: "I don't think it's funny." CBS News. https://www.cbsnews.com/news/gretchen-whitmer-trump-response-kidnapping-plot/.

Seiger, T. (2020, June 25). Coronavirus: 18 family members test positive for COVID-19 after surprise birthday party. *WSBT.* https://www.wsbtv.com/news/trending/coronavirus-18-family-members-test-positive-covid-19-after-surprise-birthday-party/YRPCJKVT3ZHWREDCT72NIYGADQ/.

Sellers, F.S., & Hauslohner, A. (2020, July 25). Houston, Miami, other cities face mounting health care worker shortages as infections climb. *Washington Post.* https://www.washingtonpost.com/national/houston-miami-and-other-cities-face-mounting-health-care-worker-shortages-as-infections-climb/2020/07/25/45fd720c-ccf8-11ea-b0e3-d55bda07d66a_story.html.

Senior, J. (2020, July 21). I spoke with Anthony Fauci. He says his inbox isn't pretty. *New York Times.* https://www.nytimes.com/2020/07/21/opinion/anthony-fauci-coronavirus.html.

Serazio, M., & Thorson, E. (2020). Weaponized patriotism and racial subtext in Kaepernick's aftermath: The anti-politics of American sports fandom. *Television & New Media, 21*(2), 151–168. https://doi.org/10.1177/1527476419879917.

Serwer, A. (2021, August 21). Greg Abbott surrenders to the coronavirus. *The Atlantic.* https://www.theatlantic.com/ideas/archive/2021/08/texas-politics-are-dangerously-broken/619725/.

Setty, G. (2020, July 27). Chief of critical care at Baltimore's Mercy Medical Center passes away due to Covid-19 complications. *CNN.* https://www.cnn.com/2020/07/27/us/baltimore-mercy-medical-center-doctor-dies-covid-19/index.html.

Shafer, E. (2021, March 7). Rita Wilson reflects on contracting COVID-19 one year ago in heartfelt Instagram post. *Variety.* https://variety.com/2021/scene/news/rita-wilson-covid19-reflection-one-year-ago-1234924332/.

Shaffer, C. (2020, June 8). The Obamas address Class of 2020 in virtual commencement speeches. *Rolling Stone.* https://www.rollingstone.com/culture/culture-news/barack-michelle-obama-class-of-2020-commencement-speeches-1011359/.

Shah, J. (2020, June 18). A comedian watched her mom die from COVID on an iPad. Her live tweets will break you. *Los Angeles Times.* https://www.latimes.com/lifestyle/story/2020-06-18/comedian-laurie-kilmarten-live-tweets-her-mothers-death.

Shapiro, M. (2021a, January 27). Asia Durr details her COVID-19 diagnosis, recovery in HBO "Real Sports" interview. *Sports Illustrated.* https://www.si.com/wnba/2021/01/27/asia-durr-wnba-covid-19-threatens-career.

Shapiro, M. (2021b, November 9). Aaron Rodgers on avoiding politics: "I'm an athlete, not an activist." *Sports Illustrated.* https://www.si.com/nfl/2021/11/09/aaron-rodgers-avoiding-politics-athlete-not-activist.

Shear, M.D., Haberman, M., & Vogel, K.P. (2020, October 2). The busy week when the president met the virus. *New York Times.* https://www.nytimes.com/2020/10/02/us/politics/trump-white-house-virus-decisions.html.

Shear, M.D., Weiland, N., Lipton, E., Haberman, M., & Sanger, D.E. (2020, July 18). Inside Trump's failure: The rush to abandon leadership role on the virus. *New York Times.* https://www.nytimes.com/2020/07/18/us/politics/trump-coronavirus-response-failure-leadership.html.

Shepherd, K. (2020, July 28). Twitter penalizes Donald Trump J. for posting hydroxychloroquine misinformation amid coronavirus pandemic. *Washington Post.* https://www.washingtonpost.com/natino/2020/07/28/trump-coronavirus-misinformation-twitter.

Shepherd, K., & Armus, T. (2020, April 20). Cuomo's advice to fathers: The answer has to be "I like the boyfriend." *Washington Post.* https://www.washingtonpost.com/nation/2020/04/20/cuomo-advice-fathers-answer-has-to-be-i-like-boyfriend.

Sherfinski, D. (2020, March 19). Surgeon General Jerome Adams calls on celebrities to get the word out about coronavirus. *Washington Times.* https://www.washingtontimes.com/news/2020/mar/19/jerome-adams-us-surgeon-general-calls-celebrities-/.

Sheth, S. (2020, June 18). Trump says he thinks some Americans are wearing masks to show they disapprove of him and not as a preventive measure during the pandemic. *Business Insider.* https://www.businessinsider.com/trump-americans-wearing-masks-show-disapproval-not-as-preventive-measure-2020-6.

Shevenock, S. (2021, May 13). Celebrities don't move the needle when it comes to vaccine willingness. *Morning Consult.* https://morningconsult.com/2021/05/13/celebrity-vaccine-covid-influencers/.

Shiffer, E. (2019, October 17). Jennifer Garner, 47, shares mammogram video on Instagram for breast cancer awareness. *Women's Health.* https://www.womenshealthmag.com/health/a29300102/jennifer-garner-mammogram-instagram-video/.

Shumow, M. (Ed.). (2015). *Mediated communities: Civic voices, empowerment, and media literacy in the digital era.* Peter Lang.

Siegel, T., Kit, B., & Gardner, C. (2021, October 6). Hollywood battle lines emerge in simmering vaccine war. *Hollywood Reporter.* https://www.hollywoodreporter.com/business/business-news/covid-vaccine-mandate-hollywood-1235026178/.

Sigman, S. (Ed.) (1995). *The consequentiality of communication.* Erlbaum.

Silver, C. (2021, March 3). Emma Samms dishes on battle with long COVID: "I haven't felt well for a year." *Daytime Confidential.* https://daytimeconfidential.com/2021/03/03/emma-samms-dishes-on-battle-with-long-covid-i-havent-felt-well-for-a-year.

Singer, J. (2021, August 17). Grading celebrities on how much they've hyped the vaccine. *Glamour.* https://www.glamour.com/story/celebrities-who-have-gotten-the-vaccine.

Singh, N. (2021, October 19). Conservative radio host Dennis Prager has Covid and claims he got it on purpose. *Independent.* https://www.independent.co.uk/news/world/americas/us-politics/radio-host-dennis-prager-covid-b1940824.html.

Sinn, D. (March 29). Seniors learning to accept end. *Journal Gazette.* https://www.journalgazette.net/sports/colleges/local-colleges/20200329/seniors-learning-to-accept-end.

Sipple, S. (2020a, August 5). One of strongest Nebraska football players in history battling COVID-19 in Lincoln hospital. *Journal Star.* https://journalstar.com/sports/huskers/football/one-of-strongest-nebraska-football-players-in-history-battling-covid-19-in-lincoln-hospital/article_c6d7b1a9-9378-53f7-a9b3-cdff0ebfd40a.html?utm_medium=social&utm_source=facebook&utm_campaign=user-share&fbclid=-IwAR3eGFR-c99QbPiB25_BKjgS-GQrMAo7xQMy40QfUsciKA7bbJg9uy-MeXM.

Sipple, S. (2020b, October 16). Former husker didn't take covid-19 very seriously until it nearly killed him. *Journal Star.* https://journalstar.com/sports/huskers/sipple/steven-m-sipple-former-husker-didnt-take-covid-19-very-seriously-until-it-nearly-killed/article_e0b7d2e4-b50e-50bb-b021-8fadef4afbe3.html?utm_medium=social&utm_source=email&utm_campaign=user-share&fbclid=IwAR3PhWAcYQofnOCmIP6lGowxZlfVxsOihEY1sTulGquAyMM6cY1_wnhdYII.

Sircar, A. (2021, August 17). Op-ed: As a doctor in a COVID unit, I'm running out of compassion for the unvaccinated. Get the shot. *Los Angeles Times.* https://www.latimes.com/opinion/story/2021-08-17/vaccinated-covid-doctor-shot.

Skinner, D. (2020, Summer). Elvis Presley gets his polio shot. National Endowment for the Humanities, 41(3). https://www.neh.gov/article/elvis-presley-set-example-getting-his-polio-vaccination.

Slavitt, A. (2020, October 2). Trump's COVID-19 opportunity: Stop mocking masks. Embrace them instead and save lives. *USA Today.* https://www.usatoday.com/story/opinion/2020/10/02/trump-positive-covid-chance-to-promote-masks-save-lives-column/5895939002/.

Slisco, A. (2021, September 20). Tucker Carlson's "vaccine misinformation" influenced dad who died of COVID, daughter claims. *Newsweek.* https://www.newsweek.com/tucker-carlsons-vaccine-misinformation-influenced-dad-who-died-covid-daughter-claims-1631009.

Sloss, M. (2021, August 25). 17 famous people who got a COVID-19 vaccine, and 7 who absolutely refuse to. *Buzzfeed.* https://www.buzzfeed.com/morgansloss1/celebrities-for-covid-vaccine-and-against-it.

Smith, A., & Alexander, P. (2020, September 16). Trump takes victory lap over return of Big Ten football: College president says it has nothing to do with him. NBC News. https://www.nbcnews.com/politics/donald-trump/trump-takes-victory-lap-return-big-10-football-college-president-n1240239.

Smith, B. (2020, March 16). Andrew Cuomo is the control freak we need right now. *New York Times.* https://www.nytimes.com/2020/03/16/business/media/cuomo-new-york-coronavirus.html.

Smith, S. (2015). *Forever red: More confessions of a Cornhusker fan.* University of Nebraska Press.

Smith-Schoenwalder (2020, June 5). CDC: Some people did take bleach to protect from coronavirus. *US News.* https://www.usnews.com/news/health-news/articles/2020-06-05/cdc-some-people-did-take-bleach-to-protect-from-coronavirus.

Snyder, M. (2020, August 24). Lina Hidalgo and Sylvester Turner appear united. But behind the scenes their styles clash. *Texas Monthly.* https://www.texasmonthly.com/politics/turner-hidalgo-coronavirus/.

Sollenberger, R. (2020, September 24). Exclusive: GOP Sen. Thom Tillis embraced QAnon conspiracy about COVID-19 death count in town hall. *Salon.* https://www.salon.com/2020/09/24/exclusive-gop-sen-thom-tillis-embraced-qanon-conspiracy-about-covid-19-death-count-in-town-hall/.

Solly, M. (2020, December 22). How Elvis helped America eliminate polio: The rock star's much-publicized vaccination inspired reluctant U.S. teens to get inoculated. *Smithsonian Magazine.* https://www.smithsonianmag.com/smart-news/how-elvis-helped-america-eliminate-polio-180976614/.

Sonkin, J., Weiss, A., & Fonrouge, G. (2021, July 7). Hometown heroes parade for essential workers kicks off amid scorching NYC temps. *New York Post.* https://nypost.com/2021/07/07/hometown-heroes-celebrated-in-nyc-ticker-tape-parade/.

Sonmez, F., Kane, P., & Dawsey, J. (2020, July 29). Rep. Louie Gohmert, who had been scheduled to travel with Trump, tests positive for the coronavirus. *Washington Post.* https://www.washingtonpost.com/politics/rep-louie-gohmert-who-had-been-scheduled-to-travel-with-trump-tests-positive-for-coronavirus/2020/07/29/3a0974f2-d1a6-11ea-8d32-1ebf4e9d8e0d_story.html.

Soukup, C. (2006). Hitching a ride on a star: Celebrity, fandom, and identification on the World Wide Web. *Southern Communication Journal,* 71(4), 319–337.

Spangler, T. (2020, May 11). Virtual graduation 2020: Selena Gomez, Cardi B, dozens more join Oprah for Facebook's livestream. *Variety.* https://variety.com/2020/digital/news/virtual-graduation-2020-facebook-selena-gomez-cardi-b-oprah-livestream-1234603291/.

Spector, J. (2020, May 8). In coronavirus response, Gov. Andrew Cuomo shows a different side: a softer one. https://www.democratandchronicle.com/story/news/politics/albany/2020/05/08/coronavirus-response-cuomo-shows-different-side-softer-one/5174405002/.

Spencer, C. (2020, December 26). My emergency room is full of patients no vaccine can help. *The Atlantic.* https://www.theatlantic.com/ideas/archive/2020/12/coronavirus-vaccines-wont-save-usyet/617492/.

Sperling, N. (2020, March 11). Tom Hanks says he has coronavirus. *New York Times.* https://www.nytimes.com/2020/03/11/business/media/tom-hanks-coronavirus.html.

Stanfill, M. (2013). "They're losers, but I know better": Intra-fandom stereotyping and the normalization of the fan subject. *Critical Studies in Media Communication,* 30(2), 117–134. DOI: 10.1080/15295036.2012.755053.

Stanfill, M. (2020). Introduction: The reactionary in the fan and the fan in the reactionary. *Television & New Media,* 21(2), 123–134.

Stanley-Becker, I. (2020, November 17). Adopting mask mandate, some GOP governors give up the gospel of personal responsibility. *Washington Post.* https://www.washingtonpost.com/national/mask-mandates-republican-governors/2020/11/17/9f0638fa-28da-11eb-8fa2-06e7cbb145c0_story.html.

Stanley-Becker, I., & Witte, G. (2020, July 20). Why Georgia Gov. Brian Kemp stands alone on masks. *Washington Post.* https://www.washingtonpost.com/national/why-georgia-gov-brian-kemp-stands-alone-on-masks/2020/07/20/2365b294-caba-11ea-bc6a-6841b28d9093_story.html.

Staurowsky, E. (2014). College athletes' rights in the age of the super conference: The case of the All Players United Campaign. *Journal of Intercollegiate Sport, 7*, 11–34. DOI: http://dx.doi.org/10.1123/jis.2013-0052.

Steaklin, W., & Rubin, O. (2020, July 9). Trump rally likely contributed to surge in COVID-19 cases, Tulsa health official says. ABC News. https://abcnews.go.com/Politics/trump-rally-contributed-surge-covd-19-cases-tulsa/story?id=71680180.

Stecklow, S., & MacAskill, A. (2021, March 18). The ex–Pfizer scientist who became an anti-vax hero. Reuters. https://www.reuters.com/investigates/special-report/health-coronavirus-vaccines-skeptic/.

Stein, L.E. (2015). *Millennial fandom: Television audiences in the transmedia age.* University of Iowa Press.

Stein, R. (2020, August 5). Fauci reveals he has received death threats and his daughters have been harassed. NPR. https://www.npr.org/sections/coronavirus-live-updates/2020/08/05/899415906/fauci-reveals-he-has-received-death-threats-and-his-daughters-have-been-harassed.

Stelter, B. (2020). *Hoax: Donald Trump, Fox News, and the dangerous distortion of truth.* One Signal Publishers.

Sternlicht, A. (2020, May 28). Nearly 300 healthcare workers have died from coronavirus. *Forbes.* https://www.forbes.com/sites/alexandrasternlicht/2020/05/28/nearly-300-healthcare-workers-have-died-from-coronavirus/?sh=295b40ca49ec.

Stevens, H. (2021, November 18). Column: Dolly Parton is the closest thing we have to a universally beloved icon. And that was before she helped fund Moderna's COVID-29 vaccine. *Chicago Tribune.* https://www.chicagotribune.com/columns/heidi-stevens/ct-heidi-stevens-why-everyone-loves-dolly-parton-covid-vaccine-1118-20201118-mrvt2qtoszb5nhpsw37hlfz6sq-story.html.

Stolberg, S.G., & Weiland, N. (2020, July 21). Facing "a lot of blowback," Trump's surgeon general steps up. *New York Times.* https://www.nytimes.com/2020/07/21/us/politics/jerome-adams-surgeon-general-trump-coronavirus.html.

Stradling, R. (2020, June 17). In one North Carolina hospital, coronavirus outbreak feels like it's just beginning. *News & Observer.* https://www.newsobserver.com/news/coronavirus/article243570332.html.

Strauss, V. (2021, February 16). The deeply distorted debate about reopening schools. *Washington Post.* https://www.washingtonpost.com/education/2021/02/16/distorted-debate-on-reopening-schools/.

"Study shows fans missing sports" (2020, May 18). Insights Association. https://www.insightsassociation.org/article/study-shows-fans-missing-sports-more-other-activities-during-covid-19-pandemic.

Sullivan, M. (2020, July 30). This was the week America lost the war on misinformation. *Washington Post.* https://www.washingtonpost.com/lifestyle/media/this-was-the-week-america-lost-the-war-on-misinformation/2020/07/30/d8359e2e-d257-11ea-9038-af089b63ac21_story.html.

Sullivan, M. (2021, September 25). The NBA's anti-vaxxers are trying to push around the league—and it's working. *Rolling Stone.* https://www.rollingstone.com/culture/culture-features/nba-anti-vaxxers-covid-1231988/.

Sun, A., & Heyward, G. (2021, August 17). American hospitals buckle under Delta, With I.C.U.s filling up. *New York Times.* https://www.nytimes.com/interactive/2021/08/17/us/covid-delta-hospitalizations.html.

Sun, L.H., & Dawsey, J. (2020, July 9). CDC feels pressure from Trump as rift grows over coronavirus response. *Washington Post.* https://www.washingtonpost.com/health/trump-sidelines-public-health-advisers-in-growing-rift-over-coronavirus-response/2020/07/09/ad803218-c12a-11ea-9fdd-b7ac6b051dc8_story.html.

Svitek, P. (2020, August 21). The Democrats' national convention shone a spotlight on Texas' emerging bench—beyond the Castros and O'Rourke. *Texas Tribune.* https://www.texastribune.org/2020/08/21/dnc-2020-texans/.

Tamir, I. (2021). The deprivation of live sports broadcasts during Covid-19: Israeli sports fans during the global pandemic. In P.M. Pederson, B.J. Ruihley, & B. Li (Eds.), *Sport*

and the pandemic: Perspectives on Covid-19's impact on the sport industry (pp. 328–340). Routledge.
Tapp, T. (2020, October 5). CNN's Chris Cuomo rips Donald Trump's choreographed return to White House: "What a bunch of bulls*t." *Deadline*. https://deadline.com/2020/10/cnn-chris-cuomo-rips-donald-trumps-return-to-white-house-bullshit-1234591942/.
Taylor, D.B. (2021, November 5). George Floyd protests: A timeline. *New York Times*. https://www.nytimes.com/article/george-floyd-protests-timeline.html.
Tetteh, D., & Upadhyaya, S. (2018). Effect of Angelina Jolie's medical announcements on American health awareness and risk management culture. In C.M. Madere (Ed.), *Celebrity media effects: The persuasive power of the stars* (pp. 67–84). Lexington Books.
Thamel, P. (2021, August 21). "We're 90% vaccinated and I'm still nervous"—As Delta variant shrouds 2021 college football season, players walk fine line. Yahoo Sports. https://sports.yahoo.com/were-90-vaccinated-and-im-still-nervous-as-delta-variant-shrouds-2021-college-football-season-players-walk-fine-line-015736765.html?guccounter=1&guce_referrer=aHR0cHM6Ly93d3cuZ29vZ2xlLmNvbS8&guce_referrer_sig=AQAAACH4zOOiFo6RoEMra-L9C_GiLOBlWRrhI_nhmQV2tSFrHzYLkdNCfSxXkvMkw4d2QJw7BiGv90GciD9ouEqkICizMMcjJkbsl4NIqguku94llhL1n_wIwPKcfqI7PwVRYffMf3lXTLUS0UbRiXdYYpg43KU4yDj_vEBfZLiaUN_J.
Thompson, J. (2020, December). Laurent Duvernay-Tardif. *Sports Illustrated*, *131*(15), 83–87.
Tillett, E. (2021, January 23). Dr. Deborah Birx, who ran Trump's COVID task force, says she "always" considered quitting. CBS News. https://www.cbsnews.com/news/deborah-birx-considered-quitting-trump-covid-task-force/.
Tollefson, J. (2020, October 5). How Trump damaged science—and why it could take decades to recover. *Nature*. https://www.nature.com/articles/d41586-020-02800-9.
Toresdahl, B.G., & Asif, I.M. (2020). Coronavirus disease 2019 (COVID-19): Considerations for the competitive athlete. *Sports Health*, *12*, 221–224. DOI: 10.1177/1941738120918876.
Torres, M. (2021, June 3). Naomi Osaka shows that prioritizing yourself over a job is still a radical act. *Huffington Post*. https://www.huffpost.com/entry/naomi-osaka-prioritize-yourself-over-jo_l_60b79ecae4b001ebd46cd31a.
Towler, C.C., Crawford, N.N., & Bennett III, R.A. (2019). Shut up and play: Black athletes, protest politics, and Black political action. *Perspective on Politics*, *18*, 111–127. DOI: 10.1017/S1537592719002597.
Treene, A. (2020, October 2). White House has no plans to mandate masks. *Axios*. https://www.axios.com/politics-policy/2020/10/02/.
Treisman, R. (2020, July 20). Dr. Anthony Fauci to throw first pitch for Washington Nationals' season opener. NPR. https://www.npr.org/sections/coronavirus-live-updates/2020/07/20/8933403343/dr-anthony-fauci-to-throw-first-pitch-for-washington-nationals-season-opener.
Treisman, R. (2021, March 3). From "Jolene" to vaccine: Dolly Parton gets COVID-19 shot she helped fund. NPR. https://www.npr.org/sections/coronavirus-live-updates/2021/03/03/973240792/from-jolene-to-vaccine-dolly-parton-gets-covid-19-shot-she-helped-fund.
Trepany, C. (2000, July 16). Jamie Foxx, Ellen Pompeo and others star in Mask Up campaign as more celebs encourage face masks. *USA Today*. https://www.usatoday.com/story/entertainment/celebrities/2020/07/16/what-tom-hanks-jamie-foxx-more-celebs-saying-face-masks/5456283002/.
Trepany, C. (2021, July 14). Olivia Rodrigo rocks Aviator sunglasses with Biden, meets with Fauci for vaccine campaign. *USA Today*. https://www.usatoday.com/story/entertainment/celebrities/2021/07/14/olivia-rodrigo-white-house-biden-fauci-covid-vaccine-campaign/7960016002/.
Troy, T., & Skalka, L. (2020, August 25). "Have at it": DeWine said he isn't concerned with impeachment attempt. *Toledo Blade*. https://www.toledoblade.com/local/

Coronavirus/2020/08/25/lucas-county-coronavirus-numbers-dropping-compared-to-others/stories/20200825122.
Trudon, T. (2021, May 9). "We feel lost in time": COVID-19 transforms teen milestones. *Salt Lake Tribune*. https://www.sltrib.com/artsliving/2021/05/09/we-feel-lost-time-covid/.
Truitt, B. (2020, July 6). Broadway star Nick Cordero dies at 41 after coronavirus struggle highlighted by wife Amanda Kloots. *USA Today*. https://www.usatoday.com/story/entertainment/movies/2020/07/05/broadway-star-nick-cordero-dies-after-coronavirus-battle/5232813002/.
Trump, M. (2020). *Too much and never enough: How my family created the world's most dangerous man*. Simon & Schuster.
Uitti, J. (2021, October). Eric Clapton releases new apparent anti-mask protest song. *American Songwriter*. https://americansongwriter.com/eric-clapton-releases-new-apparent-anti-mask-protest-song/.
Umeri, S. (2021, March 3). How elite athletes have struggled with the long-term effects of Covid. https://sbnation.com/nba/2021/3/3/22292213/athletes-cofid-recovery-stories-jayson-tatu-mo-bamba-asia-durr.
Van Dijck, J. (2013). *The culture of connectivity: A critical history of social media*. Oxford University Press.
Van Driel, I.I., Gantz, W., & Lewis, N. (2019). Unpacking what it means to be—or not to be—a fan. *Communication & Sport*, 7, 611–629.
Van Zoonen, L. (2004). Imagining the fan democracy. *Journal of Communication*, 19(1), 39–52. DOI: 10.1177/0267323104040693.
Victor, D., Serviss, L., & Paybarah, A. (2020, October 2). In his own words, Trump on the coronavirus and masks. *New York Times*. https://www.nytimes.com/2020/10/02/us/politics/donald-trump-masks.html.
Vielkind, J., Palazzolo, J., & Gershman, J. (2020, September 11). In worst-hit Covid state, New York's Cuomo called all the shots. *Wall Street Journal*. https://www.wsj.com/articles/cuomo-covid-new-york-coronavirus-de-blasio-shutdown-timing-11599836994.
Viglione, G. (2021, November 3). Four ways Trump has meddled in pandemic science—and why it matters. *Nature*. https://www.nature.com/articles/d41586-020-03035-4.
Villegas, C.M. (2020). Performing rituals of affliction: How a governor's press conferences provided mediatized sanctuary in Ohio. *American Journal of Cultural Sociology*, 8, 352–383. https://doi.org/10.1057/s41290-020-00116-9.
Vlessing, E. (2020, April 20). Celine Dion, Shania Twain, Michael Buble and more team for TV special fighting COVID-19. *Hollywood Reporter*. https://www.hollywoodreporter.com/news/general-news/celine-dion-shania-twain-michael-buble-set-coronavirus-tv-benefit-1290859/.
Voght, K. (2020, October 3). How the GOP turned Washington, D.C., into a COVID hotspot. *Mother Jones*. https://www.motherjones.com/politics/2020/10/how-the-gop-turned-washington-dc-into-a-covid-hotspot/.
Wade, S. (2020, March 31). Tokyo Olympics rescheduled for July 23-August 8, 2021. Associated Press. https://apnews.com/article/sports-asia-sports-middle-east-virus-outbreak-olympic-games-tokyo-4ee76147929e50c7ed5787d40eb8227e.
Wagner, J., Costa, R., & Gowen, A. (2020, July 30). Herman Cain, former Republican presidential hopeful, has died of coronavirus, his website says. *Washington Post*. https://www.washingtonpost.com/politics/herman-cain-former-republican-presidential-hopeful-has-died-of-the-coronavirus-statement-on-his-website-says/2020/07/30/4ac62a10-d273-11ea-9038-af089b63ac21_story.html.
Waldrop, T. (2021, November 13). Scientists react to Aaron Rodgers' comments on Covid-19 vaccine and treatments. CNN. https://www.cnn.com/2021/11/13/us/aaron-rodgers-covid-vaccine-scientists/index.html.
Wallis, A. (2020, June 17). Katy Perry, Adam Lambert and more to unite for LGBTQ2 benefit show, "Can't cancel pride." *Global News*. https://globalnews.ca/news/7075084/cant-cancel-pride-coronavirus-benefit-lgbtq2-katy-perry-adam-lambert/.

Wallis, C. (2020, June 12). Why racism, not race, is a risk factor for dying of COVID-19. *Scientific American.* https://www.scientificamerican.com/article/why-racism-not-race-is-a-risk-factor-for-dying-of-covid-191/.

Walsh, S. (2020, May 15). How to watch "#Graduation 2020: Facebook and Instagram celebrate the class of 2020." *Elle.* https://www.elle.com/culture/celebrities/a32477050/how-to-watch-facebook-instagram-virtual-graduation-ceremony/.

Walton, A. (2021, August 30). From the COVID frontlines: TMH ER nurse tells WCTV about daily reality amidst new peaks in hospitalizations, deaths. WCTV. https://www.wctv.tv/2021/08/30/covid-frontlines-tmh-er-nurse-tells-wctv-about-daily-reality-amidst-new-peaks-hospitalizations-deaths/.

Wanshel, E. (2020, May 20). Dr. Fauci's #passthemic campaign will take over Julia Roberts' social media accounts. *Huffington Post.* https://www.huffpost.com/entry/coronavirus-julia-roberts-celebrities-passthemic-fauci-experts_n_5ec56fcbc5b689d9fl4be4c9.

Warren, T.H. (2021, September 26). The limits of "my body, my choice." *New York Times.* https://www.nytimes.com/2021/09/26/opinion/choice-liberty-freedom.html.

Weiner, M. (2020, March 31). Digital views for Cuomo's daily coronavirus briefings set records. https://www.syracuse.com/coronavirus/2020/03/digital-views-for-cuomos-daily-coronavirus-briefings-near-1m-a-day.html.

Weise, E., & Weintraub, K. (2020, September 13). Scientists outraged by White House appointees' meddling with coronavirus information: "Outright egregious." *USA Today.* https://www.usatoday.com/story/news/health/2020/09/13/covid-scientists-white-house-meddling-cdc-mmwr/5787230002/.

Weisholtz, D. (2021, April 2). Rita Wilson explains why she and Tom Hanks haven't gotten COVID-19 vaccine yet. *Today.* https://www.today.com/popculture/rita-wilson-why-she-tom-hanks-haven-t-gotten-covid-t213876.

Wertheim, J., & Apstein, S. (2020, July). Game changed. *Sports Illustrated, 131*(7), 22–29.

West, J. (2020, July 27). Dr. Anthony Fauci baseball card sets TOPPS record. *Sports Illustrated.* https://www.si.com/mlb/2020/07/27/dr-fauci-baseball-card-sets-print-run-record-topps.

West, J. (2021, January 27). The disinformation pandemic is real: Fighting it will require compassion. *Mother Jones.* https://www.motherjones.com/politics/2021/01/the-disinformation-pandemic-is-real-fighting-it-will-require-compassion/.

Wheeler, M. (2013). *Celebrity politics: Image and identity in contemporary political communications.* Polity.

White, A. (2021, August 20). Melissa Joan Hart "disappointed with herself" after "getting lazy" and contracting Covid. *Independent.* https://www.independent.co.uk/arts-entertainment/tv/news/melissa-joan-hart-covid-instagram-b1905832.html.

Wilder, E. (2020, December 7). Navajo Nation enters COVID-19 "crisis mode." *USA Today*, pp. D1–2.

Wilentz, A. (2020, October 3). Trump thought he'd never get it. *The Atlantic.* https://www.theatlantic.com/ideas/archive/2020/10/thought-rules-applied-suckers/616605/.

Williams, A., Martin, T., & Allen, R. (2015). Communicating through fitness: An examination of the use of athletes to communicate fitness in print media. *International Journal of Interdisciplinary Studies in Communication, 10*(4), 9–19. https://doi.10.18848/2324-7320/CGP/v/10i04/53566.

Williams, P. (2020, November 2). How American can avoid dual cataclysms. *The New Yorker.* https://www.newyorker.com/news/us-journal/how-america-can-avoid-dual-cataclysms.

Williams, P., & Gregorian, D. (2020, June 19). Oklahoma Supreme Court denies legal challenge to Trump's rally. NBC News. https://www.nbcnews.com/politics/2020-election/oklahoma-supreme-court-denies-legal-challenge-trump-rally-n1231564.

Williams, T.C. (2020, July 2). Do Americans understand how badly they're doing? *The Atlantic.* https://www.theatlantic.com/ideas/archive/2020/07/america-land-pathetic/613747/.

Wilson, J. (2011). Playing with politics: Political fans and Twitter faking in post-broadcast democracy. *Convergence: The International Journal of Research into New Media Technologies, 17*(4), 445–461.

Witte, G. (2020, May 18). Ohio's Amy Acton inspires admiration, and a backlash, with tough coronavirus response. *Washington Post.* https://www.washingtonpost.com/national/a-white-coated-hero-or-a-medical-dictator-ohios-amy-acton-inspires-admiration-and-a-backlash-with-tough-coronavirus-response/2020/05/17/fa00cd1c-96d4-11ea-82b4-c8db161ff6e5_story.html.

Witte, G., & Zezima, K. (2020, March 16). Ohio Gov. Mike DeWine's coronavirus response has become a national guide to the crisis. *Washington Post.* https://www.washingtonpost.com/national/coronavirus-ohio-dewine-outbreak/2020/03/16.

Witz, B. (2020, May 27). With or without the say of players, college football moves toward a return. *New York Times.* https://www.nytimes.com/2020/05/27/sports/ncaafootball/coronavirus-college-football.html.

Witz, B. (2021, October 10). A coach's vaccine refusal generates discord at Washington State. *New York Times.* https://www.nytimes.com/2021/10/10/sports/ncaafootball/rolovich-vaccine-status-washington-state.html?smid=tw-nytimes&smtyp=cur.

Wolfe, R. (2010). *For Husker fans only.* Rich Wolfe and Lone Wolfe Press.

Wong, B. (2020, October 7). People who lost loved ones to coronavirus reaction to Trump's tweet. *Huffington Post.* https://www.huffpost.com/entry/people-lost-loved-ones-coronavirus-trump-tweet_l_5f7dfa01c5b62e45eed529ba.

Wong, N.C.H., Lookadoo, K.L., & Nisbett, G.S. (2017). "I'm Demi and I have bipolar disorder": Effect of parasocial contact on reducing stigma toward people with bipolar disorder. *Communication Studies, 68*(3), 314–333. https://www.tandfonline.com/doi/abs/10.1080/10510974.2017.1331928.

Wood, M. (2020, April 16). DHD Films launches #HealthCareHeroes campaign with $100,000 gift announcement. *Dallas Regional Chamber.* https://www.dallaschamber.org/dhd-films-launches-healthcareheroes-campaign-with-100000-gift-announcement/.

Woodward, B. (2020). *Rage.* Simon & Schuster.

Wootson Jr., C. R., Stanley-Becker, I., Rozsa, L., & Dawsey, J. (2020, July 25). Coronavirus ravaged Florida, as Ron DeSantis sidelined scientists and followed Trump. *Washington Post.* https://www.washingtonpost.com/national/coronavirus-ravaged-florida-as-ron-desantis-sidelined-scientists-and-followed-trump/2020/07/25/0b8008da-c648-11ea-b037-f9711f89ee46_story.html.

Wright, L. (2020). *Star power: American democracy in the age of the celebrity candidate.* Routledge.

Wu, C. (2012, September 27). A leading lady: Betty Ford's candor about her breast cancer diagnosis helped bring a private issue out of the shadows. *Cancer Today.* https://www.cancertodaymag.org/Pages/Fall2012/betty-ford-yesterday-and-today.aspx.

Wu, K.J. (2020, July 6). In Nick Cordero's death, a reminder of Covid-19's unknowns. *New York Times.* https://www.nytimes.com/2020/07/06/health/coronavirus-nick-cordero-underlying-conditions.html.

Wulderk, N. (2020, September 25). Stars align for 45th NIAF gala to honor Dr. Anthony Fauci. https://www.orderisda.org/culture/news/stars-align-for-45th-niaf-gala-to-honor-dr-anthony-fauci-2020/.

Yahr, E. (2015, October 2). What Robin Roberts said to Amy Robach that convinced her to get a mammogram on live TV. *Washington Post.* https://www.washingtonpost.com/news/arts-and-entertainment/wp/2015/10/02/what-robin-roberts-said-to-amy-robach-that-convinced-her-to-get-a-mammogram-on-live-tv/.

Yahr, E. (2020, December 28). Country music's pandemic year: Frustration, backlash and a sad ending. *Washington Post.* https://www.washingtonpost.com/entertainment/music/country-music-covid-charley-pride-2020/12/26/ac51bd2e-4566-11eb-975c-d17b8815a66d_story.html.

Yamaguchi, M. (2021, August 5). Tokyo logs record 5,042 cases as infections surge amid games. *AP News.* https://apnews.com/article/2020-tokyo-olympics-lifestyle-sports-coronavirus-pandemic-business-0b250f40128b0892863bc55067a4ba39.

Yang, R. (2020, May 21). All My Children cast reuniting in EW's weeklong celebration of iconic soap for #UnitedAtHome series. EW. https://ew.com/tv/ew-reunites-all-my-children-cast/.
Yee, N. (2021, September 16). As COVID-19 pandemic wears on, demand increases for deworming drug ivermectin. *Cronkite News*. https://cronkitenews.azpbs.org/2021/09/16/ivermectin-covid-19-deworming-drug-demand-increases-pandemic-continues/.
Yong, E. (2020, August 4). How the pandemic defeated America. *The Atlantic*. https://www.theatlantic.com/magazine/archive/2020/09/coronavirus-american-failure/614191/.
Yong, E. (2021, November 16). Why health-care workers are quitting in droves. *The Atlantic*. https://www.theatlantic.com/health/archive/2021/11/the-mass-exodus-of-americas-health-care-workers/620713/.
Yost, M. (2020, June 16). Editorial: Dr. Amy Acton delivered a winning prescription. *Columbus Dispatch*. https://www.dispatch.com/story/opinion/2020/06/16/editorial-dr-amy-acton-delivered-winning-prescription/42130241/.
Young, R. (2020, December 24). Rudy Gobert reflects on last season's COVID-19 microphone incident: I was trying "to liven the mood." Yahoo. https://www.yahoo.com/lifestyle/utah-jazz-rudy-gobert-microphone-incident-coronavirus-covid19-pandemic-015904350.html.
Yuan, S., & Lou, C. (2020). How social media influencers foster relationships with followers: The roles of source credibility and fairness in parasocial relationship and product interest. *Journal of Interactive Advertising*, *20*(2), 133–147. https://doi.org/10.1080/15252019.2020.1769514.
Zavaleta, L. (2020, October 2). Gayest & greatest 2020: People part 1. *Outsmart Magazine*. https://www.outsmartmagazine.con/2020/10/gayest-greatest-2020-people-part-1.
Zillgitt, J. (2020, October 13). Meet the eight key figures who helped make the NBA bubble a success. *USA Today*. https://www.usatoday.com/story/sports/nba/2020/10/13/nba-bubble-succeeded-because-eight-key-figures-adam-silver/3640236001/.

Index

AARP 114
Acton, Amy 61–65, 68
Adams, Bryan 103
All My Children, cast of 104
Aniston, Jennifer 120–121
Antetokounmpo, Giannis 106
Arnett, Will 103
As the World Turns 113
Ashe, Arthur 40
athletes, health advocacy 35–54, 49, 133
Atwood, Margaret 103

Bamba, Mohammed 47
Banus, Camila 94–95
Barkley, Charles 131
Barrymore, Drew 106–107
Beyonce 108
Biden, Joseph, administration of 121, 124, 129
Bieber, Justin 103
Birx, Deborah 83–84
Blunt, Emily 110
Brady, Tom 103
Bravery and Hope: 7 Days on the Front Line 141
BTS 111
Bundy, Laura Bell 115–116
Burch, Tory 120
Burnstein, Danny 97
Burton, Steve 129–130
Bush, George W. 70

Cain, Herman 84–85
Camp, Anna 95–96
"Can't Cancel Pride" 103
Cardi B 111
Cavuto, Neil 128–129
Christie, Chris 85
celebrity fandom, influence of 3, 13, 16, 17, 20, 28–34, 39–41, 49, 91–134; health narratives 2, 23–24, 31–34, 40–41; health practices 16–17, 20, 49, 91–92, 114–133; politics 56–60, 69–72, 80–81, 91–92; raising awareness of Covid-19 16, 49, 91–102; support regarding Covid-19 16, 91–92, 102–114
Centers for Disease Control (CDC) 4, 11, 82–85, 98
Chang, David 111
Charles, Tina 48
Cheney, Liz 82, 85
Clapton, Eric 125
Clinton, Hillary 111
Cobert, Stephen 105
commencement celebration 110–112
conspiracy theories 11, 12, 77, 126–127
Cordero, Nick 7, 19–21, 23
Couric, Katie 32, 111, 123
Covid-19: alternate remedies 117–119, 126–127; bleach 77, 126–127; chlorine dioxide 77; Ivermectin 118–119, 126–127
Covid-19, death toll 2, 4, 7; discrepancies 3, 9–14, 28, 33–34, 44, 56–60, 70 88, 126, 147–148 (*see also* narratives, competing master); disparities 6–7; disruptions because of 4–6, 108–109; division 7, 44, 56–60, 126–130; framing 16, 28, 33–34, 44, 72, 83–84 (*see also* narratives, celebrity health); mask-wearing 9, 10–12, 28, 77, 82, 85, 87, 90, 94–95, 97, 98, 101, 107, 119–122, 125–126, 130; parties 14; politicization 12, 16, 33, 55–88, 90; scientific approach 9, 12–13, 33–34, 56, 70–88, 91, 119–124, 126–133; skepticism of 3, 9, 11–14, 33–34, 38, 56, 58–60, 72–88, 91, 119, 124–133; truth, disputing 9–14, 33–34, 83–84, 119, 147; U.S. mishandling 4, 73–88
Covid-19, vaccinations 86, 88, 119, 122–134; "My Body, My Choice" campaign 126; Operation Warp Speed 86, 117–118
Covid-19 Physicians Memorial 138
#CreateThanks 139
Crystal, Billy 103
Cuban, Mark 124
Cuomo, Andrew 2–3, 65–70, 119–120

Index

Cuomo, Chris 100; *see also* Cuomo, Andrew
Curry, Stephen 106

D'Amelio, Dixie 111
Day, Ryan 52
Delle Donne, Elena 48
Dempsey, Patrick 121
DeWine, Mike 2–3, 61–65, 68
Dion, Celine 103
Dr. Oz 111
Dorsey, Jack 108
Durr, Asia 47–48
Duvernay-Tardiff, Lauren 135
Dynasty, cast of 103; *see also* Samms, Emma

Esiason, Boomer 40
Estefan, Gloria 103
Evans, Judi 96–97

Facebook *see* social media
facts, disputing 13; *see also* Covid-19, truth, disputing
Fallon, Jimmy 104, 111
fandom, implications 3, 13–14, 16–17 (*see also* celebrity fandom); anti-fandom 16, 27–28, 58–60; communities 25–26, 58–60; identities 25–28; relationships 26–27, 29–30; *see also* parasocial relationships
Fauci, Anthony 1, 13, 70–72, 76–77, 79, 81–84, 87
Feeding America 104
Fey, Tina 104
first responders 107
Food Banks Canada 103–104
Ford, Betty 31
Foster, David 103
Fox, Michael J. 33
Fox & Friends 12, 74
Fox News 12, 74, 128–129, 145
Freeman, Freddie 46

Gaga, Lady 105, 111
Garner, Jennifer 123
General Hospital 129–130
Gobert, Rudy 35–36, 41
Gomez, Selena 111
Graduate Together: America Honors the High School Class of 2020 112
Grahn, Nancy Lee 129–130
Guiding Light, cast of 104, 113

Hamilton, cast of 110
Hamilton, Scott 40
Handler, Chelsea 111
Hanks, Tom 2, 16, 93, 102
Hannity 12, 74

Hart, Melissa Joan 98–99
Hathaway, Anne 121
health care professionals 17, 107, 135–148; compassion fatigue 146–148; doctors 136–142; fandom 136–142; implications of Covid skepticism 136–148; nurses 136–142; public health officials 8–9, 12–13, 16, 55–56, 84–85; shortages 136–138, 145; tributes to 136–142
"HealthCareHeroes" 140
Heroes Act 139
Hildago, Lina 55–56
Hobson, Mellody 111
Hometown Heroes Parade 141
#HonorHeroes with Creativity During Covid-19 140
Hudgens, Vanessa 92
Hydroxychloroquine 11–12, 77, 79

identification 28–29
Instagram *see* social media
intensive care units 7
interpretive communities 10, 14, 17, 24–27, 28, 33–34, 56–60, 91
Irving, Kyrie 131

James, LeBron 112
Joel, Billy 104
Johnson, Dwayne 116–117
Johnson, Jimmie 46
Johnson, Magic 33, 40
Jollie, Angelina 32
Jovie, Jon Bon 104, 106

Kardashians 91–92
Kennedy, John F. 56–57
Kilmartin, Laurie 89–91
Kimmel, Jimmy 105
Kloots, Amanda 19–21, 23, 28–29
Krasinski, John 109–111
Krzyzewski, Mike 111

Lambert, Adam 103
Lara Logan Has No Agenda 145
Lavigne, Avril 103
Lawrence, Trevor 52
Levy, Dan 103
Levy, Eugene 103
Lightner, Keven 37–39
Limbaugh, Rush 12–13, 79
The Locker Room 112–114
long-haulers 99–102
Longoria, Eva 124
Lucas, William 121–122
Lucci, Susan 114

Madonna 91
mainstream media 12, 80

Index 191

Mandel, Howie 103
Manning, Eli 111
Manning, Peyton 103
"Mask Up America" campaign 119–120
McChrystal, Stan 111
McConaughey, Matthew 107, 111
McLauchlan, Sarah 103
Menzel, Idina 104
messages, Covid-19 see Covid-19
Mickelson, Phil 103
Milano, Alyssa 100–101, 117
Miranda, Lin-Manuel 104, 110
Mitchell, Jadan 52
"My Body, My Choice" campaign 126
Myers, Mike 103

narratives: celebrity health 2, 20, 23–24, 31–34, 40–41, 91–92, 133–134 (see also celebrity fandom and fandom, implications of); competing master narratives 12, 16, 33–34, 56, 73–88, 91–92, 126–127, 136–148; Covid-19 16, 33–34 (see also Covid-19); health 21–24, 33; narrative paradigm 21, 147; narrative theorizing 21–23; public health 12–13, 16 (see also health professionals, public health); trustworthiness 61–70
Nicklaus, Jack 46
1918 Influenza 3, 4, 8–9, 70
No Kid Hungry 107
"Nurse Heroes Live" 103
Nye, Bill 119

Obama, Barack 111–112
Obama, Michelle 111
Ohai, Kealia 106
"One World: Together at Home" 105
Osaka, Naomi 49

parasocial relationships 16, 29–31, 93; see also celebrity fandom and fandom, implications of
Parks and Recreation, cast of 104
Parton, Dolly 122, 127–128
Perry, Katy 103
Peters, Russell 103
Pink 107
Plandemic 11
postmodern era 10, 12. 20, 33
Powell, Colin 128
Praeger, Dennis 125–126
Presley, Elvis 123–124, 127
Pride, Charley 125
Priestley, Jason 103

Rademacher, Ingo 129–130
Ray, Rachel 106

realities, multiple of 9–13, 20, 34, 60; see also Covid-19
Reality TV 30–31, 57–58
Rexha, Bebe 114
Reynolds, Ryan 103
Rice, Condoleeza 111
"Rise Up New York" 104, 105
Robach, Amy 123
Roberts, Julia 1, 13, 71
Roberts, Robin 123
Robertson, Robbie 103
Rodgers, Aaron 132–133
Rodrigo, Olivia 124
Rolovich, Nick 132
Roosevelt, Franklin D. 56–57
Roosevelt, Teddy 56–57

Saban, Nick 52
Samms, Emma 101–103; see also *Dynasty*, cast of
Schwarzenegger, Arnold 126
Seacrest, Ryan 107
#SnackinwithActon 2, 61–62
social construction of reality 13, 16, 69
social media, implications of 2, 10–11, 12, 15, 30, 35, 49, 57–59, 74–75, 79, 81, 84, 87–88
Solomon, David 111
Some Good News (SGN) 109–111
Spanish flu 3–4; see also 1918 Influenza
Spencer, Octavia 107
Spielberg, Steven 111
Spielman, Chris 40
sports, importance of 16, 35–54; desire for normal 44–46, 49–53; economic impact of Covid-19 45–46, 49–53; importance to fans 44–45, 49–51, 53
sports organizations, response of 16; Big 10 51; college football 49–53; March Madness 41–42; MLB 35, 42–43; MLS 35, 42–43; NBA 35, 42–43, 45, 47, 106, 131; NCAA 41–43, 45; Nebraska Cornhuskers 37–39; NFL 106, 135; NHL 35, 42–43; Olympics 43–45, 53; Washington Mystics 48; WNBA 47–48
Springfield, Rick 104
Stewart, Jon 111
"Stronger Together, Tous Emsemble" 103
Summitt, Pat 40
Sutherland, Kiefer 103

Teherán, Julio 46
"Thank a Healthcare Hero Campaign" 139–140
Theron, Charlize 107
Thomas, Peter 95
#TogetherForHer 108
Trump, Donald J. 2, 7; administration

response 4, 11, 12, 73–88; allies 12, 79; bleach 77, 126–127; celebrity status 57–60; college football 51; followers 57–61, 72–75, 79–81, 90; framing of 12, 16, 90; hospitalization 13, 78–80; Operation Warp Speed 86, 117–118 (*see also* Covid-19, vaccinations); ratings 2, 72
Twain, Shania 103

Usher 111

virus *see* Covid-19
Volvano, Jim 40

Wambach, Abby 111
Watt, J.J. 106
Wayne, Jennifer 115
"We Can Do This" campaign 124
Westbrook, Russell 47

White House *see* Biden, Joseph; Trump, Donald
"Who Am I? Mask Challenge" 121–122
Williams, Allison 131–132
Williamson, Zion 106
Wilson, Russell 106
#WineWithDeWine 2, 61–62
Winfrey, Oprah 103, 108, 111
Witherspoon, Reese 121
Witmer, Gretchen 81
Wonder, Stevie 103
Woods, Tiger 103
World Health Organization (WHO) 4, 12, 105–106

Yousafzai, Malala 111

Zakaria, Fareed 93–94